Religion, Death, and Dying

Religion, Death, and Dying

Volume 3: Bereavement and Death Rituals

Edited by Lucy Bregman

PRAEGER PERSPECTIVES
PRAEGER
An Imprint of ABC-CLIO, LLC

A B C 🔅 C L I O

Santa Barbara, California • Denver, Colorado • Oxford, England

Library of Congress Cataloging-in-Publication Data

Religion, death, and dying / edited by Lucy Bregman.
   p. cm. — (Praeger perspectives)
   Includes bibliographical references and index.
   ISBN 978-0-313-35173-0 (set : hc : alk. paper) — ISBN 978-0-313-35174-7 (ebook) —
ISBN 978-0-313-35175-4 (vol. 1. : alk. paper) — ISBN 978-0-313-35176-1 (ebook) —
ISBN 978-0-313-35177-8 (vol. 2 : alk. paper) — ISBN 978-0-313-35178-5 (ebook) — ISBN
978-0-313-35179-2 (vol. 3 : alk. paper) — ISBN 978-0-313-35180-8 (ebook) 1. Death—
Religious aspects. 2. Bereavement—Religious aspects. 3. Death. 4. United States—Religion.
I. Bregman, Lucy.
   BL504.R43   2010
   202'.3—dc22   2009028725

ISBN: 978-0-313-35173-0
EISBN: 978-0-313-35174-7

14 13 12 11 10   5 4 3 2 1

This book is also available on the World Wide Web as an eBook.
Visit www.abc-clio.com for details.

Praeger
An Imprint of ABC-CLIO, LLC

ABC-CLIO, LLC
130 Cremona Drive, P.O. Box 1911
Santa Barbara, California 93116-1911

This book is printed on acid-free paper ∞

Manufactured in the United States of America

Copyright Acknowledgments

Excerpts from Nadine Pence Frantz and Mary T. Stimming, eds., *Hope Deferred: Heart
Healing Reflections on Reproductive Loss* (Cleveland: The Pilgrim Press, 2005). Reprinted with
permission.

Moravian Book of Worship, 1995, p. 543 (Interprovincial Board of Communication, Moravian
Church in North America, www.moravian.org). Used with permission.

Excerpts from Research Report: "Beyond the Death of a Child: Social Impacts and Economic Costs Following the Death of a Child" by Dr. Jon Stebbins and Dr. Trevor Batrouney.
Reprinted with permission by The Compassionate Friends Victori Inc., July 2007. ISBN No:
978-0-646-47444-1. www.compassionatefriendsvictoria.org.au.

CONTENTS

PREFACE TO SET

Lucy Bregman

These volumes intend to inform and provoke thought regarding religion, death, and dying. The focus is on the United States today, but to study religion is to study that which is "handed down" and what is experienced now. Therefore to understand it, we must look at its roots, history, and depth in time. Meanwhile, to study death and dying today is to examine a human universal experienced under very novel conditions. As many of the authors in the volumes of this anthology insist, there were traditional ways to face death and die, but by and large, these have been displaced today in this country by the hospital setting and the "medicalization" of death. Indeed, so overwhelming is this new setting and context that to retrieve any of the wisdom of the past, or of alternative perspectives, is daunting. Finally, the face of America has changed, so that increased diversity and increased public awareness of it require attention to religious and cultural traditions long considered exotic and "other." It is this total situation, and openness to discussion of it, which has prompted Praeger to publish this anthology.

This new setting for many discussions of dying and death led us to devise the framework and organization of the anthology. The basic ground plan of this set is to start with understanding the human meanings and implications of medicalized death, then with particular religious responses to it. These concerns constitute Parts I and II of Volume 1. We then turn to special issues and topics of contemporary interest, which for a wide range of reasons do not fit snugly within the parameters of that "medicalized death" umbrella. These are the "special issues" of Volume 2. Finally, because bereavement and the rituals surrounding death are also an important element in religious responses to it and yet seem to escape the medical framework so dominant in the first volume, Volume 3 covers these concerns. Yet even here, some of the dominance of medicine, in the form of public health regulations and a psychiatric stance toward grief, often appear in the background. Some of the principles that have guided our understanding of what to include and how to organize it are important to state here at the very start.

Religious diversity is a fact of American life. Whatever one's personal commitments, it is important for contemporary Americans to recognize and learn something about how different world religions deal with important human concerns, including death, of course. At the most pragmatic level, hospital chaplains, hospice volunteers, and others with direct contact with the dying must accommodate the diverse religious beliefs and practices of their clients and patients, whenever this is possible. Moreover, because religion has a dramatically increased public presence over the past few decades—it is in the news a lot more than before—many persons are rightfully curious about how members of different religions believe and practice. Some of this curiosity may be filled with apprehension: "Do Muslims really advocate suicide for the sake of holy war?" "What happens to unbaptized children, according to Christian teachings?" "Does religion interfere with medical care when it seeks to impose its teachings on terminally ill patients?" Not all questions about religions are motivated by this kind of fearful concern, of course, but we should acknowledge it as a behind-the-scenes motive. However, given the presence of many relatively new immigrants who brought their religious commitments with them to America, curiosity about how Hindus or Buddhists or Jains have retained or accommodated or transformed their faiths once here is an important part of the story for all of us to hear.

Religion matters, but so do other factors and forces. Religion was once predicted to be an illusion that had no future, a leftover from the past that would simply wither away as people became more educated and scientifically oriented. This has not happened. All of the contributions dealing with medicalized death reveal how religion continues to be an element in the specialized setting of the intensive care unit, the emergency room, the hospice program, and so forth. Even those contributors who avoid use of the term "religion" in favor of some more experiential concept of "spirituality" do not deny that such dimensions of human beings as meaning-making creatures really do matter, but it would be ridiculous to ignore other social and psychological factors. That is why, for example, we have a chapter on the impact of inequality of health care for understandings of end-of-life issues of African-Americans. In some of the other chapters, such as the one about caregivers for Alzheimer's patients, gender appears to be a dominant factor because women are the assigned caregivers in our society. Race and gender also appear as important elements of the story in the two chapters on homicide in America and the death penalty. Although there are some disputes about whether the concept of "religion" as a category is useful in all situations, the inter-relations among religious meanings, symbols and rituals, and all the rest of the lives of people are what the contributors to these volumes stress.

Information about religion, dying, death, and bereavement can be presented for general readers by scholars, without demeaning either those readers or ideals of scholarship. Perhaps this is the philosophy behind all Praeger anthologies, but it needs to be stated explicitly here. "The curse of specialist expertise" is one of the problems with contemporary medicine, according to many critics of its dehumanizing effects, but this desire to create and employ a specialist vocabulary that requires translation back into ordinary English has also infiltrated the liberal arts, within which the study of religion, theology, and ethics belongs. What we do as scholars may require long years of training and practice, but we cannot say to nonscholars: "You will have to take on trust that we know what we are talking about, even if it is too obscure and difficult for you to understand." This does not work; in the college classroom, for the media, or for the reading public, this is not an intellectually or morally worthy stance. Some of us are more adept at sharing what we know with others, but in the long run, scholarship is a trust, given to us by society as a whole or by the world community as a whole. We are obligated to return that trust by making available what we know in a form that actually communicates with those who want or need to know. This is why all of the authors writing for this anthology, whatever their scholarly credentials, are able and willing to do what they are doing here. Even when there is necessary technical vocabulary, it is explained carefully, highlighting the context in which it was developed.

Also, religion is not too holy, too "off-limits" to be written about in an academic, scholarly manner. Clearly, there is a difference between "knowledge about" and deep personal "knowing" and experience when it comes to many of the topics covered in this anthology. There are many different types of religious literature and purposes for writing. In this anthology, the assumption is that religion is open to investigation and discussion and, therefore, scholarly inquiry, especially as it makes its presence available in situations of dying, death, and bereavement.

Although it would have been ideal to aim for total coverage, a chapter on every religious tradition and every possible death-related issue, this ideal remains difficult to achieve at this time, within the framework of an anthology of manageable size. We wanted contributions that included a wide range of religious perspectives, but it is apparent that the understandings of some specific religious groups are left out. The same holds for the "coverage" of issues in Volume 2. For example, there is a chapter on homicide and one on "reproductive loss," but there are no chapters specifically about abortion.

Two other principles also need to be stated. Passionate commitment is compatible with good scholarship. We do not ask for "neutrality" on topics such as the death penalty or equal access to healthcare. Our contributors often show how concerned they are about issues of justice, blaming, cruelty, and discrimination. They reveal compassion, indignation, and advocacy of particular solutions over other pathways, but they aim for fair and adequate presentation of the evidence for their views and for an understanding of positions that differ from their own. This stance is particularly apparent when it comes to topics that have a long history of controversy, such as suicide and war. Each contributor writes so that there is room for intelligent disagreement over some choices and so that the full complexity of some of the problems can be appreciated.

There is something about focus on death that brings out a personal dimension in response. Throughout these essays, however scholarly the presentation and arguments, the personal voices of the authors emerge repeatedly. This is most apparent in the chapter on "Navaho (Diné) Narratives of Death and Bereavement," where the primary author retells the stories of the deaths of his relatives. However, the personal voices can be heard in many other contexts. The authors of the chapters covering medicalized death include vignettes of patients whose dying challenged them personally, for instance. The authors of the chapters on AIDS and suicide include personal information about themselves that they will be the first to admit has drastically shaped their approach toward these topics. Scholars today—more than they did a generation ago—accept that this "personal voice" can be relevant and compatible with a truly scholarly presentation. Death and loss seem especially suited to bring this forth, and the editor has honored this and not tried to suppress it.

BRIEF SURVEY OF CONTENTS BY VOLUME

Volume 1 begins with an "Introduction," situating the post-1970s discussion of death and dying in America. It emphasizes the medicalized setting and understandings for encounters with death and, therefore, stresses discontinuities with past worldviews and experiences. This is followed by four chapters that examine this medicalized context from different perspectives. Gelo looks at "The Role of the Professional Hospital Chaplain," whose congregation is often the patients and staff of the intensive care unit or other extraordinary environments. Klink's chapter on "Knowledge-Seeking Wisdom: Health Care Professionals, Religion, and End-of-Life Care" dovetails with this, focused on the explicit and implicit religious factors at work in those who preside over medicalized death. Anderson, on the other hand, writes on "Hospice and Spiritual Needs of the Dying" as a challenge to this environment and its ethos and the efforts of those who see themselves as advocates on behalf of the dying as spiritual beings. Finally, Payne raises issues of social justice and inequalities in health care, particularly as these affect the end-of-life experiences of African-Americans.

Once this portrait of medicalized death has been established, the more explicitly religious responses to it are the subject of the second part of Volume 1. Dorff and McLean, working from within Jewish and Christian traditions, respectively, present accounts of the highly developed medical bioethics approaches found therein. In the case of Hussain's chapter on Muslim approaches, it is clear that some steps also have been taken in North America to move into a similar encounter with the factors and forces depicted earlier in the volume. In contrast, the stories told by Williamson on Hinduism, Mullen on Buddhism, and Chapple on Jainism are stories of relatively recent arrivals, coming here with very rich and long-standing traditions about death and accommodating to utterly new situations. The final chapter in this collection, by Lefler and Wiethaus on the Eastern Band of Cherokee, takes on the question of "Cultural Revitalization and Demedicalized Death," as people long underserved by the health-care system attempt to restore some control over their lives and dying by a rediscovery of their own indigenous resources.

Volume 2 is intentionally a collection of "special issues" that do not seem to fit directly within the frameworks of "medicalized death." Klass's in-depth treatment of the spirituality of bereaved parents in "The Death of a Child" is an example where psychiatric perspectives, and even those of traditional theology, seem deeply inadequate to uncover the realities of this kind of bereavement experience. Related to this is the material covered by Stimming, in "Hope Deferred," that deals with miscarriage, stillbirth, and infertility. The material from this chapter appeared in published form earlier and is far more explicitly theological than are the rest of the chapters in the anthology. The next two special topics are two diseases that pose very distinct and very different moral and religious questions: Alzheimer's, which in Black's chapter leads to a "Folk Morality of Caregiving," and AIDS, the history of which McGinley traces in "A Modern Plague?" In contrast to these two relatively new concerns, those discussed by Stimming in the chapter on suicide are long-standing. What is striking is the recent transformation of religious teachings and practices. The next three essays involve public and legal issues much more directly than do any of the former topics. "Homicide and American Religion" by Pahl traces the history of connections, whereas McAdams focuses on recent, post-1977 legal rulings and arguments surrounding the death penalty. Next, Steffen's discussion of "Warfare Deaths" and the just war arguments takes "death and dying" into the largest, most global context possible. The final chapter in this volume, by Moreman, does something really unique; instead of focusing on death, it examines the debates and discussions over "The Evidence for Life after Death."

Volume 3 presents what people actually do, religiously and culturally, when death approaches, and afterward. Garces-Foley's historical overview of "Funeral and Mourning Rituals in America" sets the stage for particularized religious variations on what has long been the "mainstream" pattern. Alpert's succinct presentation of a Jewish approach focuses on mourning rites as a central contribution to Jewish perspectives on death. There are three chapters on Christian rituals. A chapter by Boisclair documents the Roman Catholic and Eastern Orthodox history and practices, which are heavily sacramental. Meanwhile, Asquith looks closely at Protestantism, which has tried not to be "ritualistic" but nevertheless developed an impressive set of rituals at the time of death and after. Armstrong examines both African and African-American Christian patterns of funerals and bereavement. The remaining chapters include experiences of relatively recent immigrants with ancient traditions. Webb on Muslims in America, Murata on Hindus, and Wilson on Buddhists all show rich specific resources for coping with death and loss, within a new and sometimes confusing setting. The chapter by Shorty and Wiethaus, rich in personal narratives of Navaho (Diné) experiences and rites, shows how substantial particularity remains a feature of the totality of American religion. The final chapter in this volume, Johnson's on civic ritual, looks at public occasions of national mourning, from the death of President Lincoln to mourning the victims of 9/11. These are intended to offer symbols of unity, meaning, and hope in the face of loss.

A final word of caution is that we must all allow that the topics covered in this anthology include many difficult concerns that will not be "solved" quickly, easily, or by one agency (such as government) simply imposing its agenda on everyone else. Indeed, as many thinkers have recognized, death is not a "problem" but a "mystery," meaning that the quest for a "solution" to it may be in vain. Yes, there are specific questions that admit of "solutions," such as whether the death penalty laws should be changed and, if so, how and why. Yet, as the chapter on "Evidence for Life after Death" reveals, those who sought to turn the question of death into something that could be approached "scientifically" and empirically tested ended by floundering in philosophical waters, no matter which side of the controversy they espoused. Although I, the editor, believe that American society today is much less "death-denying" than it was forty or fifty years ago, I do not see this change as a step in an inevitable predetermined direction of "progress." The closer I look at past and present, the more uncomfortable I become with grandiose predictive scenarios of the future. In contrast, humility, compassion, charity, and a concern for justice will abide, come what may. It is with these thoughts in mind that I am honored to present this anthology.

ACKNOWLEDGMENTS

My thanks to all those who contributed to the Praeger anthology on *Religion, Death, and Dying*. I would also like to thank the following persons specifically for their help, support, and advice:

My former and current Chairs at Temple University, Dr. Rebecca Alpert and Dr. Terry Rey; the Chairs of the "Death, Dying and Beyond" Consultation of the American Academy of Religion, Dr. Kathleen Garces-Foley and Dr. Christopher Moreman; Dr. Dennis Klass, Dr. Ulrike Wiethaus, and Dr. Mary Stimming; the editorial staff at Praeger Publishers; and my sister, Emily Rizzo.

A special debt of gratitude to my students in the course on "Death and Dying" over the years.

INTRODUCTION TO SET

Lucy Bregman

Religion, death, and dying: what could be more appropriate and easy to link together? It must seem obvious that religions have always and everywhere been concerned about death, even in prehistoric times when what we now call "religion" was not yet institutionalized. Ancient peoples buried their dead, leaving them grave goods that suggest a hope for rebirth or at least for continued existence. Beliefs about the soul, why death happens, and what comes after: aren't these the core of what religion is really about? And if we focus on America—North America and, in almost all cases in this anthology, the United States of America—we will find a particular geographical and historical setting for this universal link between religion and death.

Unfortunately for those who like universal generalizations, these volumes will not be welded to them, and the above perspective is not going to carry the day. Perhaps it is true that "religion" has always had something to say about "death," but in this introduction, and in what follows, we are going to lay aside terms such as this and proceed to look at *religions* and at death and dying in the current, contemporary context here and now. We will do what religion scholars call contextualizing and historicizing, namely, place our very general terms in specific settings and see how they are used and what stories lie behind these uses. Even the title of our anthology, as we will soon show, has a specific history that defies, to some extent, the assumption that "religion" and "death" always and everywhere belong together.

The structure of the anthology's volumes, as outlined in our brief preface, witnesses to this approach. Volume 1 deals with death *now*, in the context within which it is most often studied and most often occurs. What we will call "medicalized death" can be examined for its religious meanings and implications from the perspectives of various professionals who cope with it and for the particular and startlingly new dilemmas it poses for moral decision making. It can be set up as the new context within which religious traditions—plural—must find a way to continue saying something about death's broader and deeper meanings. The plural is really important, really central to this project. There is not necessarily one entity called "religion," but there are certainly a variety of religious traditions that structure the human encounter with death and dying, each based on its own norms and precedents.

Volume 2 collects a range of topics and issues, all of which have been seen as having some religious implications but which do not necessarily cohere together. Each special topic now has its own history of debate, its literature, and its special contexts. A volume on religion and death in America ought to include such "nonmedical" topics as the debates over capital punishment, homicide in America, and warfare. Not all of these topics are "nonmedical," but the material on AIDS, for instance, includes religious debates relatively unique to discussions of that disease and its spread. The relevant literature on suicide or the deaths of children, likewise, is sufficiently distinct to warrant separate chapters for each one of these three topics.

Finally, there is to be considered what religions have done to ritualize death and to structure and guide the experiences of the bereaved. The third volume deals exclusively with rituals, funerals, and mourning; therefore, this volume would seem to be not only less medical, but also more practical. What do religious people do when a death occurs? Do their actions always reflect perfectly their beliefs and doctrines, or, in many cases, is there no such consistency (nor any demand for it)? Even here, though, a false universalism can hide more interesting stories. True, peoples everywhere, even in prehistoric times, held some rituals at the time of death and showed care and respect for the dead in the manner of burial. However, within our own society and its unusual neglect of public mourning (see below), how do specific religions practice funerals and bereavement, and how much room is given them to express particularities and past traditions?

These three volumes are not meant to be read cover to cover but to be used, we hope, as reference sources for those who want to learn about the wide range of topics and traditions included. However, it would be futile to reintroduce a common topic repeatedly in each and every chapter; therefore, we have tried to cut down on overlap and point readers toward extended discussions that appear earlier in the set. Moreover, not all of the contributors share common assumptions and definitions of terms, and readers should note this. It represents the state of discussions in the fields of both religion study and death studies. What we hope is that the individual chapters will be readable, useful, and exemplify the best current scholarship in these fields.

The title of our anthology is less obvious than it might sound. The topic of "death and dying" is a relatively new one, if we look at the use of this to cover discussions of the human experiences of terminally ill hospital patients. Indeed, the phrase itself is easy to date because it comes from the title of Elisabeth Kübler-Ross's 1968 classic *On Death and Dying*, which began the modern Death Awareness Movement, as it became known.[1] This movement became not just an endeavor of researchers or professionals but as "death education" engaged the imagination of the wider public, including the media. Because the experiences of the dying had received so little attention before this, and because these were swallowed up in the medical understanding of their condition and future prognosis, the Death Awareness Movement continued to focus on what it felt like to be dying within the setting of contemporary high-tech medicine. Along with this went the experiences of the family and friends of the dying, so that a better phrase might have been "dying and bereavement." About death in itself, this body of literature was comparatively reticent, and followed Kübler-Ross, in trying not to ponder what seemed beyond the scope of psychological or therapeutic perspectives. Something was certainly said about death—that it is "a natural part of life" stands out as one of the themes of this literature[2]—but what really became the center of attention were dying and mourning. Once again, we are not just thinking of professionals here, although the very interdisciplinary nature of the Death Awareness Movement has always been one of its strengths. We are thinking too of the many autobiographies focused on terminal illness experiences, on made-for-TV specials that did the same, and on open-to-the-public conferences on death and loss.

Was this focus absolutely new? It felt new, and it was presented as new, especially in contrast to the silence and denial that immediately preceded it. Surprisingly, it was not as new as the Death Awareness Movement made it seem. Particularly because the whole interest seemed to correlate with the rise of high-tech in medical care (for example, intensive care units, which began in the 1960s), it seemed easy to find the Death Awareness Movement's beginnings in the human reaction to the extreme dominance of medical models and understandings. When Marilyn Webb wrote about the movement in her account, *The Good Death: The New American Search to Reshape the End of Life*, this was the cause-and-effect sequence she assumed.[3] Also, the date of *On Death and Dying* is significant; 1968 is the era of the Vietnam War, the counterculture, and the rise of "expressive individualism." Much of the death awareness literature can be placed within the "post-Vietnam ethos" (according to Samuel Southard),[4] which stressed feelings and experiences over rationality, power, and technique. Suspicion of the overly rational, and of the power of "experts" to control the rest of us, marked some of this ethos.

However, there were earlier examples of this protest against the medical model of how to understand illness, suffering, and dying. It may surprise most of us that a book written in 1936, by Cabot and Dicks, *The Art of Ministering to the Sick*, reveals exactly the same portrait of the ultraspecialized medical environment, the powerlessness of the patients, and their inability to make anyone in that environment to attend to what it was like to be a suffering, sick human being.[5] Even by 1936, before the introduction of modern antibiotics (let alone all the really high-tech "stuff"), the problems were in place for all of the subsequent literature to document. It was not that Cabot and Dicks were not grateful to the doctors and hospital staff or that they resented the wonderful scientific progress of medicine in the twentieth century but that progress and the environment that enshrined it proved costly to the humanity of patients, in ways Americans were reluctant to acknowledge. It was a hidden cost. People lived longer and recovered from what earlier would have killed them, but dying as human experience became somehow worse. It was now burdened with the meaning of "medical failure," for which too often the patient seemed to bear the blame.

Moreover, everyone who thought about this situation at all knew that it was new and that things had once been very different. I say "once," but perhaps I should write "once upon a time." As decades passed, memories of "traditional" or old-time dying grew more distant and became tinged with the nostalgia reserved for all things small-town and old-fashioned. Kübler-Ross illustrated this with a vivid scene from her childhood in a Swiss village, where a farmer died at home, surrounded by his family and community.[6] This was the way most people *used* to die, and there was something good about it which is now gone, even though no one seriously wished to reverse the history of medical advances. "Old-time dying" made death "a natural event," a part of life rather than its negation, and was a community experience. Every individual who died left a hole in the social fabric; therefore, bereavement, too, was a part of life rather than repressed or silenced or denied. (To use the specialist term, bereavement was "enfranchised" and required, as opposed to today's "disenfranchised" grief.) This picture of premedicalized death permeates the death awareness literature. Whether the location is a Swiss village, a farm in Minnesota, or indeed anywhere outside the range of Western high-tech medicine almost does not matter. "Traditional dying" was essentially more human than what we have today, the argument goes.

That is why the phrase "death and dying" is not neutral or merely descriptive. It contains within it this contrast between then and now and, therefore, carries a challenge to the dominant medical perspective on illness and death. Although as we will see, doctors, nurses, chaplains, and many other professionals have taken up this challenge and worked very hard over the last forty years to make space for the humanity of their patients, the challenge and the discrepancy remain. Medicalized death means not just death within the hospital or hospice or nursing home building. It means the whole social and cultural context within which medical categories and meanings rule, and other perspectives are squeezed out, or must find some very restricted marginalized space in which to appear at all. The many stories in Volumes 1 and 3, told about patients from backgrounds where other sets of categories and other worldviews reign, bring this disjunction vividly to life for readers.

How has religion appeared or not appeared in this situation? Obviously, the first claim to make is that religions have always dealt with death, have said something about its meanings, and have always been involved in the disposal of the dead. (Note that the latter topic was never a part of Kübler-Ross's approach, and the whole question of funeral rituals has been within the Death Awareness Movement more or less subsumed under studies of mourning and "the grief process.") What is astonishing, however, is that after this claim is made, the contribution of religions to contemporary discussions of dying under medicalized conditions is very limited. The reason for this is definitely not that the Death Awareness Movement was hostile to religion or militantly secular. From its inception, some of its strongest advocates were chaplains. Even when conventional religion was criticized for aiding in "denial of death," those who voiced this often did so on behalf of a more courageous, full-bodied faith. For example, an early anthology edited by Kübler-Ross included contributions by spokespersons from religions who chimed in with the dominant theme that death was to be "accepted" as "a natural part of life."[7]

However, the new problems and issues did not seem to mesh at all well with the traditional resources and wisdom of religion. Yes, major religions had a lot of say about death and its ultimate eschatological (literally, "last things") meaning, but how did that really relate to the fears, decisions, and denials of the terminally ill hospitalized patient? Significantly, even in that 1936 book, the role of the hospital chaplain is to become "patient advocate," counteracting "the evils of specialism" (reliance on extreme technical expertise) rather than a specialist in religious doctrines or rites.[8] The chaplain as patient advocate is the least likely staff member to be bound to medical jargon, is able to see and honor the patient as suffering person rather than diseased organism, and to deliver what is now known as "spiritual care," whether or not this occurs within the framework of traditional religious categories. We will see, within the chapters of these books, how the shift toward language of "spirituality" helps those who fulfill this role. Within the setting of medicalized dying, the preference for "spirituality" over "religion" loses much of its usual either/or edge and becomes a way to place the chaplain on the side of the patients rather than as one more specialist expert (see especially the chapter by Florence Gelo in Volume 1).

Yet, surely religions have had resources that could be drawn upon to address just this plight of the patient as person? Even though the setting is utterly different from that of "traditional dying," does that make the specific teachings of various religions irrelevant? We will see that the answer to this question is "no, but." Note that this manner of posing the question treats religions as storehouses of ideas, images, rites, and practices, storehouses that can be mined or drawn upon very selectively. To use another, more frequently appearing image, modern American religion can be a kind of supermarket, where consumers wander down the aisles and pick and chose what they personally at the moment need or want. Nowhere is this more evident than in the way bits and pieces of Christianity, Buddhism, and Native American traditions are mixed-and-matched by the dying, whose autobiographies (and personal stories written by surviving relatives) are filled with poignant examples of this. What are the Tibetan temple bells doing at the lesbian wedding of the cancer sufferer and her partner? Why would a young and very nontraditional dying American Quaker want to hold a "Stations of the Cross" devotion for himself? A category such as "secular" or "secularization" surely does not cover what is happening here, but what does? The authors of these chapters will all have their own insights on these processes.

Scholars of religion have debated what terms to use and how appreciative or condemnatory to be toward this phenomenon. Are terms such as "syncretism" and "hybridization" better than just "consumer religion"? Is this reduction of religious traditions that once functioned as "sacred canopies" and wisdom traditions for entire societies, down to "resources" to be selected by individuals as needed in a decline or an advance, and for whom? From the perspective of the official spokespersons for religious traditions (and not all religions have such a clear-cut role), "syncretism" or "consumer religion" is often equated with "diluted religion," religion too accommodated to contemporary norms to be authentically itself. For example, one voice from the Roman Catholic tradition calls for Catholic funerals to be solely focused on the death and resurrection of Jesus Christ. They are *not* to "celebrate the life" of the deceased person, and any departure from this principle would be a betrayal of the faith.[9] Alternatively, others celebrate the "little stories" that elevate individual experience, spirituality, and life story over the norms and official narratives of any tradition. The chapter by Dennis Klass on "The Death of a Child" in Volume 2 embodies this approach, but the tension and complexity of many of the essays in these volumes come in part from their authors' awareness of this pervasive dilemma.

Even the category of "religion" has come under close scrutiny. If we start from Christianity, it looks obvious. "Religion" is based on beliefs, a community, an institution, the church, which is separated from the state, and so on. "Religion" is based on personal beliefs, and one joins or drops out depending on these beliefs (or those of one's parents). Everyone is entitled to one religion or none, but in our normal understanding, no one can truly and authentically hold two religions simultaneously. Alas, it now appears that this model does not fit all cases. Even some of our names for world religions are suspect, so that the label "Hinduism" is more or less a European concept applied to the vast and heterogenous practices and teachings of traditional India. This discovery has been used to argue against the category of "religion" and certainly against the organization of a book into chapter-by-chapter treatment of "world religions." Indeed, "world religions" could be just an invention at the original 1893 Parliament of World Religions in Chicago. Some religion scholars now spend a lot of time on this issue. For some, the whole construction imposes upon the non-Christian and non-European populations of the world (including immigrants to the United States) an understanding that violates their own conceptions.[10]

Nevertheless, we want to keep this framework, including the implication that there is a totality of "world religions," now available and active within American borders. There are two reasons for this decision. The first is that whatever the questionable colonialist origins of the "world religions" framework, it has worked well enough for over hundred years to serve as a guide for readers of these volumes. People begin from where they are coming from, and for many potential readers, questions such as "What do Muslims believe about suicide?" or "Why do Buddhists prefer cremation?" may be the most natural starting point. That is because this anthology is written for a North American nonspecialist readership, not for religious studies scholars. The latter have also learned, by and large, that exact definitions of "religion" are less important than the value of particular definitions to uncover certain interesting and valid aspects of human beings. Therefore, because the "world religions" model is what by now is familiar to most of us, that is what we will rely upon, although individual authors will surely want to challenge particular instances and applications of it.

There is a second reason to accept "religion" as a category and, along with it, the theme of diversity of religions within our contemporary society. This is the constitutional protection offered to "free exercise of religion," protection that does not stop at the hospital admissions desk. This right to free exercise of religion does not trump every other factor, but it helps patients and their families cope with the monolithic nature of the hospital environment and its dominant values. To put this very simply, we have in this country one medical system. Hospitals and insurance health coverage are not "pluralistic," there are no competing rival established philosophies/institutions. To go into the hospital means to be subject to the same universal rules and scientific frameworks, wherever. Credentials for staff, health regulations, and so on may vary as far as living up to standards, but those standards are there for all. There is no equivalent to

Democrat and Republican Party structures and candidates in American health care, nor is there any equivalent to Canadian bilingualism, where in one part of the country French is the preferred language. We have alternative and adjunctive therapies, but these do not displace our one set of large-scale, highly regulated medical institutions. No one seriously imagines that this situation could be truly different. Unlike railroads that initially were built with different gauge tracks, or the PC versus Mac situation today, the contemporary hospital and Western medical system was never the product of competing entrepreneurial business interests.

However, there *are* a plurality and diversity of religions, and to the extent that the patient remains a legal human being when he or she enters the hospital (or visits the clinic or becomes a resident in the nursing home), he or she retains the constitutional right to free exercise of religion. This right is taken for granted in almost all cases. The exceptions are what make news and have generated a probably misleading sense that religion "interferes" with or conflicts with medicine because some people will not accept medical treatment for their children or will not allow blood transfusions. Yes, these cases do exist, but the actual overall situation is rather different. Forget the much overblown "battle between science and religion" and look at the history of how public medical care developed.

Over the nineteenth century in the United States, religious groups went into the business of establishing hospitals, along with schools and colleges. There were even instances where, despite formal separation of church and state, some Western states opted to delegate all public responsibility for inpatient healthcare to orders of Roman Catholic nursing sisters! These religious organizations were the best prepared to shoulder such burdens in underfunded and underorganized municipalities. Many of the hospitals in Philadelphia, for example, have names that echo that era: Methodist, Presbyterian, Episcopal, St. Agnes. The story of how these institutions became more and more separate from their religious parent bodies may be a legitimate instance of "secularization" because no one now expects that all of the doctors and nurses at Presbyterian Medical Center are themselves Presbyterian Christians, nor is there anything distinctively Calvinist about the medical care patients receive there. This is a case, not of "religion's" interference with "science," but of the gradual "functional autonomy" of institutions, paralleled by the functional autonomy of schools and colleges with religious beginnings such as Temple University, where I teach.

However, as autonomously functioning medicine developed and created new situations that called for decisions at the levels of hospital policy, not just individual views and opinions of doctors, the contemporary specialized and secular hospital environment emerged, as it had by the time of the 1936 book of Cabot and Dicks. Within this setting, as new medical treatments led to new decisions and dilemmas—or rethinking of very traditional ones—a discipline of biomedical ethics emerged. Some of its pioneer thinkers drew on religious ethics and formulated principles and values that were intended to guide those who worked in the health care setting. Issues that have received the most publicity include how far a hospital must go to preserve the life of the patient, when the latter's condition is obviously terminal and his or her life depends entirely on artificial means of support. Even more strikingly new is the whole question of organ donation; when, if at all, is it right to deal with one nearly dead person as a field from which organs may be "harvested," so that another desperately ill person may have a chance at life? Some of the chapters in Volume 1 explicitly cover this kind of biomedical ethics and its history, but although the founders of this field in the mid-twentieth century include figures associated very explicitly with religious traditions, this religious element has faded in terms of how actual hospital policies work and how bioethics committees in hospitals function.

Instead, "religion" has been preserved in the patients' right to free exercise, in their right to refuse or insist, based on their own personal choice of religious teachings. These are the cases that are most often newsworthy. Other sorts of "free exercise" examples exist, however. Suppose as part of one's Native American heritage, smoke rituals for healing are considered vital and intrinsic to care for the sick. Once one enters the hospital, one is brought into the realm of medicalized death, where the official meanings and official health regulations hold sway. A fire in a room where oxygen is stored is a hazard. It cannot be permitted in the hospital patient's room. Period. However, "free exercise of religion" carries moral and some limited legal weight. A solution (worked out in Minneapolis, apparently) is to set aside one space in the hospital where smoke rites for healing are permitted, and Native American patients have the right to be temporarily moved there so as to give them a chance to practice their religion. In this case, it may not matter that such peoples originally had no separate concept of "religion;" today, in Minnesota, "religion" as a constitutionally guaranteed freedom can work to their benefit. It carries moral credibility to honor and permit otherwise dangerous practices to grant the patients not just their legal rights but perhaps more basically the human dignity for which the Death Awareness Movement has struggled. Religion's free exercise is not an absolute right anywhere; it can be overridden in a variety of settings, but the importance of keeping the right in mind means that concerned hospital staff (including Christian chaplains, in this example) will try to work out something that permits religious practices even in the home realm of medicalized death. We will find many examples of this in the chapters that follow.

There are, however, two places or areas where this very American special niche for "religion" becomes important for many of our contributions. Perhaps those who question the category of "religion" as appropriate for the sacred traditions of India and elsewhere are really trying to suggest that the roles and spaces for these traditions were always so different than what Westerners used to Christianity might expect: that confusion results when we impose the category itself. The role of religious specialists is one source of such confusion. Christianity's clergy are priests and pastors, and they appear through many of the chapters that follow, in all sorts of situations befitting these roles. They advise the daughter of a suicide, for example, that the church no longer will refuse to bury her mother and provide counsel and guidance for her. They join together in organizations to issue statements on questions such as the morality of capital punishment. They are visible community leaders in local activities, such as Memorial Day celebrations. However, not all religious specialists from other traditions take on these tasks. The Hindu priest is a ritual specialist, not a pastor or community leader. Yet, here in America, the pressure is on such specialists to fit more and more within the model conveniently provided of "Christian minister." We will note how this works at the time of death, at the occasion of funeral and mourning rites, but also in preparation for death and in dealing with hospitals, funeral homes, and other professionals. When traditional ritual specialists cannot or will not fit into this expected role, lay leaders fill in, and the tradition itself is subtly transformed. Indeed, the very categories of "clergy" and "lay" must be scrutinized to watch these transformations occur.

The second point is that "religion" was learned in diffuse ways when it worked as the "sacred canopy" of an entire society. It was learned everywhere, but maybe nowhere in particular. At homes, in the local community centers, in temples or mosques; it was learned in ways closer to the way children acquire language, than to any method of formal instruction. I am tempted to say "by osmosis." Just by growing up as a member of a society, one absorbed it. Perhaps specialized expertise required something more deliberate, such as an apprenticeship or becoming a disciple, but the average person did not experience this, nor did he/she feel it was needed. However, in our society, it appears this method does not work, and virtually all religious groups have had to adapt to new understandings of how religion is transmitted across generations. Most, at least as seen through these chapters, have followed the Protestant Christian Sunday school model. This means children are given intentional instruction, perhaps combined with language and cultural history, probably taught not just by "clergy" but by lay volunteers. These are likely to be women, whatever the official traditional views on gender and religious leadership. Although there may be all sorts of advantages and positive outcomes to this pattern for "teaching religion," it is very unlikely that such Sunday schools will include direct acquaintance with death. Dying and funeral preparations will happen elsewhere, but they will not necessarily even be able to include children. The home deathbed scene witnessed by Kübler-Ross as a child back in Switzerland will not be duplicated in an American Sunday school, even when all the adults are committed to overcome societal denial of death. This is the kind of situation so taken for granted today that all of our authors tacitly assume it. What "death education" means in this new religious setting is more likely to resemble school discussions about grief and loss, now common when a classmate dies, than the kind of day-to-day familiarity with dying and death an older generation took for granted.

I have written as if the hospital (and nursing homes) were the only home of medicalized death, but of course, that is misleading. Medicine and medical categories for understanding illness and death are part and parcel of our entire society's way to face mortality. Any other language is subordinate, permitted only on the margins, or used by individuals in that pick-and-choose shopping mode. As I write this, Ted Kennedy's brain cancer is, of course, a political story, but the first on the spot to deal with it is the medical reporter for the local all-news radio station. What kind of cancer, and what are the treatment options and survival rate? These are the kinds of questions raised first, even in the absence of any specific information from the senator's doctors, and this information is what goes on the news immediately. It is, however, a sign of the success of the Death Awareness Movement in supplementing if not challenging this language, that the next part of the news story dealt with Senator Specter, who is himself a brain cancer survivor, and his encouragement to his fellow legislator. This is what is different now from when Kübler-Ross wrote, for fellow patients speak up, tell their stories, and contribute to the awareness that life-threatening illness is a human experience better faced with others than alone.

What is very significant is that this current news story is in no way a "religion story." Senator Kennedy may have been visited by his parish priest, just as a Native American patient in the same hospital might request to be moved to the "smoke room" so that the family could perform a ritual of healing there, but the free exercise of religion by individuals does not make this a "religion story," and the role of religion in interpreting illness, death, and bereavement seems minimal or obscure. When a public figure dies, the stock phrase "He lost his battle with cancer" reveals our medicalized conception of what matters, but that individual's spiritual struggles in the hour of his or her death (or, more likely today, in the months or weeks leading up to this) go unrecorded by the media in all but a very few cases. How did this happen? Is this a true case of "secularization"? When did religion lose its ground to be the mainstream interpreter of public events or of any events in the lives of public figures? Put this way, we assume that once upon a time, religion did have this role and that its ideas and images and performed rites were the primary language for coping with the same realities now covered in medicalized terminology. Is this assumption accurate? Or is it closer to the nostalgic portrait of "traditional dying," which captures something true but hides a lot as well? Maybe the questions themselves are wrongly phrased, and we need to step back and say: what do we know has changed? When? Why? Many of the contributors to these volumes will have their own answers and, indeed, their own ways to re-pose such questions. Here, however, are some of mine.

I am convinced that one very un-nostalgic fact about "traditional" versus "modern" dying is that the demographics were utterly different. Regardless of whether medical or religious categories or both were relied upon by ordinary persons or specialists, the bottom line is that up through the 1870s in North America (and a lot longer elsewhere), the most likely group of persons to die were infants and young children. When a preacher presiding at a funeral in 1920 stated that one-third of the human race dies before leaving childhood, he was already out of date, but he might be excused because the shift had occurred only a few decades before. Some time during this fifty-year period, death went from being associated with extreme youth and vulnerability to a fate linked with old age. Did this make death more "natural" or easier to accept? Obviously, based on what most writers believe, the answer is no, but it changed the pervasiveness of death, its nearness to all the living, and, of course, it changed the experiences of parenting and family life. Death was closer to the midst of daily life, not just because it happened in homes rather than hospitals but because it happened to the young and the old. Even the "old" were not so "old" as we now take for granted. (There is a lot of evidence that people in the past were already more debilitated by their thirties than modern persons by their fifties and sixties; that is, of course, for the adults who survived childhood.)

Death also happened more quickly. Not always, of course, but the kinds of bacterial diseases kids died from did not usually span the months and sometimes years of contemporary terminal illnesses such as cancer or AIDS. Diaries from one hundred and fifty years ago or more reveal tragic patterns, when families experienced the deaths of several children all in the course of a few weeks. Yes, tuberculosis killed young adults slowly, but the suddenness of many deaths really was part of the normal picture. Add to this memories of epidemics, where out-of-control death rates left unburied corpses and social networks in ruins. Some of these epidemics happened in far-off places (yellow fever at the Panama Canal diggings), but others happened in American cities; for example, cholera in Philadelphia. Sudden death, against which medicine could do almost nothing, was part of the cultural scene, even as memory by 1900 when the infant death rates were dropping. The story of that era is often excluded from the Death Awareness Movement, and the transition out of it was due not to what we would consider high-tech medical advances but to relatively simple public health measures such as protected drinking water and central heating for homes.

Sudden death was not considered a kind of blessing, a shortcut, or a relatively painless exit without all the mess of extended illness. Today, it has these meanings and is, in fact, the preference of about 95 percent of the population. When a local politician running for mayor dropped dead mid-campaign, the universal reaction was that, if he had to have died now, he was fortunate to have died in the midst of doing something he loved best. In the past, sudden death was not necessarily so instantaneous, nor was it painless. (Remember, a high proportion of those dying were small children.) However, it had one additional feature that was genuinely frightening: it caught persons "unprepared," unable to stand before God at the moment of death with their lives and failures sorted out and cleared up. Dying "unprepared" meant a missed opportunity for adults to die as full, conscious, morally aware human beings. Some ideal of the well-prepared-for death continued to dominate persons in this country, right up through around that period in the 1920s when the medicalized framework began its ascendancy. Such an ideal still lingers; it has not totally vanished. Elderly Roman Catholic nursing home patients in Stearns County, Minnesota, say their rosaries and prepare for death and do not need Kübler-Ross and specialized death education to help them, but they now stand out, lingering remnants of "traditional dying" that included this element of religious preparation and the ideal of a life lived and about to be completed face-to-face with God.

These background factors, I believe, have to be considered when one looks at how religion appears to have receded in contemporary life or lost its moorings and visibility in public space. There are countless examples of persons finding God, or learning the truth of Buddhist nonattachment, in hospital settings now. What is missing is the sense of a shared cultural ideal pattern, implicit in hopes that death could be meaningful and dignified, but also in fears of dying suddenly and unprepared. As with Tony Walter's discussion of *The Eclipse of Eternity*[11] among the English, it is not so much personal belief that has diminished, it is the shared social space in which it might have found a home and a voice. Even when more and more "public space" has been granted to religion—amid great contention in some areas—the silence of religious voices and perspectives in regard to death so far remains. Remember that "he lost his battle with cancer" and not "he made his peace with God" is the normal way a death is announced today. Even if many of us will agree privately that the latter statement is of more ultimate importance and has eternal meaning for the individual person who died (the cancer is merely temporal), this dimension of contemporary dying and death remains off limits for public view. For our topic, this fact appears tied not just or even primarily to high-tech medicine but to changed demographics and patterns of experience with death.

Additional support for this comes from tracing the patterns and practices of one area shunned by medicalized death: funerals and mourning rituals. Medicine deals with the living and the recently dead insofar as they are resources for organ donation or dissection. It does not cover nonpatients, who in this case are surviving friends and family members. Funerals and mourning are the entire subject of our Volume 3, and as "bereavement" or "the grief process," this has held its place in the scope of the Death Awareness Movement. However, the background story for funerals and mourning lies untold in most death-awareness treatments, especially those that focus exclusively on the psychology of grieving. When medicalized death became the primary language of mainstream American society, it is hard to see what happened to those aspects of death that could not be encompassed or directly encountered by medicine and its categories.

As with "all religions deal with death," all cultures and historical eras feature some rites of funeral and some mourning practices. This generalization has, however, a special edge to it which needs explaining. Premodern funerals and mourning were sometimes stark and simple, sometimes really elaborate. In fact, ours—and that means contemporary postindustrial Western society as a whole—is just about the *only* historical example of a culture that has eliminated obligatory mourning rites. These did not disappear totally, but they disappeared massively—and fast. Just at the same time when death rates for the very young dropped precipitously, so too did the "standard traditional American funeral" become a fixed pattern. For Gary Laderman, in *The Sacred Remains*, the standard pattern is in place by 1883. His sequel to this book, *Rest in Peace*, charts controversies about funerals, but that pattern retains its hold.[12] Meanwhile, everything else changes: gone are elaborate mourning clothes, restrictions on activities of the bereaved, and the specialized social role of "mourner." Today, look out at any group of Americans, and no one could tell from our dress or even our demeanor which of us are among the recently bereaved.[13] This change happened right after World War I and was often perceived at the time as cultural liberation. It was also tied to feminism because the most burdensome restrictions of mourning had fallen upon women, and to discard these was a sign that one was modern, progressive, and future-oriented. Lack of public mourning was no longer a sign of disrespect for the dead because no amount of mourning would bring them back. This major shift left the funeral as the only site of traditional grief and the only place where thinking about death at all was obligatory. As Laderman and some of the authors in these books will point out, funerals are and have been for decades the sources of certain contentions, but they are, for mainstream Americans, over quickly. The chapter on American funerals by Kathleen Garces-Foley that introduces Volume 3 reviews and expertly interprets this story of relative continuity and specialized sites of contention.

This leaves any mandatory traditional religious or cultural expression of extended mourning in some conflict with the normal pattern (which, remember, is historically and cross-culturally as abnormal as one can imagine!). Pressure to get on with life, to shorten mourning periods such as

Judaism's Shiva and its equivalents in other traditions, are immense and all-pervasive. If the old-time role of public mourner was a matter of social convention and control, grief as private psychological process—what we now are left with—is intensely policed. Grieving that is too extreme, too disruptive of social requirements such as employment, and grieving that lasts too long: again and again, there are warnings about such problems in the clinical literature. The Death Awareness Movement has, however, opened up space for the voices of the bereaved; increasingly, these voices have asked, "Who sets the boundaries for length and depth of mourning?" and "Why should 'get on with it' be the only message mourners hear from nonmourning others?" The disappearance of mourner as a public, shared social role goes hand in hand with the story of the triumph of medicalized death.

What was religion's role in this shift? Did religious leaders fight tooth and nail to retain public mourning and all the practices of the mid-nineteenth century that embodied it? No, not at all. In this case, far from religion taking on the task of unqualified endorsement of "traditional" values, the Protestant Christian clergy often found themselves in the role of critics of elaborate, "pagan" funerals.[14] The American way of death, as in place by 1883, was ostentatious, overburdening the poor with the show of costly funerals, and glorified and exalted the body over the soul. These same criticisms were repeated for at least the next eighty years, sometimes with more emphasis on consumer movement values and less on Plato, but even so, religion is and was an uncertain ally in the battles over funerals and mourning. The paradox is that what had come to seem "traditional" in the way of funerals had little intrinsically to do with Christian theological norms and much more to do with personal bonds and memories between the recently deceased and the mourners.

Curiously, however, despite religious and cultural and ethnic diversity in North America, the standard traditional funeral and the disappearance of the role of the public mourner affected all newcomers and immigrant groups, whatever their religious heritage. Just as hospital rules about what rituals might not be performed because of safety reasons impacted how the right to free exercise of religion might operate, so public health regulations about bodies and the practices of funeral homes left some traditional practices impossible to perform legally. For example, any rite that requires the sacrifice of animals on the spot as an element in a human's funeral will be performed clandestinely, if at all. Crematoria in this country must use certain technologies, regardless of how cremation was handled in India or the Far East. New immigrant groups may hold as their ideal burial or cremation back in their homeland, but the expense and trouble—it is extremely complicated legally to ship human remains across international borders—means that such nearer-to-hand choices and restrictions are a pervasive part of how "immigrant religion" works.

So far, I have addressed the question of medicalized death as the contemporary context for death and dying in America now and have said something about the nonrole of public mourning and the potential conflict this creates for all religious and cultural traditions. However, there are obviously a lot of matters left out. Kübler-Ross dealt only with slowly dying hospital patients, not with the murdered, or suicides, or those who die in battle. The Death Awareness Movement has addressed dying and grieving as psychological conditions, but not adequately as legal issues. Moreover, although the movement attempted to teach that "death is natural," this never worked for certain types of death. Not just homicides, but deaths that are in any way human-caused create special challenges to any model of death as natural event. In addition, the psychological model (such as all "stages of grieving" assume) cannot cope well with the disintegration of psyche itself, such as in Alzheimer's disease. These threaten our very idea of a coherent "self" with memories and identity, a "self" that psychological perspectives normally take for granted. Finally, some deaths are widely perceived as morally problematic and bitterly contested. Is capital punishment a "death and dying" issue, a legal issue, a moral issue? In some respects, it is all three. The chapters in Volume 2 of this anthology are intended to cover these specialized topics, but they do not all become separate topics for the same reasons. What may mark them off is how unrelated the literature on these particular topics is to the more widespread discussions of the Death Awareness Movement. Debates over capital punishment, for example, are specialized and depend on arguments and precedents going back way, way before modern methods of inflicting capital punishment and are overwhelmingly unrelated to the "medicalized death" concerns that permeate Volume 1. AIDS, on the other hand, is clearly a medical topic, and the literature on this includes discussions of viruses and T-cells. However, AIDS—almost alone among current life-threatening diseases—has been argued in the recent past as a moral issue, using categories of guilt and responsibility that make it closer to car accident deaths (where the driver is responsible, but he/she and all the passengers may suffer death). Although there are lots of separate topics covered in Volume 2, others were left out. Once again, I believe the topics here have no necessary similarity or connection to one another.

Is the study of death, dying, and religion in America a moving target? Are we the contributors to this anthology telling a story whose plotline is still in progress, and are we unaware of how it will shift in the near future? Remember how often narratives of religion in the century just past were fixed by a scenario of "secularization," with the expectation that religion was now an illusion with an ever-shrinking future? I think the background belief of many who told the story this way was that religion would become like horse racing: once the sport of kings, but today of interest to very, very few. So far, as of now, this is not the way the story of religion in

America turned out. This may be its condition in Western Europe today, but not here or in most parts of the world from which new immigrants to North America originate.

Nor has the story of death and dying turned out as Kübler-Ross and the early advocates of the Death Awareness Movement hoped: we have not transformed our hospitals or our social attitudes toward death sufficiently to make the entire topic simply "a natural part of life." Indeed, imagery of "natural" seems among the most problematic of ways to understand or change American practices. "Natural" seems both universal and somehow "scientific" or at least biological, but again and again, we find stories of decisions, choices, and human tinkering intrinsic to the contemporary scenes of dying. This is not "inauthentic" and "unnatural," it is part and parcel of responsible behavior in the face of medicalized and other human deaths today. People make choices, and just as surely attempt to live up to those choices, to become the kind of persons whose characters can abide by what they as moral agents have chosen. The clearest example of this may be the caretakers of Alzheimer's disease patients, whose moral dilemmas and sufferings are depicted in Helen Black's chapter in Volume 2. Religions clearly contribute to this process of sustaining and enriching the spiritual lives of those dying and mourning, but to see this at work and explain it carefully and thoughtfully, we must acknowledge that it is a work of cultural activity, where some ideal of a "natural" baseline is a deceptive dead end.

Yet, as we will see from the chapters in the anthology, some things have changed, and some trends remained relatively continuous. To write the history (of religion or death) of the future is beyond any of us. The AIDS epidemic stands as one warning to those who predict a future of linear medical progress toward longer, healthier lives for all. Another limit might be the changing patterns of immigration, affected by global economic conditions as much as by one country's laws. Imagine an American future in which the continuous presence of immigrants had ceased, not through tough legislation but for other reasons. Should this happen, the stories of Hindus, Buddhists, and Muslims as told in some of our chapters will be once-upon-a-time tales of a unique era, rather than a sign of the way things will continue to be for future generations. These are only two possible forces or factors to keep in mind before we project our hopes toward the future. Those of us who study death ought above all modestly to recognize that limitation on our powers of prediction.

NOTES

1. Elisabeth Kübler-Ross, *On Death and Dying* (New York: Macmillan, 1968).

2. Lucy Bregman, *Beyond Silence and Denial: Death and Dying Reconsidered* (Louisville, KY: Westminster John Knox, 1999), 43–76.

3. Marilyn Webb, *The Good Death: The New American Search to Reshape the End of Life* (New York: Bantam Books, 1999), 28.

4. Samuel Southard, "Development and Direction of Thanatology Literature," *Death and Dying: A Bibliographical Survey* (Westport, CT: Greenwood Press, 1991), xxx.

5. Richard C. Cabot and Russell L. Dicks, *The Art of Ministering to the Sick* (New York: Macmillan, 1957 [1936]).

6. Kübler-Ross, *op. cit.*, 5.

7. Elisabeth Kübler-Ross, ed., *Death: The Final Stage of Growth* (Englewood Cliffs, NJ: Prentice-Hall, 1975).

8. Cabot and Dicks, *op. cit.*, 7.

9. Archbishop John Myers, "Reports and Policies for Funeral Liturgies Need Clarification," Roman Catholic Archdiocese of Newark, http://www.rcanorg/archbish.

10. For example, see Manuel A. Vasquez, "Historicizing and Materializing the Study of Religion: the Contribution of Migration Studies," in *Immigrant Faiths: Transforming Religious Life of America*, ed. Karen I. Leonard et al., (Lanham, MD: Rowan & Littlefield, 2005).

11. Tony Walter, *The Eclipse of Eternity* (Houndsmith, UK: Macmillan Ltd., 1996).

12. Gary Laderman, *The Sacred Remains: American Attitudes Toward Death, 1799-1883* (New Haven, CT: Yale University Press, 1996) and *Rest in Peace: A Cultural History of Death and the Funeral Home in Twentieth-Century America* (New York: Oxford University Press, 2003).

13. I am indebted to Terry Tafoya for this observation.

14. Andrew Blackwood, *The Funeral: A Sourcebook for Ministers* (Philadelphia: Westminster Press, 1942), 76.

CHAPTER I

Funeral and Mourning Rituals in America: Historical and Cultural Overview

Kathleen Garces-Foley

Given the diversity of people who have claimed America as their home over the last five hundred years, it should not surprise us that their funeral rites and mourning practices have varied tremendously throughout those centuries and across the land. Although many scholars have tried to identify an "American way of dying," borrowing the title of Jessica Mitford's 1963 best-selling tirade against the funeral industry, it is the goal of this volume to resist the simplifying appeal of such a claim. Instead, the contributing authors provide rich descriptions of the diversity of religious responses to death—the diversity between and within religious traditions—as they have been enacted in the American cultural context. Religious traditions from all reaches of the globe are now practiced in America, but trying to pin down what is meant by the "American cultural context," we find ourselves again on shaky ground. Even if we narrow our focus to the death practices common among the majority of Americans (middle-class, white Protestants), these have changed considerably since the European colonization of America to today. A comprehensive understanding of funeral and mourning practices in America must take into account these historical developments and the experiences of those outside the middle-class majority. On the other hand, the diverse experiences of American culture were shaped by such factors as religion, ethnicity, nationality, region, class, and gender.

The focus of this volume is the postmortem activities of religious practitioners stretching from the preparation of the body for disposal and ending with mourning rituals. Readers seeking to learn more about religious approaches to the dying process, medical issues, and the like should consult Volume 1 about medicalized death. The task of this introductory chapter is to provide an overview of the breadth and depth of American religious responses to death. Working chronologically, we begin with the first peoples on the land before turning to the European colonizers and waves of immigrants that followed them and are still coming. Their traditional ways of dealing with death have been adapted to varying degrees to the American culture by choice and fiat. By the twentieth century, a powerful funeral industry had taken the preparation and burial of the dead out of the hands of their families and religious communities. In recent years, Americans have sought to reclaim some control from the funeral industry and to reassert personal values, religious and otherwise, into funerary practices. In the subsequent ten chapters, the reader will discover in greater detail how followers of specific religious traditions have responded to death in the American context. Taken together, these chapters provide a comprehensive account of American *ways* of dying, or more accurately, American funeral and mourning practices.

DEATH IN NATIVE AMERICA

One often hears today about the religious diversity of the United States of the twenty-first century but very little about the religious diversity that existed at the time of the European invasion. Historians have identified at least 550 societies in North America with distinct languages and cultures. When Europeans first encountered Native Americans, they considered them "heathens" lacking any sense of religion. For example, Christopher Columbus wrote in 1492, "I believe that they would easily be made Christians, for they appear to me to have no religion."[1] In reality, Native Americans then and now have complex religious systems thoroughly integrated into their everyday cultural traditions rather than differentiated in a category of "religion." Consequently, they did not hold their beliefs and practices to be universally true but expected different peoples to have their own religiocultures. Another source of misunderstanding between Native Americans and Europeans was the concept of divinity. Indians had a wide range of beliefs in supernatural beings and sacredness, which missionaries and early scholars often translated into a monotheistic framework for evangelistic and analytic convenience. Although many tribes did have a concept of a creator god, they also understood themselves as inhabiting a world imbued with sacredness. Christian notions of a spiritual/material divide were foreign to the native worldviews. Most importantly for our focus on death, Native Americans utilized ritual as a primary means of interacting with the sacred world surrounding them. This world included the ancestors or living dead who remained integral to sustaining communal life. The ancestors are called upon to provide assistance in hunting, fertility, and healing and to intervene with other spirits. In exchange, the living offered veneration and material gifts.

Before the arrival of Europeans, the funeral rites of Native Americans varied widely from large-scale communal ceremonies to smaller family rituals. There is evidence of burial, cremation, and exposure often on raised burial platforms. Burial could be earth burial or entombment in a cave or clay container, and in some cases, groups engaged in "secondary burial." For example, the Algonquin of the Northeastern region hunted in small family groups and buried their dead immediately after death. They believed that the souls of the dead remained close by the grave until the body had decomposed and the bones had been reburied in a communal grave. The reburial occurred every eight to twelve years when groups gathered to perform the feast of the dead. In preparation, family members would disinter the remains, clean the bones, and dress them in new clothes for the feast. Only when all the bones were reburied together in a central grave were the souls finally released to travel to the world of the dead.[2] On the California central coast, Chumash Indians interred their dead in a sitting position within a burial pit containing everyday objects needed for survival. The Chumash covered the eyes of the dead with poppy flowers so they could see on their journey to Shimilaqsa, the land of the dead. Chumash burial was accompanied by a feast thrown by the family, but like the Algonquin on the east coast, the Chumash joined together for a collective mourning ceremony every few years. Instead of reburying the remains, Chumash families would throw images of the recent dead into a large fire. Both the small and large ceremonies were accompanied by processions, dances, and songs.[3]

DEATH IN THE COLONIES

From the beginning of European colonization of the "new world," attitudes toward death, beliefs about the afterlife, and funeral practices were important markers of identity separating native from colonist, Protestant from Catholic, African from European, and rich from poor. The Catholics arrived first, bringing with them elaborate liturgical and sacramental practices that depended on the availability of a priest to perform them. On the West Coast, Spanish soldiers were accompanied by Franciscan priests who established missions, but on the East Coast, Catholics settled in Maryland with little institutional support. Ideally, Catholics would receive the sacrament of the last rites before death and take advantage of this last chance to repent and receive forgiveness before their postmortem journey. Although necessary for the forgiveness of sins and eventual reception into heaven, the sacrament did not guarantee a direct entry into heaven. Apart from the saintly, most were destined to spend time in the state of purgatory expiating their sins. After a death, the faithful gather for a funeral mass and burial designed to aid the souls on their heavenly journey by asking that God mercifully shorten the duration of this purification period.

After the Reformation, Protestant Christians defined themselves in opposition to much of the Catholic belief system and how it was expressed in ritual practices. With regard to death, they rejected the existence of purgatory claiming it lacked a Biblical basis. Without a purgatorial way station, souls of the dead were immediately judged and sent to heaven or hell. This meant the living could not affect the destiny of the dead through prayers or other meritorious acts designed to shorten their purgatorial punishment. Thus, there was no need for an elaborate funeral ritual, and Protestants were directed to carry the body to the place of burial and immediately inter it without any ceremony.[4] The first colonists in America arrived from England and were by law members of the Church of Anglican, which walked a middle road between the elaborate funeral mass of the Roman Catholics and the simplified liturgy of the Protestants. Within the Anglican tradition, the Puritans were dissatisfied with this compromise and followed the more radical reforms of John Calvin, who expressly forbid any forms of ceremonialism. Because of their importance in the founding of the colonies and lasting impact on the United States, the Puritan approach toward death deserves greater elaboration.

Puritans

The Puritans who settled in New England followed the Calvinist belief that humans are utterly depraved because they are inheritors of Adam's guilt. Consequently, there was nothing they could do to warrant salvation, and damnation was the appropriate punishment for their sins. Those that will be saved would be so through God's unconditional mercy. Calvin also taught the doctrine of predestination. Through God's pure gift of grace, a select group had been elected for salvation, but the knowledge of who was elected was utterly beyond human capacity. Together, the doctrines of depravity and predestination made it impossible for Puritans to rest assured that salvation awaited them. Instead, they lived in anxious fear of damnation. Puritan ministers encouraged this anxiety by describing death in ghastly images of decomposition and hellfire. Educated in the terrors of hell and unable to discern their predetermined fate, Puritans were understandably terrified of the destiny awaiting them. They were taught to constantly assess themselves, critically searching for sinfulness they could repent for. Only those sufficiently humbled by their own wretchedness could fully depend on God's grace. Any Puritan who dared to claim righteousness was surely among the damned.

In the early years of the English colonies, death was a frequent event because the average life span was forty years. Like their English brethren, and in keeping with Calvin's rejection of all things "Papist" or Roman

Catholic, Puritans in New England buried their dead in an austere but dignified manner. The deceased's family would prepare the body and dress it in a simple white shift or shroud and lay it out at home for a few days before burial. At the tolling of the bell, neighbors gathered to solemnly carry the dead to the graveyard to witness the burial. The early colonists buried their dead in simple wooden coffins with no prayers or funeral sermon. Excessive displays of emotion, even the wearing of black garments, were forbidden. Often, they were buried in a central, unmaintained graveyard with no permanent grave marker, in keeping with their disdain for monuments to the dead and iconography.

Within a few decades of settlement, however, Puritan death practices began to change as funeral and mourning rituals emerged first among the upper class in the growing towns. For example, by the 1650s, it became customary among the wealthy to send a mourning glove with the funeral invitation, which mourners wore to the funeral along with mourning ribbons and cloaks. They also purchased lined coffins made from expensive woods and hired a coach to bear the coffin that was decorated with dark cloth and pinned-on funeral verses. The burial service itself was expanded to include prayers and a sermon. This ceremony was designed to remind the living of the dreadful judgment awaiting them, but on occasion, it also included a eulogy, although this, too, served as a warning. In speaking at the funeral of his friend, the Rev. John Bailey, Puritan preacher Cotton Mather opined, "His Thoughts were continually swallowed up, with the Vast Concern of not being Deceived, about the Marks of a Regenerate and Sanctifying Soul."[5] After the burial, the funeral procession gathered for a funeral feast at the deceased's home or at the church.

The growing elaboration of Puritan funeral practices was also apparent in their graveyards. By the 1660s, burial plots were marked with gravestones engraved with the deceased's name and images of bones, hourglasses, coffins, and winged death's-heads.[6] These symbols served to warn the living of the judgment awaiting them, but the ubiquitous winged skull also suggested the possibility of transcendence. In addition, tombstones began to contain epitaphs such as the following, which was routinely used until the nineteenth century.

Remember me as you pass by
as you are now so once was I.
As I am now you soon must be.
Prepare for death and follow me.[7]

Despite efforts to retain the simple but dignified farewell of the early Puritans, death practices among white, middle-class, urban New Englanders had grown considerably more elaborate and expensive by the eighteenth century. Nonetheless, Puritans, and their successors known as Congregationalists, continued to fear the judgment awaiting them, which

Congregationalist minister Jonathan Edwards poignantly described in his 1741 sermon, "Sinners in the Hands of an Angry God." Edwards's focus on depravity and the need for conversion was echoed throughout the Christian communities of this time period. The rhetoric of "hellfire and damnation" was at the center of the enthusiastic revivals that swept through the colonies before the Revolutionary War. However, beyond the terror, rhetoric signs of an emerging hope in salvation can be found in the graveyards where tombstone engravings changed almost universally from skulls to cherubs by the 1760s.[8] If the winged skulls hinted at the possibility of transcending death, the cherub clearly expressed a hope of salvation. The revivals combined with the successful revolution and birth of democracy created a sense of optimism in human abilities and the future fundamentally incompatible with the Calvinist worldview. Naturally, such profound theological changes found expression in American funeral practices.

FROM FEAR OF DAMNATION TO HOPE OF SALVATION

In the early decades of the United States, anxious fear of damnation had given way to a hopeful anticipation of heavenly rewards. In addition to angelic images engraved on tombstones, this new optimistic attitude was expressed in a variety of forms, ranging from the rationalistic treatises of Unitarian ministers to the letters and diaries of middle-class white women. Because the mortality rate remained high, there was a strong awareness of the precariousness of life, and death continued to be seen as a warning to turn away from worldly attachments and sin.[9] Although God and death continued to be a central occupation of Christians in the nineteenth century, they were no longer thought of as inscrutable. Instead, God, death, and salvation were open to human reason and amenable to human agency.

No longer was salvation limited to the elect. The evangelical revivals of the early nineteenth century opened up the possibility of salvation to any repentant sinner. God was pictured as loving and merciful, and the only ones who continued to fear Him or their awaiting judgment were the unrepentant. In addition, heaven was now described in the familiar and sentimental terms of home and hearth so prevalent in the nineteenth-century imagination. Clearly influenced by writings of Swedish philosopher Emanuel Swendenborg, Americans longed for a heavenly home where they would be reunited with family and friends.[10] Enslaved Africans and their African-American descendants had long professed that after death, the soul traveled "home," either to their ancestral home in Africa or home with Jesus and their loved ones. The segregated cemeteries of the nineteenth century only heightened their longing for this homecoming. Now, European Americans shared their confidence that death was a peaceful homecoming. We can also see the influence of Romanticism in the "naturalizing" of death. Death came to be seen as a natural process that liberates the living from their worldly suffering. Now demystified, the dying experience was no longer to be feared, anymore than what awaited those who had been born-again in Christ. Similarly, heaven was no longer a remote destination, but familiar and close by, just as the dead themselves were kept in close communication through the spread of spiritualist practices.

As in previous centuries, death in antebellum United States occurred within the local community of family and friends who understood the experience through their Christian faith, but gone was the anguish of the Puritan on his deathbed. Instead, the faithfully departing expressed confidence in their awaiting homecoming and family, and friends gathered around the bedside to witness the release of the soul as an edifying experience.[11] Family members continued to prepare the dead for burial at home by laying the body on a board or table for washing and then dressing it in a shroud before laying it out, in the parlor when possible, for the vigil. In the warm months, ice was tucked around the body to slow decomposition until it was carried on foot or by carriage to the graveyard, sometimes with a stop at the church for a funeral service, for a burial service. Coffins were built by hand or purchased from a local cabinetmaker.

The vigil and viewing of the body before burial allowed family and friends time to travel to the home, pay their last respects, and gaze one last time at the visage of their loved one. Many valued the peace of mind that the deceased was really dead and would not be buried alive, a common fear at this time. Irish Catholic immigrants had their own version of the wake which combined praying the Rosary with food, drink, and sharing stories about the deceased. The gathering continued after the funeral with greater gusto, although rarely with the drunken revelry of the stereotypical Irish wake.[12] Loved ones gathered back at the family home after the burial for a funeral feast that sometimes lasted several days. This domesticated death was beyond reach of poor and enslaved Americans and those suffering from war or epidemics that demanded immediate and, thus, unceremonious and detached disposition of the dead.

For the upper classes, funeral and mourning practices became increasingly elaborate and expensive. Historian David Stannard describes the nineteenth-century approach toward death as characterized by self-indulgence, sentimentalization, and ostentation.[13] Those who could afford to do so would purchase a coffin from an undertaker, rather than make their own, and some even paid for metal ones rather than the traditional wooden model. Undertakers became more than coffin makers as wealthy families hired them to assist in the preparation and transportation of the body by specially designed carriages called hearses. Undertakers became the first funeral professionals to make house calls and assist in the preparation of the body for burial such as replacing ice blocks as needed to slow decomposition.

Not surprisingly, the sentimentality of this period and emphasis upon the domestic sphere and family bonds was expressed through public mourning. During the vigil, the funeral service, and burial, public grieving, and displays of sentimental affection, such as wailing, were expected from women. At the same time, women were increasingly barred from funeral services and expected to remain in seclusion. Mourners wore black clothes and cherished such *momento mori* as locks of hair and posthumous mourning pictures of the deceased. Public mourning was also signified by the hanging of black crepe at the family home and lowering the curtains. Encouraged by the readily available mourner's manuals, the period of public mourning was extended from a few days to a year or more.

The changing forms of graveyards and tombstone iconography give us additional insights into the changing attitudes toward death during the early decades of the nineteenth century. Beginning in the eighteenth century, a growing chorus of voices called for the reform of graveyards. Whether church graveyards or public graveyards, these spaces were rarely enclosed, allowing cattle to roam over them. Upkeep of individual gravesites was usually the responsibility of the family, and any unused land was left wild. When families moved or stopped grooming the gravesite, the entire graveyard became neglected and unkempt. Because of a lack of space, gravesites were commonly reused, even if it required exhuming skeletons, and entire graveyards were developed over as cities grew. Lacking organization, grave markers were placed haphazardly and left in disrepair. This was especially true of the local potter's field, where the poor, insane, enslaved, and criminal were unceremoniously interred. Enslaved Americans were often buried in unmarked graves, whereas free blacks who could afford a gravesite were typically segregated from white gravesites. Urban crowding gave rise to epidemics and crowded graveyards that emitted foul odors and, many believed, a gaseous substance or "miasma" that was injurious to public health. More important than the issue of unsightliness, it was these health concerns that propelled the creation of modern cemeteries.[14] The goal of cemetery reformers was to establish supervision of graveyards so as to avoid overcrowding, maintain a dignified space unsullied by roaming animals, grave robbers, or unearthed bones, and protect the gravesites in perpetuity. The first modern cemetery, known as the "New Burying Ground," was opened to great acclamation in New Haven, Connecticut, in 1797. It served all the desired functions of a modern ceme-tery but lacked the aesthetic appeal of the rural or garden cemeteries that quickly overshadowed it.

Rural cemeteries protected the living by moving the dead outside city limits, while also protecting the dead from the encroachment of city development. They were designed as park-like settings that memorialized the cultivation of nature. Mt. Auburn Cemetery, the first rural cemetery, opened in 1831 four miles outside of the city of Boston. Like all rural cemeteries, Mt. Auburn was designed to ensconce the dead in a beautiful garden, which, as the Greek root of the newly named "cemetery" indicates, would be a place for sleep. The dead and, thus, death were integrated into a romanticized natural setting intended to portray the paradisiacal beauty of heaven. Mt. Auburn became the model for the rural cemetery movement that spread across the country and included the bucolic burial grounds of Laurel Hill Cemetery in Philadelphia (1836) and Green-Wood in Brooklyn (1838). With regard to the tombstone images, the earliest engravings of crossbones and heads of skulls had already begun to disappear by the 1760s. In their place, tombstones bore willow branches and cherubs, crude portraits, and personalized epithets. Rather than warn of the impending Judgment Day, the new tombstone engravings served to soften death by keeping the living connected with their beloved dead.

With their cultivated landscape, ornamental plantings, walking paths, ornate mausoleums, monuments, fountains, familial engravings, and cherubic statuaries, rural cemeteries attracted crowds of visitors who came to picnic and nap and the mourners who came to visit with the dead. They served as the first public park-like spaces in the United States and became the model for the creation of public parks such as New York's Central Park. When Mt. Auburn opened in 1831, it immediately became a major tourist destination, and local families, even those in the lower classes, were able to purchase family plots that would ensure their eternal togetherness. The poor could not afford to rest eternally in urban or rural cemeteries and continued to be buried in potter's fields. People of color were often denied burial in urban and rural cemeteries, prompting the creation of modern African-American cemeteries such as Mount Auburn in Baltimore (1872).

Funeral Directors and the Making of the Modern American Funeral

After the Civil War, a cadre of death professionals emerged to assist the grieving family and take charge of the disposition of the dead. The successful marketing of embalming was key to this change. Before the war, the vast majority of Americans of all religions rejected embalming as unnatural and irreligious because it encouraged clinging to the body that the soul had already departed. These attitudes changed during the Civil War when soldiers died too far away from home to be transported for burial without the preservation of embalming. The desire to see their beloved dead one last time and bury them near home outweighed religious rejections and distaste of embalming. During the Civil War, embalming was performed on the battlefields by technicians, many but not all of whom were surgeons, who used a variety of substances until formaldehyde was discovered in 1866. The embalming of President Lincoln and the public procession of his body across the country added greatly to the esteem of embalming.

After the war, undertakers became the primary practitioners of embalming because they were already involved in selling caskets and transporting bodies. With the war over, demand dropped sharply, except in frontier areas where the dead were still likely to be transported to the East for burial in a family plot. With less need for transporting bodies, undertakers had to create demand for embalming. This was all the more important because coffins began to be mass produced in the 1870s by the Stein Manufacturing Company, taking a significant source of income away from the undertaker.[15] To bolster acceptance of embalming, undertakers portrayed themselves as medical professionals, known as funeral directors. They marketed embalming as a scientific advancement over traditional burial by appealing to growing concerns about disease caused by overcrowding in urban areas. Proponents claimed that embalming disinfected the body, thus protecting the living from disease. In addition, embalming improved the deceased's appearance, which became the most important selling point of the technique. Embalmers worked to make the body look natural and lifelike. To this end, they dressed the dead in their own clothes rather than a shroud. The use of make-up, which was increasingly available in the late nineteenth century, made it even easier to enliven the dead and create the image of peaceful slumber. Ultimately, embalming and the professional services of funeral directors became accepted because they allowed bodies to be transported, sanitized them, and improved their appearance, enabling mourners to enjoy a last gaze of their loved one before burial.

In keeping with the emphasis on the body and concern for aesthetic appearances, coffins were replaced with caskets—a term used for containers of precious goods. The two types of containers differed in more than name. Coffins were quickly constructed out of available lumber to fit the shape of the body, with greater width at the shoulders and tapering toward the feet. Caskets, in contrast, are rectangular in shape and thus less obvious markers of death. In addition to changing the shape, caskets were made with greater ornamentation and finery to match the greater attention being given to the viewing of the deceased. Before the Civil War, only the very wealthy would pay for a lined coffin made of fine wood, but funeral directors aggressively marketed upgraded caskets to middle-class customers increasingly anxious to provide a "respectable" farewell. Casket makers also created sturdier caskets made from metal or wood with metal hinges and marketed these models as the best protection possible against decomposition. They also marketed "grave liners," which had originally been designed to protect against grave robbers, as a further layer of protection against the elements.

Undertakers formally organized themselves as professionals in 1882 with the creation of the National Funeral Directors Association (NFDA). The NFDA aimed to provide education for members in the best methods of "mortuary science" and to enhance their professional standing. Toward this goal, members were advised to be well-groomed and well-dressed and to carry themselves as gentlemen. According to historian James Farrell, "The required traits of the undertaker included mastery of self and situations, delicacy and tact, urbane manners, the ability to be all things to all people, to all classes, quietness and quickness, and a temperament of assured equanimity."[16] In addition to being perceived as a medical professional, many funeral directors hoped they would be perceived as equally capable as clergy in handling funeral matters and given like respect.

Over the course of a few decades, Americans came to accept and value the services and products offered by professional funeral directors. This change happened first among the upper classes in urban areas in the North, who had surplus money and wanted to express their refinement in death as in life. They were encouraged by experts on decorum to entrust care of the dead with experts, and middle-class Americans followed suit as soon as they could afford to do so. Funeral directors insisted they were not merely selling services and products but a dignified farewell, which was beyond the ability of family members to provide. This complete package required shifting preparation of the dead out of the home into specialized facilities. "Funeral parlors" or "funeral homes" were designed to resemble the family parlor of the Victorian home, where important life events such as marriages and funeral vigils were held. The familiar but formal environment of the funeral home helped smooth the transition as the dead were taken out of the control of the family and friends and placed into the care of professional funeral workers. In many cases, the funeral home was designed to include a nondenominational chapel to negate the need to transport the body to the family's place of worship, while also allowing the funeral director to maintain control of the body during the religious service and challenge the authority of the clergyperson officiating at the service.

Cemeteries also changed considerably after the Civil War as the prominence of the rural cemetery declined, and the lawn cemetery became the preferred model. Lawn cemeteries were also park spaces but much simpler in design. Lacking ornamental plantings, fenced family plots, and fountains, they offered an open expanse of undulating meadow. Striving to create an uncluttered vista, lawn cemeteries rejected tombstones in favor of uniform plaques placed flush to the ground that were difficult to see unless up close. Regulations, enforced by the cemetery superintendent, forbade the installation of individual memorials to the dead as they detracted from the uniform dignity of the whole. As a result, the lawn cemetery had removed most of the symbolic reminders of death so prominent in early burial spaces. The first lawn cemetery, Spring Grove Cemetery in Cincinnati, actually began in 1845 as a rural cemetery, but after the Civil War it made modifications, such as the removal of all fencing around family plots, to create an open expanse.[17] Forest Lawn mortuary-park, which opened in 1906 in Los Angeles, is the best known twentieth-century example of a lawn cemetery. Modern lawn cemeteries were also designed to run efficiently as any modern business.[18] The open lawn and flush plaques reduced the time and, thus, expense of lawn care. In addition, cemeteries required the use of grave liners or vaults to ensure the surface of each gravesite would not sink or settle after an interment.

RESISTERS AND INNOVATORS

The modern funeral caught on first in the Northern cities and was much slower to be accepted in rural areas and the Southern states, where families continued to care for the dead in the context of the local community and traditional Christianity. Some resisted the cost, whereas others were pained to relinquish their traditional role in caring for their own. In both rural and urban areas, however, there were groups who resisted the modern funeral on religious grounds, particularly the practice of embalming. American Jewry provides an interesting case as an example. Like Christians, Jews had long been opposed to it as a violation of the sanctity of the body. Unlike Christians, Orthodox Jews saw no benefit in the procedure designed to slow decomposition because by Jewish law, they were commanded to bury the body within twenty-four hours. Likewise, they saw no benefit in purchasing elaborate caskets designed to protect the body because they sought to return the body to the earth as soon as possible. Rather than purchase the services of a funeral director, Orthodox Jews continue to rely upon their own burial societies, known as the *Chevra Kadisha*, to care for the dead. The *Chevra Kadisha*, or burial society, is a group of volunteers trained to prepare the dead for burial. When a death occurs, they gather quickly to ritualistically wash the body as they say prayers over it. The body is dressed in a simple white shroud and, when required by the cemetery or zoning laws, buried in a simple pine coffin with no metal. From the death and until burial, the deceased is accompanied by a pray-er who reads the psalms. Not all American Jews continued to follow these traditions, however. Reform Jews were more likely to utilize the services of a funeral home for embalming and viewing of the body and purchasing an expensive casket and flower arrangements. In urban areas with high Jewish populations, Jewish funeral homes were established to provide various combinations of traditional and American funeral forms for the diverse Jewish community. Over time, Jewish funeral directors formed relationships with the *Chevra Kadishas* who used their facilities.[19]

As discussed above, after the Civil War, most American Christians accepted embalming with little resistance because it improved the appearance of the body for the final viewing, preserved its life-like appearance for an indefinite future in the grace, and sanitized the body of infectious diseases. Theologically, the soul had departed from the body, but these pseudomedical interventions done for the benefit of the living had no effect on the postmortem journey of the soul or the future resurrection of the body. On the other hand, Christians and Jews reacted quite differently to another nineteenth-century innovation that served as an alternative to the modern funeral practice marketed by the funeral industry—cremation. Cremation is an ancient practice practiced all over the world, including North America, but it was transformed into a modern means of disposal in the late nineteenth century. Cremation had been banned officially by Emperor Charlemagne in 789 as a capital offense and was generally perceived as a pagan practice antithetical to Christianity. In the United States, a group of culturally elite Americans—many of whom had ties to the Theosophical Society—introduced the practice to Americans in the 1870s.

Cremation advocates argued for cremation on two grounds: sanitary and spiritual.[20] From a public health perspective, cremation was more hygienic because it removed the threat of disease harbored in decomposing bodies. From a religious perspective, they argued that cremation was purifying and resonated better with belief in the soul, rather than worship of the body. Cremationists also sought to replace antiquated burial rituals with their more refined religious sensibilities. Charles De Palm, a Theosophist, was cremated in 1876 in Pennsylvania in a well-publicized event designed to demonstrate the scientific benefits of the practice and its respectability. Although scientists, clergy, and public reformers were invited to observe, crowds of reporters and locals also arrived and turned it into a spectacle. As described by Stephen Prothero, the event was replete with religious symbolism and ritual, including a solemn procession of the body into the crematory and adornment of the body with spices, flowers, and evergreens before setting it ablaze.

The first cremation was sufficiently respectable to satisfy many social reformers who applauded its sanitation benefits and low cost, but it failed to gain the approval of most Americans, who continued to view it as less civilized than burial and clearly un-Christian. Cremation advocates continued their campaign, nonetheless, and the numbers grew slowly, from sixteen cremations in 1884 to 1,996 in 1899.[21] For the majority of Americans, cremation did not become a viable alternative to the "embalm and bury" model until the 1960s, when it took off quickly. Until then, cremation, like traditional burial perform by the *Chevra Kadisha*, remained an exceptional practice resisting the hegemony of the funeral industry.

THE TWENTIETH-CENTURY "AMERICAN WAY OF DYING"

By the 1920s, funeral professionals had successfully convinced most Americans that they needed professional assistance to give their loved ones a proper and dignified farewell. The successful entrenchment of the modern funeral was attributable to many factors. For one thing, many more Americans were living in cities by the early twentieth century, and urbanization disrupted the traditional practices maintained in local, rural communities. In their place, experts in various fields offered their specialized services as modern improvements over traditional practices based on local knowledge. We can see this shift clearly in the emergence of modern medicine and hospitals. As effective medicines and therapies for disease became available, care of the sick moved out of the home and into the hospital, where it could be treated efficiently. With their traditional caregiver role supplanted by doctors and nurses and the increase in life expectancy modern medicine provided, twentieth-century Americans had little direct experience with dying and dead bodies. Just as Americans became reliant on doctors to define illness and heal the sick, they became reliant upon funeral directors to guide them in the unfamiliar territory of death and prescribe the form of the proper funeral.

Stephen Prothero has aptly labeled the modern funeral the "embalm-and-bury" regime, but there was much more involved in the modern funeral. It began with a call to a local funeral home to retrieve the body. In addition to embalming, families paid to have the visage of the deceased naturalized with the aid of cosmetics and, as needed, facial reconstruction. Simi-larly, in keeping with the emphasis on the appearance of the body, a beautifully crafted casket was purchased for the final memory image. In addition to appearance, caskets were designed of the toughest metals with air-tight sealants, ostensibly to protect the body from the natural process of decomposition. Such finery and protection could cost as much as $10,000. Beyond assisting the family in selecting the casket, the funeral director guided them through all the details: getting the obituary published in the local paper, purchasing of flowers, picking out clothes for the deceased, selecting pallbearers, and, at times, creating prayer cards displaying the name and dates of the deceased along with an appropriate prayer or poem. The actual funeral service was often a two-day event, beginning with an open-casket viewing and praying the Rosary for Roman Catholics. The next day, a funeral would be held either at the deceased's place of worship or in the funeral home chapel. Led by a clergyperson, the funeral service combined prayers of consolation with a sermon reflecting on theological teachings and a eulogy. Typically somber in tone, the service was followed by a formal procession to the cemetery, where more prayers were said before the burial or entombment. At a considerable cost, the funeral director orchestrated this entire ritual drama from the open-casket viewing, the funeral service, and procession to the cemetery with fluid ease to unburden the grieving family.

Together, the removal of the body from the home and family's control, the practice of embalming and the use of make-up, and the body-preserving caskets served to protect the mourners from the reality of death by masking it. The funeral director arranged all the details of the funeral for the family, who could grieve free of disturbing images of decay or stressful organization details. The cemetery superintendent, likewise, did his part by shielding the grievers from intimacy with the burial itself. Graves were opened and closed without the family present. Artificial turf was placed around the grave to hide the unsightly evidence of grave digging, and pulleys were used to lower the body into the grave rather than the awkward efforts of the pallbearers. All this served to keep the family from a close encounter with the burial.

At the start of the modern funeral movement, critiques expressed concern that it masked or denied death, while glorifying the body. These concerns took on a new urgency as public mourning practices declined significantly after the First World War. Rather than encourage sentimental attachment to the dead, the emerging field of psychology urged mourners to "let go" of their grief by severing ties with the dead and exercising emotional restraint. No longer were the loved ones of the deceased awarded a special social status with clear rules for the social role of mourner.[22] Instead, excessive grief, from wearing mourning clothes to seclusion, was now seen as a sign of psychological distress. As historian of death Philippe Aries noted, "It is no longer correct to display one's grief, nor even to appear to feel any."[23] The elimination of obligatory mourning rites, apart from the funeral, was not a sign of disrespect or lack of affection for the dead but a sign of emotional maturity and the triumph of reason over sentimentality. Funeral directors took on the role of grief counselors and marketed their services and products as beneficial, if not essential, for healthy grief facilitation. They "unburdened" the mourners by beautifying death both physically and symbolically through the industry's euphemisms for everything death-related. As public mourning was condensed into a one- or two-day funeral service, it was all the more important that every detail be perfectly orchestrated. Although critiques decried this trend along with all aspects of the modern funeral, overall, there was a societal silence on the topic—a taboo on death—as it was called.

REFORMING THE INDUSTRY

While some would argue that the taboo on death still continues, critics of American death practices, from the depersonalization of the modern hospital to the expense of the modern funeral, began to gain a wider audience in the 1960s. The first major publication attacking the funeral industry to gain attention was Leo Bowman's *The American Funeral: A Study in Guilt, Extravagance, and Sublimity* (1959). Bowman argued that funeral directors pressured families into purchasing elaborate service and products by exploiting their grief. He advocated a reform of the industry and return to earlier customs that were more dignified and in keeping with the desire of the mourners. Bowman's book was quickly overshadowed by journalist Jessica Mitford's 1963 sensational best-seller, *The American Way of Death*. Mitford called the modern funeral a "new mythology" created and marketed by the funeral industry and paid for by the American consumer who has few alternatives. Mitford made many of the same charges against the industry as Bowman but did so in a humorous and salacious tone. She poked fun at the euphemisms used by funeral directors and their exploitative pretense as grief counselors masking their for-profit goals. Her sharpest barbs were saved for embalming. She described the embalming process in detail and chastised Americans for this bizarre mutilation of the dead, which is rarely practiced outside the United States. Mitford's sympathies clearly lay with the consumer who suffered as a victim of exploitation in the clutches of the funeral industry. In his survey of the American funeral industry, historian Gary Laderman reminds us that although some funeral directors surely exploited their costumer's grief, consumers willingly handed their dead over to the funeral industry because they liked the result. Most of all, they liked the way embalming and cosmetics enlivened the dead, masking the disturbing signs of decomposition, and gave them a lasting memory to cherish.[24] Nonetheless, Mitford's book had a profound effect on American assessment of these practices and led to major changes in American death practices.

Awakened and inspired by reformers like Mitford, Americans demanded federal oversight of the funeral industry. The Federal Trade Commission (FTC)'s Consumer Protection Bureau did enact a "trade rule" to protect the consumer from exploitative funeral directors in 1985. The new rules required funeral directors to provide in writing itemized costs rather than a package price. Funeral directors were also forbidden from telling families that embalming or caskets were legally necessary. With regard to caskets, they were forbidden to claim that any casket sealer could preserve the embalmed corpse for an extended or indefinite time. The FTC dropped additional rules in response to intense lobbying from the NFDA. These changes had a noteworthy impact on the industry, but there was almost no enforcement of the trade rule. More substantial reforms came not from government regulations but grassroots organizations that offered a viable alternative to the funeral industry.

Cremation was an available alternative to the embalm-and-bury regime, and in the 1960s, cremation rates began to soar in Hawaii and the West Coast, where rates of religious affiliation were lowest. Membership in local burial and cremation societies, such as the Bay Area Funeral Society founded by Jessica Mitford's husband Robert Treuhaft in 1952, also increased. These non-profits negotiated discount rates for members with the local crematoriums for direct cremations, meaning no embalming, viewing, or funeral service with the body present. Likewise, consumer groups negotiated low-cost direct burials with local cemeteries. These no-frills, no-ceremony means of disposal appealed to nonreligious Americans seeking to save money. The rise of cremation in the United States clearly corresponds to the weakening of religious ties in the 1960s, but few Americans wanted to forgo ritual and communal gathering altogether. In keeping with the spiritual-seeking mood of the 1960s, they sought meaningful and authentic rituals that expressed their personal beliefs rather than doctrinal certainties. Although cremation had long been perceived as antireligious and specifically anti-Christianity, it did not evolve as such in the American contexts where belief in God and desire for ritualizing remained strong into the twenty-first century. As the demand for cremation rose, new ritual forms were developed to suit the trend. Before turning to the new forms of funeral rituals they developed, it is important to understand how revolutionary the turn toward cremation has been.

Although the first cremation took place in 1876, the cremation rate had only grown to 4 percent in 1950. By 2005, the number had risen to 32 percent and was well over 50 percent in some states. In contrast, cremation rates were under 10 percent in the Bible Belt states of Alabama and Mississippi. The 2006 cremation rate in the United States is substantially lower than in other Westernized countries: 72 percent in the United Kingdom and 56 percent in Canada. Despite Jessica Mitford's efforts, the majority of Americans remain committed to the embalm-and-bury model, but not for long. The U.S. cremation rate is projected to reach 57 percent by 2025.[25] The success of cremation created a crisis for the funeral industry that consumed its attention in the 1980s and 1990s. Direct cremation (and direct burial) requires no embalming, no facial reconstruction, no refrigeration, no casket (other than a cardboard box), no formal attire, no burial plot, and no memorial tombstone. Although the funeral industry had long been the staunchest opponent of cremation, it had to find a way to incorporate the practice to survive.

The funeral industry has adapted to the demand for cremation in creative ways. Many funeral homes have built crematoriums on the premise or contracted with nearby crematoriums for the service. In this way, funeral directors can continue to control the disposal of the body and charge for refrigeration and transportation services and a cremation container. By law, bodies must be cremated in at least a cardboard box, but some families are willing to purchase a beautiful wood casket for the cremation. After the cremation, they will receive the ashes (or cremains as the industry calls them) in a cardboard box unless they purchase a more attractive urn, varieties of which are displayed in the casket showroom. The funeral industry also has been innovative in offering families a variety of services and products to memorialize the dead. In fact, funeral directors express great concern that some kind of memorialization is necessary for healthy grief facilitation. For this reason, memorial services are strongly encouraged. Like a funeral service, but without the body present, memorial services held at the funeral home will require the orchestration of a funeral director to oversee everything from the floral arrangements to a guest book. To make up for the lost revenues from casket sales, savvy funeral directors sell video recording services and live webcasting. Funeral directors will also encourage the family to purchase their assistance for the disposal or dispersal of ashes. In the mid-twentieth century, most cremation remains were buried in cemetery plots and marked with a headstone. Today, the options are rapidly expanding as funeral directors and independent entrepreneurs offer creative ways for families to personalize a final farewell. New funeral-related industries have arisen to fill this hole, offering everything from diamonds made with ashes to a fireworks dispersal.

Although the number of religiously unaffiliated Americans has grown sharply in the last decade, to 16.1 percent, a strong majority continue to have a religious affiliation.[26] Not surprisingly, when faced with a death, they turn to their faith community for support and guidance. Because Judaism, Christianity, and Islam have traditionally required the dead to be buried, the post-1960s demand for cremations has directly challenged those traditions. Some religions have maintained their prohibition against cremation without hesitation. The largest of these in the United States are Orthodox Judaism, Orthodox Christianity, Islam, and the Church of Jesus Christ of Latter-day Saints. American Protestants and Catholics have mixed opinions on the practice and have pushed their denominational bodies to allow for the choice. Many Protestant denominations have acquiesced but continue to encourage the faithful to have a funeral service (with the body present), even if they intend to do a cremation afterwards, on the grounds that this ritual helps to acknowledge the reality of death and, thus, is an important counter to the death-denying culture.[27] Although the Roman Catholic Church has had an absolute ban on cremation since the eighth century, it also bowed to pressure from the laity and lifted the prohibition in 1963, allowing cremation after the full funeral liturgy. The church requires that the body be present for the funeral liturgy, but because all funeral homes require embalming and a casket for the funeral, many Catholics proceed with direct cremation to save money. Rather than continue to deny the funeral mass in these cases, the church officially permitted the Catholic funeral liturgy to take place with the cremated remains instead of the body in 1997.[28]

Just as embalming opened the door to the professionalized care of the dead, the practice of cremation has pushed the funeral industry and religious bodies to adapt. Some have resisted or refused to do so, but others have found new opportunities to make meaningful connections with individuals. Funeral directors emphasize their skills in "grief facilitation" and offer grief support groups that are appreciated by families not ready or willing to cut ties with the dead. A growing number of Protestant and Catholic churches have adapted to cremation demand by creating a scattering ground, such as an attractive rose garden and columbarium on church property. This trend is a modern twist on the ancient Christian practice of burying the dead inside the church or next to its walls. In effect, by binding the dead to the particular church, it serves to build a lasting bond with the survivors, who, as a result, may be less likely to church shop. The accommodations made by funeral directors and religious leaders all have served to meet the demand of Americans seeking death rituals that are more personally meaningful than those they inherited from their parents.

RITUALIZING DEATH

Scholars point to the 1960s as a significant turning point in American religion. Denominational and congregational loyalties declined significantly, and many American began to seek authentic religious experiences both inside and outside of religious traditions. Like weddings, funerals have become an opportunity to express authentic feelings and personal truths rather than go through the motions of a ritual prescribed by either the funeral industry or religious authorities. Eschewing a traditional script, families try to personalize the funeral by adding to and modifying inherited traditions. Rather than do this ritual creation on their own, most rely on help from clergy, funeral directors, and ample resources now available in print and on the Internet. Thus, the final decisions are made through the interactions of family members and these professionals. Like the Roman Catholic Church, many denominations revised their funeral rites in the 1980s and 1990s to allow for personalization within limits. For example, a traditional church funeral can be personalized by adding a contemporary song that the deceased loved or a poem written by a family member. With a little more work, a slide show biography can be viewed during the service, as can personal artifacts from photos to trophies. As noted above, there are now "theme" funerals designed around an activity that the deceased loved, like golf or Disney.

Contemporary funerals are not designed to only express the values, lifestyle, and personality of the deceased; they also allow for active participation on the part of the mourners. The most common means of participating is through a shared eulogy. Rather than only the clergyperson or close family member deliver the eulogy, a shared eulogy offers everyone an opportunity to pass on an endearing anecdote. Eulogies have long been a feature of American funerals, but in many cases today, they are the central feature overshadowing the theologically focused message delivered by the clergyperson. In response, clergy try to retain the religious purpose of the ritual and frame the biography of the deceased in a larger story of sin and redemption. In fact, some funerals are purposely unreligious, with the only "message" being the story of the deceased. The focus on the life of the deceased has the benefit that everyone who attends the service can relate to this story, and none will feel excluded by a theological belief system they do not share. This leads some observers to interpret the eulogizing trend as a sign of religious decline. The Rev. Thomas Long writes, "When the larger story of God and humanity loses its power over our religious imaginations, then we tell the only holy narrative left to tell—the biography of the deceased."[29]

Long may well be right that some Americans find little meaning in traditional religious stories, but there are equally compelling explanations for the appeal of the shared eulogy. For one thing, the United States is quite religiously diverse, and in the absence of a shared sacred story, the life of the deceased is an obvious common focus of those gathered at the funeral. The shared eulogy is also well-suited to American love of self-expression, or what sociologist Robert Bellah termed "expressive individualism."[30] Thanks to entrepreneurial ventures, self-expression can now continue long after the funeral by cyber-memorials that allow photos, videos, and personal postings into the indefinite future. The ascent of self-expression and focus on the life of the deceased has displaced the theological focus of the funeral fundamentally altering its traditional purpose to publicly articulate "words against death" and reinforce a shared belief system that offers hope in life after death.[31]

New death rituals are being created to express the personal values and beliefs of modern Americans. For those who feel a strong connection to nature and are concerned about environmental issues, green burials are an obvious choice. Green burials combine the ancient practice of simple and immediate burial with the modern need to protect open spaces and undeveloped land. Although there is still disagreement about what qualifies as a green burial site, in general, they forbid the use of embalming fluids, metals, precious woods, and concrete. Burial sites may be marked with simple engraved stones or buried GPS locaters. The cost of the burial site for one hundred years supports conservation of the land and management designed to encourage the growth of natural plant species and wild animals. Families who choose green burial usually handle the entire burial themselves. They will transport the deceased in a cloth shroud or biodegradable casket, dig the burial site, and hold a graveside service. This personalized service may or may not express religious beliefs and involve clergy, but it most certainly expresses the deceased's commitment to and connection with the earth. Green burials are very popular in Great Britain, and within the last ten years, thirteen green burial sites have begun operating in the United

States, with many more cemeteries claiming to have created a green burial section alongside their traditional burial site.

Green burials are one of many new death forms being developed to meet the changing tastes of twenty-first-century Americans. For those who choose cremation, there are dozens are new rituals designed to personalize the final disposition of the ashes. Some are very expensive, like the space burial, which shoots a few ounces of the remains into space. Ashes can be incorporated into a painting, jewelry, or a reef ball submerged off the Florida Keys. They can be released in a helium balloon, set off with a volley of fireworks, shot from a cannon, buried at the local golf course, or scattered at sea. As noted above, the funeral industry is rapidly expanding its services to accommodate these kinds of requests and maintain control over the marketplace of American death practices. Clearly, there is a great deal of flux at the moment as ancient religious traditions are being personalized and new death rituals are invented. For the time being, Americans have a wide range of choices in how they ritualize death, from traditional practices, to the modern "embalm-and-bury" regime, to innovative new forms chosen to express the values and lifestyle of the deceased.

NOTES

1. Christopher Columbus, *The Four Voyages of Christopher Columbus*, trans. J. M. Cohen (New York: Penguin Classics, Harmondsworth, 1969) quoted in Sam Gill, 1983, *Native American Traditions: Sources and Interpretations*, 3.

2. See Robert L. Hall, *An Archaeology of the Soul: North American Indian Belief and Ritual* (Chicago: University of Illinois Press, 1997), 36–38.

3. See Dennis F. Kelley, "The politics of death and burial in native California," in *Death and Religion in a Changing World*, ed. Kathleen Garces-Foley (Armonk, NY: ME Sharpe, 2006), 3–22.

4. David E. Stannard, *The Puritan Way of Death: A Study in Religion, Culture, and Social Chang* (Oxford, UK: Oxford University Press, 1977), 101.

5. Cotton Mather, *A Good Man Making a Good End* (Boston, 1698), 8.

6. Edwin Dethlefson and James Deetz, "Death's heads, cherubs, and willow trees," in *Passing*, ed. Charles Jackson (Westport, CT: Greenwood Press, 1977), 51.

7. Ibid., 56.

8. Ibid., 58.

9. Lewis O. Saum, "Death in the popular mind of pre-Civil War America," in *Death in America*, ed. David E. Stannard (University of Pennsylvania Press, 1975).

10. See Colleen McDannell and Bernhard Lang, *Heaven: A History* (New Haven, CT: Yale University Press, 1988).

11. Lewis O. Saum, "Death in the popular mind of pre-Civil War America," in *Death in America*, ed. David E. Stannard (Philadelphia: University of Pennsylvania Press, 1975), 41.

12. Jacqueline S. Thursby, *Funeral Festivals in America* (Lexington, KY: University Press of Kentucky, 2006), 63.

13. Stannard, *Puritan Way of Death*, 171.

14. Stanley French, "The cemetery as cultural institution: The establishment of Mount Auburn and the 'Rural Cemetery' Movement," in *Death in America*, ed. David E. Stannard (Philadelphia: University of Pennsylvania Press, 1975), 74.

15. James Farrell, *Inventing the American Way of Death, 1830–1920* (Philadelphia: Temple University Press, 1980), 149.

16. Ibid., 152.

17. French, 84.

18. Farrell, 121.

19. Gary Laderman, *Rest in Peace: A Cultural History of Death and the Funeral Home in Twentieth-Century America* (New York: Oxford University Press, 1991), 159.

20. Stephen R. Prothero, *Purified by Fire: A History of Cremation in America* (Berkeley: University of California Press, 2001), 17–23.

21. Ibid., 107.

22. Geoffrey Gorer, "The Pornography of Death," *Encounter*, October 1955: 49–52,

23. Philippe Ariès, "The reversal of death: Changes in attitudes toward death in Western societies," in *Death in America*, ed. David E. Stannard (Philadelphia: University of Pennsylvania Press, 1975), 146.

24. Gary Laderman, *The Sacred Remains: American Attitudes Toward Death, 1799–1883* (New Haven, CT: Yale University Press, 1996), xli.

25. Cremation Association of North America, *Final 2005 Statistics and Projections to the Year 2025* (Chicago: CANA, 2007).

26. Pew survey 2008.

27. Lizette Larson-Miller, "Roman Catholic, Anglican, and Eastern Orthodox approaches to death," in *Death and Religion in a Changing World*, ed. Kathleen Garces-Foley (Armonk, NY: ME Sharpe, 2006), 103, 111.

28. H. Richard Rutherford, *Honoring the Dead: Catholics and Cremation Today* (Collegeville, MN: Liturgical Press, 2001), 9.

29. Thomas G. Long, "The American funeral today: Trends and issues," *Director* 69 (1997): 14.

30. Robert Bellah, *Habits of the Heart: Individualism and Commitment in American Life* (Berkeley: University of California Press, 1985).

31. Douglas Davies, *Death, Ritual, and Belief: The Rhetoric of Funerary Rites* (London: Cassell, 2002).

BIBLIOGRAPHY

Davies, Douglas. *Death, Ritual, and Belief: The Rhetoric of Funerary Rites*. London: Cassell, 2002.

Farrell, James. *Inventing the American Way of Death, 1830–1920*. Philadelphia: Temple University Press, 1980.

Garces-Foley, Kathleen, ed., *Death and Religion in a Changing World*. Armonk, NY: M. E. Sharpe, 2006.

Grimes, Ronald. *Deeply into the Bone*. Berkeley: University of California Press, 2000.

Harris, Mark. *Grave Matters: A Journey through the Modern Funeral Industry to the Natural Way of Burial*. New York: Scribner, 2007.

Jackson, Charles O. *Passing: The Vision of Death in America*. Westport, CT: Greenwood Press, 1977.

Laderman, Gary. *The Sacred Remains: American Attitudes toward Death, 1799–1883*. New Haven, CT: Yale University Press, 1996.

——————. *Rest in Peace: A Cultural History of Death and the Funeral Home in Twentieth-Century America*. New York: Oxford University Press, 1991.

McDannell, Colleen and Bernhard Lang. *Heaven: A History*. New Haven, CT: Yale University Press, 1988.

Mitford, Jessica. *The American Way of Death*. New York: Simon & Schuster, 1963.

Prothero, Stephen R. *Purified by Fire: A History of Cremation in America*. Berkeley: University of California Press, 2001.

Rutherford, H. Richard. *Honoring the Dead: Catholics and Cremation Today*. Collegeville, MN: Liturgical Press, 2001.

Stannard, David E. *The Puritan Way of Death: A Study in Religion, Culture, and Social Change*. Oxford: Oxford University Press, 1977.

——————, ed. *Death in America*. Philadelphia: University of Pennsylvania Press, 1975.

CHAPTER 2

Grief and the Rituals Surrounding Death: A Jewish Approach

Rebecca Alpert

The Jewish approach to death and dying is based on three basic concepts.[1] First, in Judaism, death is seen as a natural part of life. Second, Jews understand the body to belong to God and as something to be treated with honor and respect even after death. Jews do not agree about what happens to the soul, but this is also not so important in Jewish teaching. Last, the human community is obligated to mourn for the dead and to carry their memory. The key factor in understanding the Jewish approach to grief and mourning is to understand that Judaism is focused more on practice than belief. As such, this chapter will examine what Jews do when someone dies and how they mourn, rather than what Jews believe about what happens to a person after death.

Jews date their origins back to the Ancient Near East, approximately one thousand years before the time of Jesus. The early history of the Jews is chronicled in the Hebrew Bible (known to Christians as the Old Testament). The Hebrew Bible is the root of later Jewish legal and cultural traditions, but Judaism as we know it today is based fundamentally on the writings of the rabbis (200 BCE–500 CE) and the books known collectively as the Talmud. Although these teachings were codified in the medieval era and adapted and modified during modern times, they remain the central traditions of Jewish practice and thought until today and contain most of the ideas about Jewish practices and rituals related to death and mourning.

Jewish traditions emphasize the values of learning, prayer, living properly, and doing good deeds. Jews view study as a holy endeavor. They focus on the Hebrew Bible and Talmud, which are the sacred texts, but have always been interested in the knowledge to be gained from philosophical, literary, and scientific sources as well. Jews pray, traditionally, three times daily and also have special holy days. The Sabbath, which is observed each week from sundown Friday to sundown Saturday, is the most important Jewish holiday. It is a time for refraining from worldly activities to concentrate on sacred study and spend companionable time with family and friends, eating and singing. Other significant holy days are Passover in the spring and the Days of Awe in the fall. On Passover, Jews celebrate the liberation from Egypt and their beginnings as a people in the land of Israel in ancient times. The ten "Days of Awe" begin with the Jewish New Year, Rosh Hashanah, and end with Yom Kippur, a day of fasting and self reflection. Jews also emphasize the importance of daily behavior and living properly. Jews are required to "keep kosher," which means to observe certain dietary rules including not eating pork or shellfish and not mixing foods that contain milk with those that contain meat. Jews are also expected to promote the values of peace, caring, and justice in their communities and toward all human beings.

DEATH AND LIFE

When the first Jews came to America in the seventeenth century, the first thing they would do was purchase land for a cemetery. Although this may be surprising, Jewish law and custom require that Jews be buried in a Jewish cemetery, and ensuring that the dead have a proper resting place is as important as caring for those members of the community who are living. Jewish customs require that you be prepared for your death and the death of your relatives in a variety of ways. In addition to being sure that financial and personal obligations are in order (the stuff of making wills and purchasing burial plots), it has been a Jewish custom to write what has come to be known as an ethical will. In addition to leaving your loved ones material objects, Jews are supposed to reflect on the values that they would like to be sure their children and grandchildren, and others to whom they want to leave a legacy, follow.[2]

Another way that Jews prepare themselves for the inevitability of death during their lives is through the celebration of the holiest day of the Jewish calendar, Yom Kippur (the Day of Atonement). On Yom Kippur, the individual takes account of his or her life and makes restitution with God and with humans for misdeeds of the prior year. Many of the rituals associated with this practice are meant to remind Jews of the ultimate point of atonement, the one we face when we die. In one sense, Yom Kippur can be viewed as a rehearsal for death. On Yom Kippur, one has the opportunity to be both the *met* (the dead person) and the *avel* (the mourner) simultaneously and then to reemerge into life renewed when the day ends, reminded both of the fragility of life and of the possibility life offers of beginning again.

Most people are aware that Jews fast on Yom Kippur. Jews also refrain from having sex and wearing leather or jewelry (signs of affluence and beautification). These acts of self-abnegation symbolize one's own death as a retreat from life. They are also the customs one observes in mourning. Wearing white and dressing in a *kittel* (a plain white gown) are other examples of how Yom Kippur functions as a symbolic death. You literally dress in the clothes you will wear to the grave. White is the color of the shroud one is dressed in after death, and the *kittel* is placed over the shroud. Finally, and most important, one of the prayers that is recited on Yom Kippur as part of the atonement ritual is called the *Viddui*, or confession. In this prayer, a Jew catalogues the wrongs that he or she has done during the year and asks for forgiveness. It is obligatory that Jews recite a form of this prayer on our deathbed and one that the most ritually observant Jews also recite daily.

We are also mourners on Yom Kippur, as we light candles for all of our family and friends who have passed away. The Yom Kippur ritual also includes a special memorial service (one of four during the year) to honor and remember those who have died. There is also a service on Yom Kippur called the Martyrology, when we remember not only our friends and relatives but all Jews who lost their lives in the past *al kiddush ha shem*, to honor God's name, as martyrs. At this point in Jewish history, we particularly remember those, Jews and others, who died in the Holocaust, and the Israelis and Palestinians who have lost their lives in the violent clashes in the Middle East, but we also remember those who were martyred during the Crusades and the Inquisition and in earlier eras.

K'VOD HA MET: HONORING THE DEAD

Although other traditions ponder the significance of the soul, Jewish teaching about death focuses mostly on the body. Jews do not doubt the existence of the soul, but most Jewish philosophers see body and spirit inextricably connected during life, and Jewish texts do not provide a clear picture of what happens to the soul after death. With the exception of the medieval Jewish philosophical tradition, which does ponder the fate of the soul, the focus of Jewish law and custom around death is primarily about how to treat the body of the deceased. Jews see the body as a holy vessel, a gift from God. Jews are instructed to take good care of the body to preserve its health in life and its honor after death. When rituals and customs around death are focused on the body, it is understood that although the soul or spirit (or breath or life force) may have departed, the body still retains the individual's holiness and must be treated with honor and respect.

A story from ancient rabbinic literature will illustrate this point. Rabbi Meir had two sons whom he loved very much. They died on the Sabbath, and his wife, Beruriah, concealed this fact from him for a day so that he would enjoy his Sabbath rest unperturbed because Jews do not bury or mourn on the Sabbath. At the end of the Sabbath, she asked him what he would do if a king entrusted his most precious jewel to them and then asked for it to be returned. He responded that he would care for it and return it, and he rented his clothes at that moment, knowing that his sons had passed away. The story illustrates the idea that our lives are a gift from God, and our bodies are merely on loan to us, to go back to God when the time comes.

Jewish tradition prescribes a variety of customs to help people deal with the reality that death is part of life and to make sure that we respect the body of the dead person as a vessel of holiness. The customs and beliefs described below are based on Jewish legal tradition. Given what we know about "the American way of death" that has sanitized and medicalized the experience of dying, it should not be a surprise that many Jews do not follow these customs or even know about them. Yet, with increased interest in encouraging people to pay more attention to death and grief as a result of the death awareness movement, many of the customs are undergoing a renaissance in contemporary Jewish life. Because people in society have become more interested in ancient rituals and customs in recent years, observance of traditional Jewish practices around death and mourning have become more common. It is also true that even Jews who define themselves as secular (who are Jews because they see Jewishness as an ethnic rather than a religious heritage) find themselves wanting to learn about and observe customs related to death. This may be because death is something we all fear or because it reminds even the nonreligious of the power and utility of Jewish ritual practices or because they want to honor the wishes and customs of parents and grandparents. Jewish funeral directors, who for many years offered standard American funerals without regard to Jewish custom, are now likely to make the families of the deceased aware of traditional practices. Additionally, funeral directors are more willing to cooperate with communal organizations that want to help Jews observe these customs. Yet, it also remains the case that for many Jews who are not Orthodox, many of these customs are unknown and unobserved. Jews are still frequently buried according to American custom, which derives primarily from Protestant tradition. The differences will be clear as these customs are described below.

When a Jew dies, the first act that takes place is to place the body on the floor. This symbolizes the return to the earth that is a hallmark of Jewish practice surrounding death. "From dust you come, and to dust you return" (Genesis 3:19) is a key to understanding the goal of Jewish practice. Of course, this ritual cannot take place if death occurs in a hospital setting. This act assumes a death at home, surrounded by family, and immediately reminds us of how the medicalization of death affects the ability to observe traditional religious customs. However, those present at the time of death, regardless of the location, are required to do two additional things. First, they should tear their clothing, an act that is part of the ancient mourning practices in the Hebrew Bible. Second, those present recite a blessing, *Baruch ata Adonai, Elohenu Melech HaOlam, dayan ha emet* (Blessed are you, Adonai our God, Ruler of the World, whose judgments are righteous). They do this out of respect for being in the presence of a dead body. Of course, it may seem strange to the modern sensibility to praise God's righteousness at the moment of someone's death, but this too is in keeping with the idea discussed above that death is a natural part of life and that even at this terrifying moment when someone is in the presence of the body of a loved one who is no longer alive, Jews are obligated to remain mindful of the gift of life. The most important thing is to remember that death is not to be feared but is part of a natural process.

Jews also honor the dead through a series of acts in preparation for the funeral and burial. From the moment of death until the body is placed in the ground, the deceased is never to be left alone. A person called a *shomer* (guard) remains with the body during that entire period. The *shomer* may recite Psalms, especially Psalm 23, although contemporary custom suggests that the *shomer* may also read other poetry or literature that the deceased person might have appreciated or found meaningful.

A group of volunteers from a local synagogue or community called a *Chevra Kadisha* (holy society) then prepares the body for burial. Members of the *Chevra Kadisha* are never paid because this act is considered a great *mitzvah*, a good deed for which remuneration would make no sense. The *Chevra Kadisha* ritually washes the body (*taharah*). There are separate *Chevra Kadisha* for men and women, and the body is washed in segments while the rest of the body remains covered. Both factors are to preserve the modesty of the deceased. Water renders the body pure (which is the meaning of the word *taharah*). The process is done in silence out of respect to the *met*, who is also asked for forgiveness by those who are handling his or her body. The *met* is then dressed in simple linen shrouds (*tachrichin*). Dressing everyone in the same simple garments rather than fancy clothing reminds us that, rich or poor, we are all equal in death. *Tachrichin* for men and women are made up of shirt, pants, a belt, and a cover that goes over the head. Men (and today women) are also dressed in their own *tallit* (prayer shawl) and then in the *kittel* (gown) they have worn on Yom Kippur. In Israel, the body is wrapped only in these garments. In the United States and other European Jewish cultures, the body is placed in a coffin. The coffin should be made only of wood, preferably plain pine, and not include any metal. These customs insure that the body will decay quickly and return to dust. Some like to include a packet of soil from Jerusalem in the coffin as a reminder of the Jewish connection to the land of Israel, but otherwise it is not customary to place objects in the coffin.

Once the *tahara* has taken place the coffin is sealed, and the *met* is left to rest in peace until the funeral, which takes place as soon as possible and preferably within twenty-four hours of the death. Immediately preceding the funeral, official mourners repeat the ritual that takes place at the time of death, known as *keriah* (tearing the garment). They tear their clothes (for a parent, over the heart; and for spouses, siblings, and children, over the right breast) and recite the blessing, "Blessed are You, Adonai our God, Ruler of the Universe, Righteous Judge." The rending of clothes (more often a small black ribbon that is affixed to the clothing) expresses their grief; the blessing formula reminds them that even at this moment of grief, they still must praise God, who created a world that includes death as a part of life. Judaism does have categories of official mourners who are obligated to participate in the various rituals. You are an official mourner if the person who died is your parent, child, spouse, or sibling. These individuals are the ones who participate in the *keriah* ceremony and who sit in the front row at the funeral service. In recent times, the partners of gay and lesbian people and other members of extended family and friendship networks (especially grandchildren as people live longer and grandchildren are themselves adults) have been included as official mourners, although this is not the universal custom.

Although in some communities it is the custom that those attending the funeral greet mourners beforehand in an effort to offer comfort, according to Jewish tradition, the actual mourning process does not begin until after the burial. The focus of the funeral continues to be honoring the deceased and not comforting the mourners. Until the time of the burial, the mourners are not technically in a state of mourning but are in a category called *aninut*. It is understood that during this period, those who have lost a loved one are in shock (even when the death has been long awaited). In that state, they may not be able to carry out their normal duties, so they are excused from them. During *aninut*, those close to the deceased have only one obligation, and that is making sure the arrangements are made to prepare the body of the deceased for burial.

The funeral is usually quite simple. There is no set liturgy required for the funeral, but certain rituals have become customary. The funeral continues to focus on honoring the dead. The ceremony is most often conducted by a rabbi but need not be according to Jewish law. It is simple and usually takes no more than twenty minutes. In keeping with that simplicity, Jews generally do not have flowers or music at the funeral. The ceremony consists of reading a few psalms and perhaps some poetry (or music if that was important to the deceased) that the deceased might have liked. The main focus is on the *hesped* (eulogy). The goal is to present the person who died in a positive but also realistic light. The eulogizer is expected to describe the good that the deceased did, but not to exaggerate it. The funeral ends with a recitation of *El Mohle Rachamim*, the memorial prayer, which asks that God, who is full of compassion, grant a perfect rest to the spirit of the person who died and to bind up their souls with the souls of the people of Israel.

Often, the funeral takes place in a chapel at the funeral parlor, but for a respected member of a synagogue community, the funeral can also take place in the synagogue. Still others hold the funeral ceremony at the cemetery, either at the site of the grave or in a chapel on the premises. The body is carried to the burial site by pallbearers, although their role is mostly symbolic. They accompany the coffin to the hearse and carry the coffin at the cemetery to the grave. This custom is also in keeping with honoring the dead. The *shomer* who has been reading psalms from the moment of death also continues his or her accompaniment of the body to the grave.

The ceremony at the grave is also very brief. It consists of reading a few psalms and recitation of the *Kaddish*, the Jewish memorial prayer that mourners will continue to recite throughout the period of mourning that will be described in greater detail below. The most important custom that takes place at the grave is the actual burial. It is Jewish custom for the mourners to fill the grave after the coffin is lowered. Many do this symbolically by placing several shovels full of dirt on the coffin, but it is becoming more common to observe the traditional practice of filling the grave completely. This is the final act of honoring the dead person. From here, Jewish custom begins to focus on the mourner. To symbolize that transition, those attending the funeral form two lines, through which the mourners pass upon leaving the grave. As the mourners pass, those on line greet them with the words, "May the One who has comforted mourners comfort you in the midst of the gates of Zion."

Jewish tradition considers attending the funeral and burial of people with whom you are acquainted, whether you know them from synagogue or other communal organization, from work or your neighborhood, to be very important. The Talmud teaches that accompanying someone to the grave is the greatest of all *mitzvot* (good deeds) because that person cannot repay the kindness. It is also appropriate to give a donation to a cause (*tzedakah*) that the deceased cared about to honor their memory. These donations are the preferred way to honor the deceased; Jews generally do not expect or welcome flowers at a funeral.

After the acts for honoring the dead are completed, the attention then turns to comforting the bereaved (*nihum avelim*). Before we look at mourning customs, however, it is important to mention several practices that are popular in American culture that raise issues for Jews given the focus on honoring the dead and centering on the fact that humans are dust and return to dust: cremation, embalming, or viewing the body before the funeral.

Embalming and Viewing

Jews believe that to respect the body involves a process that recognizes that the body should not be preserved in any way. Therefore, embalming is not a common Jewish practice. The body should be buried quickly[3] and placed directly into the ground so that it can, as suggested in Genesis, return to dust. The process of embalming (like the idea of creating hermetically sealed coffins made of things like metal that do not quickly decay and will preserve the body) is not in keeping with Jewish custom. Yet, embalming is also understood as a necessity in some circumstances. For example, if a body needs to be transported to its burial place, the law requires embalming for health and safety reasons. Also, if the funeral cannot take place within the appropriate twenty-four hours because it is necessary to wait for family members to travel back for the funeral, their needs take precedence. Refrigeration is preferred to embalming for preserving the body when necessary, but there are circumstances that require embalming, and it is an acceptable alternative. The custom of viewing the (embalmed and cosmetically prepared) body the night before the funeral is also discouraged by Jewish tradition for similar reasons. The body when prepared in keeping with Jewish tradition is dressed in a shroud, with the face covered, and is not meant to be viewed. The viewing of a cosmetically restored body is not considered respectful of the dead because it is thought to allow people to avoid the reality that death is a process of decay. Jews neither embalm nor permit viewings to help the mourners come to terms with the fact that their loved one is no longer among the living and so that they will remember the deceased as a living human and not a beautified corpse.

Cremation

Cremation is another act discouraged by Jewish traditional practice. The body should be allowed to decay in a natural process, and burial underground is understood to provide that process. Burial in a mausoleum or vault is also discouraged because these forms also impede the natural process of returning to dust.

The generations after the Holocaust also saw burning bodies as too close to the experience of the Jews who were sent to crematoria, but as evidence of Jews being buried in mass graves by the Nazis as well comes to light, and as younger generations are more removed from this experience, this explanation becomes less important. Many Jews are persuaded by the ecological advantages of cremation over burial, and Jewish cemeteries and religious leaders have become more willing to perform funerals and memorial services for those who choose cremation and also to allow the burial of the cremains in Jewish cemeteries. Yet, it is still the case that burial is much more common than cremation among Jews today.

Other practices based on medical technologies (organ donation, euthanasia, and autopsy) that do not seem to be in keeping with the Jewish ideals of honoring the body, and seeing the body as belonging to God and therefore not to be tampered with by human endeavor, need to be examined. The Jewish approaches to these things and also to suicide have undergone much rethinking over time.

Euthanasia

Jewish tradition has always taken a positive attitude towards medicine, and Jews have been in the forefront of medical research. Ancient Jewish texts support the idea that humans are partners with God in creation, and human beings are obligated to seek health and healing. The body belongs to God, so the individual has a strong obligation to take care of the body and to promote health. One consequence of that idea is that Jewish texts oppose any act by a human being that would hasten death. Therefore, Jewish law does not promote euthanasia under any circumstances. In recent times, however, many Jewish scholars have rethought this position. New technologies can keep the body alive in some circumstances way past any time when the person would be considered alive by the traditional Jewish criterion of breathing. In those cases, Jewish scholars have argued that it is in some cases appropriate to remove those technologies or, as it is expressed in the vernacular, to "pull the plug." It is also appropriate in many cases not to begin to use those technologies in the first place but to allow the process of death to take place in a natural way. Scholars often refer to the ancient story of the death of Rabbi Judah, the author of the Mishnah, a second-century legal text of great importance. As Rabbi Judah lay dying in an upstairs bedroom, his students downstairs kept praying for him, and their prayers were thought to be keeping him alive. Knowing that Rabbi Judah was ready to die, the servant who worked in the house dropped a pitcher. The loud noise disrupted the prayers, and Rabbi Judah's soul was allowed to depart. Although this is only a story and not a legal text, it has provided a warrant for contemporary scholars to argue that in certain circumstances, humans may intervene so as not to prolong a life that was ending.

Suicide

If Jews are not generally permitted to assist in the death of another person, then it follows that taking one's own life would also be viewed in a negative light. The same principle applies: the body belongs to God, and humans are only caretakers. It is obligatory for the human being, then, to care for his or her body, and it is not permissible according to this logic to end one's own life. Therefore, traditional Jewish law does not permit a suicide to receive any rites that honor the dead. However, this rather harsh approach is almost never adopted. First, Jewish law recognized that these rules are very difficult on mourners and conflict with the important rule that mourners should be comforted. There was also an understanding that most people who commit suicide are not acting out of free will or with full mental capacity. Therefore, the law requires that for someone's death to be defined as a suicide, the person would have had to committed the act in the presence of witnesses to whom they proclaimed the act as a suicide. The definition is so stringent that almost no one falls into the category. Nonetheless, the law remains to discourage people from committing suicide, given the Jewish tradition's preference for preserving life.

Organ Donation and Autopsy

Jewish tradition also opposes organ donation and autopsy. These are both considered acts that do not honor the dead because the dead must be honored by the proper burial of all parts of the body. (This principle is so far-reaching that it includes burying body parts that were surgically removed during the person's life before their death if at all possible.) However, Jewish law has become less stringent about these practices in more recent times. Although honoring the dead is indeed an important part of Jewish tradition, saving a life (*pikuah nefesh*) is always understood to take precedence over this and other commandments. Advances in medical science make autopsy an opportunity for research into inheritable diseases, and it is permitted under these circumstances. (And, of course, autopsy is permitted if there are legal requirements in the cases of suspected suicide or homicide.) Organ donation is also now widely practiced among Jews. Although not all organs directly save lives, most Jewish teachers follow the principle that quality of life is an important concept as well, and many people will live better lives as a result of organ donation.

JEWISH MOURNING PRACTICES

Jewish mourning begins when the family and friends of the deceased return from the burial site. Often, a pitcher of water is left outside the house where the mourning observances are taking place (house of mourning, or *shiva* house) for people to wash their hands symbolically on return from the cemetery. This custom probably has its roots in magic and superstition (to wash off the experience of being in a cemetery among the dead) but also takes on the symbolic meaning of a transition towards the next important phase: comforting the mourners (*nihum avelim*).

Traditional Jewish teaching places a high value on making sure that those who are experiencing grief receive adequate support from the community. Just as it is important to attend a funeral, community members are expected to participate in mourning observances. This is so important that some members of the community do not attend the funeral so that they can make sure the house is ready when the mourners return. The first thing the mourners do is sit together and eat a meal, called, appropriately, the meal of consolation, *seudat havra'ah*. It is customary to eat round foods, like eggs and lentils, as a reminder of the cycle of life and the continuity between birth and death. The mourners light a candle that burns for the seven days of mourning. They also remove their leather shoes (symbols of luxury) and wear slippers for the duration of this phase of mourning.

The name of the first phase of the mourning process is *shiva*. *Shiva* means seven in Hebrew and indicates the number of days that this first phase of mourning is observed. Seven is an important number in ancient Jewish tradition, symbolizing wholeness and completion (like the seven days of the week), and it is not surprising that this primary mourning observance is seven days in duration. Often this is referred to as "sitting *shiva*" because one of the customs is for the mourners to sit on low benches for the duration of this period of time. Mourners are also expected not to leave the house, except for the one day during the seven when *shiva* is not observed, the Jewish Sabbath. From sundown Friday until sundown Saturday the seven-day process is interrupted, and mourners are expected to go to synagogue. Otherwise, they remain in the house. Although the length of this strict time for mourning may seem onerous, the observance is actually not a full seven days. Any part of any day counts in the seven, so the day of the funeral is always counted as day one, and Friday daytime and Saturday evening are also included, and the seventh day ends after the morning prayers take place. Still, some shorten the observance to three days to accommodate the realities (and in many cases hardship) of remaining far from home or away from work or school that the full practice requires.

It is preferable to observe *shiva* in the house where the deceased lived so that the mourners can be surrounded by things that remind them of the person who died. Where this is impractical, *shiva* can be observed in the home of one of the mourners, and if necessary mourners can observe *shiva* in their own homes individually. When not in the home of the deceased, mourners often bring photographs and other keepsakes to display to remind them of the life of the person who has died.

Mourners observe various other customs in addition to sitting on low benches as a symbol of their grief. They keep doors unlocked to welcome everyone who has come to bring them comfort. They often cover the mirrors in the house to help them keep their attention focused away from themselves (and probably as a result of old superstitions that the spirit of the dead might appear in the mirror). The mourners also refrain from activities that bring pleasure: they do not engage in sexual relations, do not wear leather, bathe for pleasure, cut their hair, or wear cosmetics or perfume, as we observed was the case during Yom Kippur. As best they can, they refrain from housework and food preparation. They are also not permitted to study because study is considered a great pleasure in Jewish tradition, and they do not engage in worldly activities such as watching movies or television or playing games. Many do not use the computer, although more and more, it has become customary for people who cannot come to *shiva* to send condolence notes via e-mail. Because these provide comfort to the mourner, the prohibition against engaging in worldly activities excludes checking e-mail. These customs help the mourner to focus on the grieving process. Staying home for the seven days also promotes concentration on the mourning process.

During *shiva*, mourners primarily do two things. They have prayer services in their homes morning and evening, and they receive visitors who come to comfort them. They may also write in journals, look at photographs, or spend time resting because mourning is a deeply difficult psychological process, and rest is required to keep up their strength.

In keeping with the requirement to comfort the bereaved, members of the community are expected to make a visit to the house of mourning. It is traditional for the mourners to set the tone of the conversation and not to offer greetings to their visitors to indicate that as mourners, they stand outside the world of regular social intercourse. This gives the mourner the opportunity to experience his or her grief as he or she is experiencing it at the moment. This helps the visitor remember that the mourner is not expected to take care of the visitor's needs. The visitor can play a vital role in sharing stories about the deceased that will help the mourner in the grieving process. If a visit is not possible, a note (or an e-mail) is considered most appropriate. Mourners often reflect that these words of consolation are really helpful in the grieving process.

Visitors are also expected to participate in prayer services at the house of mourning. Jews pray three times daily, although the afternoon and evening services are often collapsed into one prayer time. For a prayer service to take place, Jews require the presence of a minyan (ten Jewish men for Orthodox Jews, ten Jewish men or women for all others). Community members come to the *shiva* house for morning and evening prayers. During the prayer service, mourners often take the opportunity to reminisce about the deceased.

They also recite the Mourner's Kaddish, or the memorial prayer for the dead. Kaddish means holy, and the Kaddish prayer is used in a variety of ways during most Jewish prayer services. For example, an abbreviated version, called the partial Kaddish, marks the place between different segments of the prayer service. The Kaddish is actually a doxology, or prayer of praise of God. Surprisingly, even the Mourner's version makes no mention of death whatsoever. Yet, it is the central prayer that is used during the period of mourning. Jews first recite the Kaddish at the end of the burial, and then continually: three times a day during *shiva*, regularly in the following month, daily for one year in memory of a parent, and at particular moments in the Jewish calendar year. It is always recited in a standing position, and normally in a "minyan" or prayer quorum, although liberal Jews may recite Kaddish even if there is not a community present. It is recited in Aramaic, the ancient language Jews spoke during the time of Jesus. Most Jews who recite Kaddish do not understand the words and read it in transliteration. In many ways, the meaning of the actual words is less important than their rhythmic cadence that holds a strong emotional power. For Jews, reciting Kaddish connects them to the Jewish community and to the past. The text follows:

Mourner:
   Let God's name be made great and holy in the world that was created as God willed. May God complete the holy realm in your own lifetime, in your days, and in the days of all the house of Israel, quickly and soon. And say: Amen.
Community:
   May God's great name be blessed, forever and as long as worlds endure.
Mourner:
   May it be blessed, and praised, and glorified, and held in honor, viewed with awe, embellished, and revered; and may the blessed name of holiness be hailed, though it be higher than all the blessings, songs, praises, and consolations that we utter in this world. And say: Amen.
   May Heaven grant universal peace, and life for us, and for all Israel. And say: Amen.
   May the one who creates harmony above, make peace for us and for all Israel, and for all who dwell on earth. And say: Amen.[4]

From this, we once again learn the lesson that for Jewish tradition, death is a part of life to be accepted and for which we praise God and God's creation. At the same time that Jewish tradition emphasizes the importance of recognizing that life goes on, it also affirms that people need a process and customs to help them grieve. *Shiva* makes provisions for both aspects.

Shiva ends on the morning of the seventh day after the morning prayers. The mourners and those present walk around the block, symbolizing the end of *shiva* and their return to the everyday world. After this intense mourning period, Jewish tradition defines another period of time, *Sheloshim*, or thirty. During the month (thirty days) after a death, mourners do not attend celebrations such as parties or weddings, but otherwise, they return to their daily work in the world. It is common not to listen to music during this period of time. Musical instruments were prohibited from religious services after the destruction of the temple by the Romans in the first century of the Common Era, and this prohibition echoes that observance because music is associated with celebration and not with mourning.

Sometimes *sheloshim* closes with a public memorial service that marks the end of this time of mourning and so brings closure to the experience of this stage of grief.

After the loss of a parent, mourners extend the restrictions of *sheloshim* for one year. During this time, they also observe a daily recitation of the Kaddish. For many, this returns them to an involvement in synagogue life because they must be present for daily services to recite the Kaddish with a minyan. In traditional Judaism and in Orthodox Judaism to this day, this daily recitation is incumbent upon sons but not daughters. It was this particular imbalance that led many Jewish women to rethink their roles in Jewish life and to demand equal rights. They were particularly influenced by Zionist leader Henrietta Szold, who wrote movingly about deciding to say Kaddish for her mother rather than accepting the offer of a male friend to do it for her in the early part of the twentieth century.[5] This custom of daily Kaddish recitation and reflection on the death of a parent has led several contemporary Jewish writers including Leon Wieselthier, Esther Broner, and Ari Goldman to publish memoirs that focus on this experience and the power it had to change their lives after the death of a parent.[6] Other Jews who do not feel bound by the restrictions of traditional Jewish customs recite Kaddish publicly when they can but also recite it privately each day for the year-long period.

Between two and eleven months after death, it is customary for Jews to have a headstone prepared and then to hold an unveiling of the stone at the cemetery. The headstone is not supposed to be elaborate. It usually contains the person's name and dates of birth and death in Hebrew and English and often the traditional phrase, "may his/her soul be bound up in the bounds of eternal life" from the *El Mohle Rahamim* memorial prayer. The service for unveiling the stone is also quite brief and mostly involves removing a covering, reading the words written there, and reciting the memorial prayer and the Kaddish. These ceremonies are meant to be attended only by close friends and family but are also opportunities to give mourners some closure or to include children in the grieving process in a less charged way than at a funeral. It is also customary for the mourners to speak about their memories and feelings during these brief services. When leaving the gravesite, it is customary to place a pebble or small rock on the grave. The rock is your personal marker that indicates you have come to visit. (This differs from other traditions where it is more common to adorn graves with flowers.)

After the mourning period ends, it is still incumbent upon Jews to perform rituals to remember their loved ones. Four times a year, on Yom Kippur, and the three pilgrimage festivals (Sukkot, Passover, and Shavuot), there are communal memorial services as part of the prayer service, and these are times when Jews are reminded to visit the graves of their relatives and friends. Jews light candles that burn for twenty-four hours in memory of their dead at these points and also on the *yahrzeit*, or anniversary of someone's death. The *yahrzeit* is observed on the year's anniversary according to the Hebrew calendar, which does not correspond directly with the calendar we use in Western societies, so it is often the case that synagogues and funeral homes send out notifications to remind people about this annual ritual. Some liberal Jews also commemorate the *yahrzeit* on the secular date. For a parent's *yahrzeit*, you are also expected to go to synagogue to recite Kaddish. For many people, the observance of *yahrzeit*, although not marked with elaborate ritual, remains a significant marker of time gone by and provides a clearly marked time to focus on the memory of their loved ones or to visit their graves.

These customs were created at a time when Jews did not have much social connection with the Christians or Muslims among whom they lived, so Jewish ritual has little to say about how to bury or grieve for the people in one's life who are not Jewish. Now that intermarriage is more common, Jewish cemeteries are more accustomed to burying non-Jewish partners alongside their spouses, and converts to Judaism have begun to incorporate Jewish rituals when mourning for their non-Jewish parents, siblings, and friends.

These rituals also were created at a time when miscarriage, stillbirth, and neonatal death (up to one month old) were such common occurrences that no ritual was observed. In recent years, the Jewish community has become more sensitive to these losses and has begun to create ceremonies and, in the case of neonatal death, permit full burial and mourning customs to take place.

These new and regularly established mourning rituals indicate the most important dimension of the way Jews conceptualize the role of death. Death is not a tragedy but something that is incorporated into daily life. For Jews, individuals live on primarily in the memory of those whose lives they influenced and changed. Remembering our ancestors and loved ones is the most important element of Jewish mourning practice. It is reflected in the nature of the eulogy delivered at the funeral, the focus on talking about the deceased during shiva, requirements to visit graves and recite memorial prayers on holy days and anniversaries of the death, and the custom among Ashkenazi Jews to name their children after deceased relatives. Having your children name their children after your beloved parent, having a child to say kaddish for you when you die, and being part of a community that will perpetuate your memory is as close as Jews get to an understanding of immortal life.

There is little Jewish concern about the afterlife, although Jewish philosophy posits a resurrection (for some of souls, for others of body) at the end of days. Jewish texts also describe the *olam haba*, or world to come. These texts provide descriptions of what the world to come will be like (there will be peace in the world; every day will be like the Sabbath; the righteous will have a reward). However, these depict hopes and aspirations for a possible future world, not a definitive expectation of life after death.[7] It is in this life that Jews learn to cope with loss and find meaning through memory that forms the basis of the ritual practices described here and the Jewish way of death and mourning.

NOTES

This article is based on an essay by the author, "Jewish Approaches to Death and Dying," in *Death and Dying in World Religions*, ed. Lucy Bregman (Boston: Pearson Custom Publishing, 2004), 33–44.

1. Although different Jewish groups today approach rituals and beliefs differently, and Orthodox, Conservative, Reform, Reconstructionist, Israeli, and secular Jews will differ in the emphasis they place on each of these rituals and beliefs, this essay will present a general introduction to traditional practice.

2. See *Ethical Wills: A Modern Jewish Treasury*, ed. Jack Riemer and Nathaniel Stampfer (New York: Schocken Books, 1983).

3. Certain Jewish holy days and the weekly observance of the Sabbath take precedence over this rule, and funerals are postponed if the death falls in too close approximation to these times.

4. Translation from *Reconstructionist Rabbinical Association Rabbi's Manual*, ed. Seth Riemer (Wyncote, PA: Reconstructionist Rabbinical Association, 1997).

5. You can find Szold's remarks quoted in *The Jewish Woman: New Perspectives*, ed. Elizabeth Koltun (New York: Schocken Press, 1976) in an article by Marion Kaplan, "Henrietta Szold, Liberated Woman."

6. See Ari Goldman, *Living a Year of Kaddish* (New York: Schocken Books, 2003); Leon Wieseltier, *Kaddish* (London: Picador, 2000); and Esther Broner, *Mornings and Mourning: A Kaddish Journal* (Harper Collins Canada, 1994).

7. See Neil Gillman, *The Death of Death: Resurrection and Immortality in Jewish Thought* (Woodstock, VT: Jewish Lights, 1997) and Simcha Raphael, *Jewish Views of the Afterlife* (New Jersey: Jason Aronson, 2002).

CHAPTER 3

The Rituals for Dying, Death, and Bereavement among Roman Catholics and Eastern Orthodox Christians

Regina A. Boisclair

This chapter concerns the rituals for the dying, the dead, and the bereaved for the Catholic[1] and Orthodox Churches. The Orthodox East and Catholic West were one more or less united church from the fourth century until 1054 CE.[2] Disputes, largely based on the authority of the pope, led to their separation in the eleventh century. Today, these churches are the largest branches of Christianity,[3] with communities that continue from the time of the apostles.[4] Although Catholics and Orthodox have much in common with other Christians in their understandings of human mortality, the practices and rituals they associate with dying, death, and bereavement are more similar to one another than those of most other Christians.[5]

Rituals respond to specific understandings, and many understandings of death and features of Catholic and Orthodox rituals today are in continuity with those of the early church and later developments.[6] This chapter begins with a brief overview of early Christian understandings of death and identifies the features that we know of the early rituals, and it then indicates salient features that developed in subsequent eras before discussing the rituals for the dying, the dead, and the bereaved in the Catholic and Orthodox Churches today. The conclusion identifies the past traditions that inform present practices.

EARLY CHRISTIANITY

Although every religion includes understandings and rituals relating to death, in no religion is death as prominent as it is in Christianity. From its very inception, Christianity was and remains a religion with a dominant focus on death. Jesus' crucifixion and his followers' subsequent experience of him as resurrected shortly after his death and burial are *the* central facets of Christianity (I Cor 15: 3–4).[7] In the first centuries, BCE and CE, some Jews considered death the universal punishment for Adam and Eve's disobedience in the garden (Apocalypse of Moses, 4 Ezra, and 2 Baruch);[8] the early Jesus movement adopted that understanding of death (Romans 5:12; I Cor 15:21). Indeed, most Christians continue to speak of death as a condition inherited from Adam and Eve as God's universal punishment for their original disobedience.[9] Early Christians also claimed that the death of Jesus effected forgiveness of sins (Mt 26:28), acquittal, and salvation for those who believed (Rom 5:8–10, 15–18).

Then, as now, Christian belief is that life does not end at death but that it is changed. This was not unique. In the Greco-Roman world of the first century CE, most pagans believed in some form of life beyond earthly life— be it as a miserable shade in Hades or as Plato's ideal of a disembodied soul in the Elysian Fields. At that time, Jews had three different understandings of death. The Sadducees seem to have had no belief in an afterlife (Lk 20:27; Josephus, *Jewish Wars* 2:154ff).[10] The Pharisees and apocalyptic writers believed the dead sleep until a time when God would resurrect and restore their embodied life (Dan 12:1–3) much like the dry bones in Ezekiel's vision (Ez 37). Some sensed that after a long resurrected life and numerous progeny in a blissful kingdom on earth, the risen righteous would die again to live in a higher spiritual world (I Enoch 10:10; 25:6). Hellenized Jews, like Philo, and the Essenes believed in the immortality of the soul (Wis 3:1–9) and eternity in a place of joy for the just and virtuous (Ps 73:23–26; Ps 49:2–5).

The Jesus movement drew from these Jewish understandings of resurrection and immortality yet transformed them in response to their intense and enthusiastic faith in God and Jesus. Early beliefs can be reconstructed from sayings of Jesus, the letters of Paul, and the visions of John of Patmos in his Book of Revelation. The gospels record that Jesus spoke of resurrected life as spiritual, eternal, and free from ties of earthly kinship (Lk 20: 35–36). He taught that the righteous would go to heaven with God, whereas the wicked would be punished (Lk 13:23–30; 16:19–28). Although Paul first believed the righteous dead would sleep until Christ's second coming, when both the dead and those living would be taken up with the Lord forever (I Thes 4: 13–18), he later wrote if he were to die, he would be with Christ (Phil 1:21–23). Paul's most significant teachings on death and the afterlife are his insistence that resurrected bodies are spiritual

(I Cor 15: 36–58), that death is an image for the Christian life of the righteous, who live by the Spirit, having crucified the passions and desires of fleshly existence when they were baptized (Rom 5:5–8, 6:3–11, 8:5–13; Gal 5:1–25); and that in eternity, one experiences God "face to face" (I Cor 13:12).[11] John of Patmos described a vision of heaven where the righteous were in the presence of God and Christ (Rev 21:3–7; 22:3–5); he also portrayed the ultimate and final defeat of Satan (Rev 20:10), who manifested his influence in this world as the Roman Empire and the imperial cult. These texts indicate that in the early church, enthusiasm on the part of believers and their expectation that Christ's second coming was imminent replaced the concerns of this world such as kinship, pleasures, and power. The early Christians considered self-denial and death, especially death by martyrdom, united them with the sufferings of Christ. This ideal of martyrdom is clearly expressed in a letter to the Romans by the Apostolic Father, Ignatius of Antioch,[12] and the second-century "Epistle of the Church at Smyrna" that recounts the death of Polycarp.[13]

Roman pagans feared the dead and their funerals sought to appease the deceased to insure their "shades" would not wander and disturb the living. Generally, Romans cremated the dead, although some were entombed. Bodies or cremains were carried in processions by the bereaved outside the city walls with burning incense and hired musicians at night, lit by candles or tapers and buried in mausoleums or catacombs, whereas the urns of ashes were placed in a columbarium. Jews always entombed bodies[14] and buried them outside a city or town on the day of death, if possible. Jews considered burying the dead an obligation and work of mercy. Both Romans and Jews would wash, anoint, and lay out a corpse, pray, burn incense, and carry the deceased to its final resting place where many had a meal in honor of the deceased (*refrigerium*). In the first century, it was common for the immediate family and close friends to gather on the anniversaries of death or burial at or near the tomb for a memorial meal. Christians continued the long-established practices of their neighbors that did not conflict with Christian beliefs.[15] From the art in the catacombs, it is clear that early Christians honored the bodies of the dead. They did not cremate in antiquity,[16] their principal service was at night, and they continued the practice of the funeral meal or "refreshment." Although the practice of annual meals memorializing the departed continued, these soon evolved into a celebration of the Lord's Supper near the tomb of the deceased. What emerged from this was the belief that prayer was the fitting care for the dead. The early Christians also celebrated the triumph of the martyrs by constructing shrines or memorials at their tombs and sometimes their homes. What emerged from this was the cult of saints and belief in the communion of the saints, i.e., those in heaven who are honored and joined with the Christians on earth. The honor given to the bodies of the martyrs also led to the cult of relics that developed in the second century and played a significant role in the devotional life of the middles ages and beyond.[17]

THE PATRISTIC AND MIDDLE AGES

Between the second and fourth centuries CE, the Jesus movement grew into a gentile religion independent of Judaism. The church of martyrs and early confessors changed when Christianity became the religion of the Empire. Many new Christians had a greater interest in this world and earthly life than those who first responded to the teachings of the apostles. In response to the fact that not all Christians who died were worthy to enter the presence of God yet not deserving of the everlasting punishment, Clement of Alexandria and Origin began in differing ways to distinguish between a cleansing fire that could be temporary and an eternal fire in the afterlife. Although these Greek theologians were otherwise influential in Orthodoxy, the existence of a purgatory, toward which they were pointing, never took hold in the East.

In the West, the understanding of purgatory originated with Augustine at the turn of the fourth and fifth centuries. It emerged slowly and became enormously prominent by the thirteenth century.[18] It was ratified as official teaching at the Councils of Florence (1431–1445) and Trent (1545–1563).[19] Purgatory was and is understood as a place or condition of temporary punishment that purged unabsolved venial sins (lesser sins that would not render one deserving of an eternity in hell) and removed residual remaining punishments for sins already confessed and absolved. For those who died in a state of grievous (mortal) sin, no cleansing was possible. Most often, purgatory is imaged and imagined as a place that purges by fire, although official teachings do not require such an understanding. Catholic belief in purgatory was one issue that contributed to the schism with the Orthodox in 1053 and was soundly rejected by the Protestant reformers. It remains the major difference in the understanding of afterlife between Roman Catholics and other Christians.

The Catholic Church teaches that the souls of the dead in purgatory can do nothing to improve their own situation. However, Catholicism has and continues to believe that the living can abbreviate the required time of suffering for souls in purgatory by prayer, fasting, and charity, including monetary offerings to the priest for celebrating Masses on behalf of the dead.[20] The conviction that Masses benefited the dead led to the construction of churches with many side altars that accommodated Masses for the deceased. By the end of the Middle Ages, there were many "altarists," priests whose only job was to recite the office[21] and to say Masses for the dead at a particular altar many times every day.

Concurrent to the emergence of belief in purgatory was the development of the application of indulgences. Indulgences assigned a temporal remission from the required time of purification due in purgatory for the venial sins and residual punishments due for mortal and venial sins already forgiven. Prayers and various devotions were assigned a specific number of days, weeks, months, or years that would be removed from the time assigned to purgatory. Some practices were assigned plenary indulgences that canceled all time due in purgatory. Indulgences were and are attained for oneself or for the souls of the departed in purgatory.

Belief in indulgences was and is founded on the theory that prayers and good works bring merit and that the church has a treasury of merit, drawn from the death of Jesus and the good works of the saints known and unknown already in heaven, who did not need them. Thus, this merit was available to be applied to others. In the late Middle Ages, the assignment of indulgences to almsgiving led to the sale of indulgences; this became the immediate cause for Martin Luther to issue his 95 Theses that led to the Protestant Reformation. The Council of Trent that met in the six-teenth century to respond to the Reformation reaffirmed its understanding of indulgences but prohibited their sale as an abuse. As Paul Binski notes: "A religion whose view of the Last Things [death, judgment, heaven and hell] had been based upon the principle of uncertainty was transformed into one founded upon an absolute calculation; and it was on this basis that much of the religious institutional development of medieval Europe came in turn to be established."[22]

Christian belief in the communion of saints is expressed in the eighth-century Apostles' Creed. However, the term "communion of saints" is found in the fifth-century documents. The term links the understanding of Jesus of the reign of God, the Pauline understanding of the body of Christ (Ephesians 4:1–16), with Hebrew's great cloud of witnesses (Hebrews 12:1). Catholics understand the communion of saints as a spiritual solidar-ity binding the living (the church militant) with the dead, in heaven (the church triumphant) and the souls in purgatory (church suffering). Thus, Catholics pray to saints, seeking their intercession as friends of God for various forms of assistance. They also pray for the souls in purgatory and to the souls in purgatory who cannot ameliorate their own situation but can and do intercede to God for the living who pray to them. During the Mid-dle Ages, the Catholic Church dedicated November 1 as All Saints' Day to honor all saints in heaven, especially those who are not officially recog-nized as saints by the Catholic Church.[23] The church also determined to observe November 2 as All Souls' Day, when Catholics pray for the souls of all who had died. These two observances continue to this day.

The Orthodox understand the communion of the saints to be the saints in heaven, with whom the living join in the worship of God in cel-ebrations of the divine mysteries (Eucharist) that bring heaven to earth.[24] The Orthodox do not believe in purgatory (although some do not pre-clude the possibility of its existence). Although they reject the Catholic theory of indulgences, the Orthodox do pray for the dead and the living and, like Catholics, the Orthodox pray to the saints seeking their inter-cession to God.

Another relevant understanding that Catholics derive from Augustine is the belief that the disobedience of Adam and Eve not only brought death to all generations but also a condition called original sin. Augustine considered that original sin was transmitted in the act of procreation and that the guilt of the sin of Adam and Eve is inherited by all humanity. Although the Catholic Church rejected the theory of transmission through procreation, it came to accept original sin as a condition that inclines peo-ple towards evil. Thomas Aquinas considered original sin the inability to keep one's inferior powers submitted to reason and directed towards super-natural ends. Aquinas also recognized that the inclination to sin was not totally removed by baptism.

The Orthodox East recognizes that death and an inclination toward sin are the consequences of the sin of Adam and Eve and the fate of all humanity, but Orthodoxy rejects the idea that all humanity inherits the guilt from the first sin. The Protestant reformers accepted the theory of original sin and emphasized that baptism did not erase the power of "concupiscence," the deep desire for sensual pleasures and worldly gratifications.

At one time, Catholics assumed that all who died without baptism, which remits all sin, were damned, although they sensed that infants and young children would not suffer but spend eternity in a place called limbo. Limbo was considered a place of natural happiness where innocent children who were not baptized would spend eternity. This hypothesis was never an official Catholic teaching, although in the past fifty years Catholic theolo-gians rejected the very idea that a good God would deny children from heaven. The presumption that all those who have not been baptized are damned and the belief in limbo are no longer part of Catholic teaching.

In the Middle Ages, Catholic theologians and preachers, who encour-aged meditation on the "four last things," death, judgment, hell, and heaven, led a society in which many, burdened by terrified consciences, joined one of the many penitential confraternities that practiced self mor-tifications such as fasting, flagellation, and wearing hair shirts. Fear domi-nated much of the population, and monastic life became a popular choice in hopes of securing eternal life in heaven. Such concerns were magnified by the pandemic known as the Black Death in the fourteenth century and other plagues that ravaged Europe in each generation through to the eight-eenth century. In response to these epidemics, the ubiquity of death became the topic of plays such as *Everyman* and paintings of the *Dance of Death*. One such image is the 1484 representation in the vestibule of St. Mary's church in Berlin.[25] Fear and the ubiquity of death continued to influence music in such works as the 1849 *Totentanz* by Franz Liszt. Although Dante's *Divine Comedy* (1308–1321) was completed before the ravages of the Black Death, his three-volume allegory of hell, purgatory, and heaven is the clearest description of the Catholic understandings that dominated the medieval era.

Despite the emphasis on the last judgment with images of Christ judging the world carved above many of the central entrances to most Gothic churches, medieval pastoral practices for the dying emphasized the particular judgment that took place at death when each individual would be assessed and assigned to heaven, purgatory, or hell. To guide a "good death," manuals—(called *Ars moriendi*)—detailed the temptations to the theological virtues of faith, hope, and charity that were apt to afflict the dying: unbelief, despair, impatience, pride, and avarice. These were described or pictured with the ideals that opposed them, concluding with a representation of a good death. These manuals were produced as an effort by the church to educate the laity on sins and their remedies.[26] Many of these images were also found in the stained glass of churches. At the time, priests who attended the dying would bring a crucifix so that the person dying could fix his or her eyes on it and associate their own sufferings in solidarity with those of Christ. This pastoral concern to foster identification of the dying with the sufferings of Christ is especially clear in Matthias Grünwald's crucifixion scene of the Insenheim altarpiece for the hospital chapel of St. Anthony's Monastery because the marks of flagellation on the body of Jesus match the skin disfigurations of the patients in that hospital dying of ergotism, then called St. Anthony's Fire.

In the fourth century, liturgical practices developed differently in different locations. The earliest extant records of funerals indicate that the rituals began in the home before death with the reception of viaticum (communion for the dying)—at the last possible moment—followed by a reading of Christ's passion narrative and the recitation of Ps 42. At the moment of death, Ps 114 was recited, and during washing and preparation of the body, Pss. 139, 93, and 23 were recommended. The body was carried in procession led by candles to the church, understood as the symbol of the heavenly Jerusalem, and received with incense, prayers, and psalms, where it remained for the vigil on the night before burial during which mourners would intermittently pray and sing psalms. Although there was as yet no funeral liturgy, mourners would attend the liturgy of the day celebrated in the morning. As the body was carried to the place of burial, Pss 25 and 118 were recited. At the site of burial, Pss 51, 42, 43, and 132 were part of the final service of commendation.[27]

In the East from the fifth century CE, there was, and is, among the Orthodox significant uniformity in the Byzantine rituals attributed to St. John Chrysostom, although the rites were translated into the various vernacular languages of different places.[28] Although Charlemagne tried to consolidate and unify the Latin liturgical rites of his ninth-century Holy Roman Empire to conform to Roman practices, these took on Gallican and Gelasian elaborations and other customs that originated in various places. A Frankish-Gelasian Roman hybrid missal went back to Rome during this reform, but ritual uniformity in the West never took hold until the Council of Trent.[29] The Catholic West ignored local languages. The only unity of Catholic rituals was that they were all celebrated in Latin.

Although the celebration of the Lord's Supper is one of the earliest memories of Christian care for the deceased, a funeral or *Requiem* Mass did not emerge until the twelfth century. Because this replaced the Mass of the day, it removed the funeral rituals from the quotidian life of the church. The distinctive medieval contribution to the funeral liturgies of the West is captured by the chanting of the *De Profundis* (Ps 130) and the *Miserere* (Ps 51) and, most importantly, the inclusion of the *Dies Irea* that came to be sung as a sequence between the Epistle and Gospel. This sublime and terrifying poem pictures the "day of vengeance" and its cosmic destruction. The speaker trembles with fear and anguish, as the divine Judge appears. "Ah poor me! What shall I mutter?" he cries in self-pity and remorse for his sinfulness. Although this clearly evokes the awe and ultimacy of death and other "last things," it is not intended to console or offer a sense of hope.[30]

While the pastoral focus of the era promoted an individual's particular judgment at death, the *Dies Irae* in the *Requiem* Mass stressed the general judgment at the end of time. In the early church, the second coming was considered a consolation; and in the medieval church it was feared. By the thirteenth century, special liturgies for the burial of baptized children begin to appear. These rituals did not comfort the bereaved; they are noted for a tone of joy and thanksgiving because the deceased is considered to be in heaven.

The fifth century introduced the practice of anointing the sick with oil, blessed by a bishop, following James 5:14–15. At first, all Christians could anoint other sick Christians for healing. In the eighth century, the sense that the practice healed the sick gave way to a perception of the practice as effecting forgiveness of sins. From that time on, in both Catholic and Orthodox churches, it would be administered only by priests. Among the Orthodox, anointing was never totally restricted to individuals close to death; among Catholics, the practice of anointing persons suffering from any serious sickness continued until the twelfth century. In the late twelfth and thirteenth centuries, European theology recognized this practice as a sacrament, reserved it for the dying, and called it extreme unction (literally, last anointing). It replaced viaticum as the very last sacrament before death. Those who recovered after receiving extreme unction were called Lazaruses and according to popular piety were prohibited from engaging in sex, eating meat, making a new will, or walking in bare feet![31] Extreme unction came to be understood as the last rites, exclusively, although the rites ideally continued to include the confession and absolution of sins and the last reception of communion, called viaticum, and anointing.

Once Christianity was legalized in the fourth century, burials started to take place in or near churches. Burial inside was generally reserved for the important, and burial outside in ground near the church was generally temporary. By the fourteenth century, bones were dug up and placed in charnel houses near the church. This practice was already common among Palestinian Jews in the first century CE, and has been followed continually in some places such as at the Greek Orthodox St. Catherine's Monastery in the Sinai of Egypt. In the ninth century, it became common to sanctify the sites of burial with holy water and incense, and the practice of issuing an absolution before burial was introduced in the tenth century along with the practice of making a sign of the cross over the gravesite after burial.[32]

The early Christians reverenced the mortal remains of the martyrs and confessors. As time went on, the cult of relics led to the division of bodies of those considered saints. The head could be buried in one place and various parts of the body of a saint in others, whereas small sections were set into reliquaries that could be sent to other places and easily transported. This led to some controversy. Many in the Middle Ages felt that one's actual body would be reconstituted at the general resurrection so the practice of dividing the body would make it difficult for the person to arrive at the last judgment. The popularity of relics led to many abuses. Many were fakes. Medieval tombs of the elite placed inside the churches became increasingly elaborate. Those of saints such as Thomas à Beket in Canterbury, England, became the destiny of pilgrimages.[33]

FROM THE COUNCIL OF TRENT TO THE SECOND VATICAN COUNCIL

The Council of Trent, held in the sixteenth century in response to the issues raised by Protestant reformers, corrected many real abuses in the Catholic Church and defined Catholic views in terms that distinguished Catholic from Protestant premises. It affirmed extreme unction as one of seven sacraments and endorsed belief in purgatory and the understanding that the prayers of the living could benefit souls in purgatory. Trent approved indulgences but prohibited the practice of selling them. Trent endorsed the practice of offering Masses for the dead and that it was valid for a priest to offer Masses without the presence of others.

The most significant contribution of the Council of Trent was the stabilization of the Roman Liturgy in 1614. From this time on, local practices were dissolved, and the clergy throughout the world were required to follow the same texts and rubrics. The Tridentine Missal of 1614 became the norm for liturgical rites. The requiem Mass it established was somber and simplified according to Roman practice. It called for black vestments and included the *Dies Irae* sung as a sequence between the epistle reading and that of the gospel. This ritual set a tone that came to express both fear and grief. At the same time, this requiem, as with all Tridentine rubrics, dissolved community participation and became something the clergy did while the community watched.

The funeral rites provided for the priest to meet the body at the home of the deceased, sprinkle it with holy water, recite Ps 130, and accompany it in a procession led by candles to the church while reciting Ps 51. Over time, this rite was conducted just inside the door of the church. This would be followed by the recitation of the *Benedictus* (Luke 1:68–79) and an elaborate formula of absolution. The requiem Mass that followed sought to reinforce Catholic understandings of eschatology in opposition to the challenges of the Reformers. It was followed by prayers and blessings over the casket and a service at the cemetery where the priest would sprinkle the casket and grave with holy water, recite the Lord's Prayer, and in some places throw some dirt over the casket.[34]

The years between the Council of Trent and the Second Vatican Council held from 1962 to 1965 witnessed the development of lay devotions to compensate for the fact that few really understood Latin to follow the rituals. The devotional practices for "First Fridays" and "First Saturdays" claimed to assure practitioners a "good death." First Friday devotions were introduced in the seventeenth century based on an instruction received during a vision of Christ, by St. Margaret Mary Alocoque.[35] This devotion proposed that those who receive communion on nine consecutive First Fridays would die in a state of grace and received the last rites. The practice was understood as an assurance the Sacred Heart of Jesus would be a refuge at the time of death. First Saturdays devotions claimed that those who confessed their sins, received communion, prayed five decades of the rosary (Catholic prayer beads), and meditated on its 15 mysteries on five consecutive First Saturdays would be assured of Mary's assistance at the hour of their death. The devotion was introduced in 1917 from a report of the children who received a vision of Mary at Fatima, Portugal. Both devotions, especially First Fridays, were enormously popular in North America before the Second Vatican Council.

Christianity can be rightly accused of the cultivation of a fear of death in sermons, catechisms, hymns, and images. This tendency began to be tempered by the mid-nineteenth century as the doctrine of the communion of saints came to recognize that the dead should experience the reunion with loved ones already deceased. By the nineteenth century, there was an increasing practice to print and distribute black and white memorial cards of the deceased with a representation of Jesus or Mary or St. Joseph, the patron saint of a good death, on one side and the name and dates and often a picture of the person who had died with a prayer for their soul printed on the verso. In the mid-twentieth century, the pictures were in color, and the practice of printing a picture of the deceased ceased. This distribution of cards with the name and dates of the deceased together with a prayer continues in many places.

During this time in history, the sense that the last rites were reserved for the dying led many to delay calling a priest to come to administer the sacraments. However, there was also an increasing fervor, especially in France, to seek deathbed conversions of individuals who had abandoned the Catholic faith. By the mid-twentieth century, nearly every Catholic family had a kit with all the essentials needed for a priest's visit, and there was a gradual growing sense that these sacraments should be administered to anyone seriously ill and not necessarily dying. Between Trent and Vatican II, cannon law required that priests refuse to officiate at the services for lapsed Catholics, and even some priests refused to conduct services for those who were known to be anticlerical, even if they were devout Catholics. During this era, those who committed suicide, died from a botched abortion, or were considered public sinners would not be buried with Catholic rites or in consecrated ground, although some priests would offer Mass for the bereaved. The practice of offering Masses for the dead continued after Trent, although the practice was significantly modified.

CONTEMPORARY PRACTICES FOR THE DYING

After the Second Vatican Council, the Catholic Church changed most of its liturgical texts and sought to foster a more biblical theology. Extreme unction, one of the three "last rites" for the dying (confession, extreme unction, viaticum [final communion, understood as heavenly food for the journey]), considered the sealing of forgiveness, is now called anointing and understood as a sacrament of healing and forgiveness following James 5:14–15. It is now given by a priest to any Catholic who is ill and requests it. It is often administered two or four times a year in parishes with a general invitation to all its members with ailments to receive the sacrament. The Orthodox identify this sacrament as the Holy Mystery of Unction and have never confined this to the dying but understand the sacrament as bringing spiritual and physical healing and forgiveness. The Orthodox have a ritual for solemn public anointing that requires seven priests to administer.

Catholic pastoral care of the dying includes an opportunity for private and an often general confession of sins of a lifetime, if possible during a separate visit. In any case, after the sacrament of reconciliation is completed, others are encouraged to be present for the anointing and viaticum if reception of these sacraments is to follow. It is desirable that a Mass with white vestments be said with a small gathering in the home or hospital room and at a time when the person who is dying can participate. This should be at a different time than reconciliation and anointing. During the liturgy, there should be time for the renewal of the baptismal profession. The liturgy ends with a special blessing and apostolic pardon that remits all the temporary punishment still due for sins that have been confessed and absolved.

Because it is encouraged that one receive the sacrament of reconciliation and anointing when one is fully conscious, it is not unusual that an individual who is dying will receive viaticum several times.[36] Although confession and anointing must be administered by a priest, any Catholic may be charged with bringing viaticum because it is increasingly unlikely that a priest will be available for daily visits. When viaticum is being offered apart from a Mass, the minister of viaticum should ask the person near death to make an act of contrition, recite the Apostles' Creed, and to join with the minister and any others who are present in saying the Lord's Prayer. All who receive communion are asked to pray beforehand: "Lord, I am not worthy to receive you but only say the word and I shall be healed." After communion has been offered to all Catholics present who wish to receive, the minister of viaticum speaks directly to the person dying, saying "May the Lord Jesus protect you and lead you to eternal life," and then ends by offering a blessing.

In Orthodox practice, a priest will chant the *Office of the Sick* at the bedside of very ill persons. When death is near, and a priest is present, he will chant the *Office of the Parting of Souls* and anoint the person who is dying. It is an Orthodox tradition that the last act of one who senses s/he is dying is to make the sign of the cross on their bodies. If no priest can be available, a layman or woman should recite the following prayer from the *Office of the Parting of Souls*:

> Receive thou in peace the soul of this thy servant/handmaid [N], Lord give it rest in the everlasting mansions of the Saints; through the grace of Thine only begotten Son, Our Lord, and God and Savior, Jesus Christ: with whom also thou art blessed, together with Thine all-holy and good, and life-giving Spirit, now and ever, unto all ages. Amen.[37]

All rituals have provisions for emergency situations, and among Catholics, if necessary, the rites can be simplified to anointing and viaticum or just viaticum unless the person who is dying asks for the sacrament of reconciliation, which would be first. If the individual is unconscious but alive, the priest may anoint the body; if dead, the priest may not anoint the body. He may have to explain to the bereaved that sacraments are only for the living while assuring them that their own prayers can assist the person who has died. He will offer a prayer for the person who has died and welcome anyone present to recite with him one of the commendations of the dying, such as:

> I commend you, my dear brother/sister, to almighty God, and entrust you to your Creator. May you return to him who formed you from the dust of the earth. May holy Mary and all the saints come to meet you as you go forth from this life. May Christ who was crucified for you bring you peace and freedom. May Christ who died for you admit you to his garden of Paradise.

May Christ the true Shepherd acknowledge you as one of his flock. May he forgive your sins, and set you among those he has chosen. May you see your Redeemer face to face, and enjoy the vision of God forever. Amen.[38]

CONTEMPORARY PRACTICES FOR THE DEAD AND BEREAVED

After death, in Catholic practice in the United States, preparation of the body for a wake or viewing and the funeral is generally the work of a professional undertaker. During the interval between death and the visitations, one or more of the bereaved family should be invited to decide which rituals are appropriate and what to include among the approved options before the rites of committal.[39] "Christians celebrate the funeral rites to offer worship, praise, and thanksgiving to God for the gift of life which has now been returned to God, the author of life and hope for the just. The Mass, the memorial of Christ's death and resurrection, is the principal celebration of the Christian funeral."[40] There is an alternate rite for places without a priest and a ritual specifically designed for the funeral of a child.

There is a prepared text for a gathering in the presence of the body that is appropriate to use when a family first gathers at the body before or after the body is prepared for burial and before others come to view the body and express their condolences to the most immediate bereaved. The minister of this rite may be a priest, deacon, or layperson. This rite and that of the vigil are preferable to a recitation of the rosary,[41] a private devotion that became a popular way for Catholics to pray when all Catholic rites were in Latin. On this particular issue, although some dioceses have prohibited recitation of the rosary by priests and deacons, pastoral sensitivity is advised, and if the bereaved sense their needs demand the recitation of a rosary, it would be appropriate for a lay minister to lead the devotion that many Catholics have long associated with wakes.

In planning the funeral, the pastors and ministers must learn and keep in mind the life of the deceased and the immediate circumstance of death, the spiritual needs of those bereaved, and their psychological need to express their grief. The Tridentine funeral rites with black vestments and somber songs, especially the *Dies Irae*, served as a clear expression of grief. The new rites developed following a mandate of Vatican II express a far better theology with respect to death and Christian hope, although the funeral Mass often fails to respond to the reality of grief. Planning before a death is advised, but most often, this occurs after the death and before the wake. In conducting interviews with the family, the pastor or associate who meets the family is to remember that apart from the blessings and prayers that benefit the one who has died, the rituals seek to give comfort to the bereaved.

The vigil liturgy, which is optional, best accommodates grief and should be encouraged whether it be in the home of the deceased or the most immediate family or friend(s), a funeral parlor or chapel or, as is most ideal, in the church. It is generally celebrated on the evening before the funeral. If the vigil will be held in a church, as is increasingly more common, the body should taken to the church and provision be made to secure the coffin after the service. When this takes place, the rite of reception of the body precedes the vigil liturgy and is omitted from the funeral. The body would then be carried into the church by bearers chosen by the family. The presiding minister (a deacon or priest) and those assisting meet the coffin and its bearers at the door of the church with a greeting such as: "May the grace and peace of the Father, who raised Jesus from the dead, be always with you."[42] The coffin is then sprinkled with holy water with the words: "In the waters of baptism **N** died with Christ and rose with him to new life. May s/he now share with him eternal glory."[43] The coffin is then covered with a white pall (cloth) by family, friends, the bearers, or the presiding minister and led into the church with candles that are placed by the coffin.[44] A symbol of Christian faith such as the Book of Gospel, a Bible, or a cross or crucifix carried in during the procession is placed on the coffin. The presider then invites those assembled to pray and offers an opening prayer. This is followed by the reading of I John 3:1–2, Psalm 103 (preferably sung), and the Gospel from John 14:1–6 is proclaimed, and a homily follows. This is followed by a litany of the saints, the Lord's Prayer, and after the concluding prayer, one or more members or friends of the family may speak in remembrance of the deceased.[45] These eulogies are appropriate at the vigil service, but they should never be included in the funeral Mass itself because the Mass is celebrated by and for the living. After the eulogies, the presider concludes the vigil with a blessing.

Among the Orthodox, after death, the body is washed and clothed in new garments, often by family members, and then the body may be returned to the home, where it is laid out in a coffin with the top open to reveal the body and an icon is placed in the hands. The body is then taken to the church several days before the funeral and placed before the altar. A cross is placed in the coffin lid. The night before the funeral, there is often an all-night vigil during which close family and friends chant psalms and read selections from the gospels.

The Catholic funeral should always include a Mass. However, there are situations in which no priest is available. Apart from the offering and consecration of the Eucharist, the two rites are very similar, a priest or deacon would wear white vestments, and a lay leader would be vested in a white alb. The service begins by receiving the body if it is not already in the church. Whether or not this has occurred, the Mass or service begins with an entrance song, a greeting by the priest presiding followed by opening prayers. After one or two readings from scripture, a psalm and the proclamation of a gospel passage that may be chosen by the family or requested by the deceased, there is a homily by the presider that focuses on Christian hope. There are appropriate general intercessions prepared in the texts of the rituals, but these may be prepared by the family, with guidance as to structure and content. Catholics in attendance are encouraged to receive communion. At the end of the service, there is a final commendation, a sprinkling of the coffin with holy water, and a "song" of farewell, such as:

> Saints of God come to his/her aid! Hasten to meet him/her, angels of God. May Christ, who called you, take you to himself, may angels lead you to the bosom of Abraham. Eternal rest grant unto him/her Oh Lord, and let perpetual light shine upon him/her.[46]

Between each petition, the community would respond:

> Receive his/her soul and present him/her to God the most high.[47]

The Mass then concludes with a prayer of commendation. A procession ensues in which one or more antiphons such as the following are sung:

> May the angels lead you to paradise; may the martyrs come to welcome you and take you to the holy city, the new and eternal Jerusalem.[48]

The funeral liturgy or service is then followed by a procession to the cemetery that in the United States is in cars forming a funeral cortege. There, a rite of committal with final commendation takes place. Catholics are to be buried in consecrated ground. This is assumed at Catholic cemeteries. The ground is blessed beforehand in other places.

After the liturgy, there is often a meal prepared by members of the parish. Many families prefer that this take place in their homes; however, this is a wonderful service for a parish to offer to the bereaved and welcomed by many families for whom the expense would be prohibitive. Many parishes prepare a booklet to assist the bereaved in planning a funeral that would include the texts of the readings from which to select and a listing of appropriate songs. The Catholic service does not include nonscriptural readings and secular songs, although a musical interlude may be included as a meditation.

The Orthodox funeral liturgy includes the veneration of the deceased body in recognition that the body is a temple of the Holy Spirit. Orthodox Christians bow or prostrate themselves before the body and then kiss the cross on the coffin. The funeral service, the shortest among Orthodox services, is actually the matins service of the day followed by interment at the gravesite, in which those present drop earth on the coffin then make the sign of the cross. However, there is a full separate liturgy for the day of burial in which family and friends receive the Eucharist.

Three, eight, and forty days after the funeral, memorial services (Pani-khidi) are held where psalms and anthems are chanted. It is believed that three days marks the passage of the soul on its journey from the earth to God. Then, the soul spends five days viewing the souls in heaven and after a second appearance before God spends the next month viewing the torments of hell. Then, they come for their personal judgment.[49]

CONCLUSION

When looking at the practices for the dying, dead, and bereaved, we find that contemporary practices are drawn from the past. Clearly, both Catholic and Orthodox understandings of death are grounded in New Testament understandings. However, the crucifixion has long been sanitized; clearly, the horror of the execution of Jesus has been domesticated into jewelry crosses commonly worn by nonbelievers. As lifetimes have become longer, those who are deeply educated have gained less fear of death among twenty-first-century Orthodox and Catholics.

Catholic and Orthodox Christians continue to wash and clothe bodies of those who have died, carry them in processions with candles, incense, and prayers, hold a vigil the evening before burial, and have a meal after the service. These practices all trace their origins to the earliest church. The care of the bodies of the early martyrs evolved into the cult of relics. Although interest in relics has certainly lost the popularity it enjoyed in the Middle Ages, Catholics continue to place relics of one or more saints in a stone in or under the altars of their churches, and the Orthodox place an antimension (a rectangular cloth with a small relic sewn into it) on the center of their altars during the celebration of the Divine Liturgy.[50] What this witnesses is that Catholics and Orthodox have a sense of solidarity with those who have gone before in the faith.

The Orthodox never lost the practice of holding the vigil in their churches, a practice that stems from the time Christianity became a legal religion of the Roman Empire. Catholics are just beginning to recover the vigil tradition that was not especially fostered after the Council of Trent. Catholics continue to believe in original sin and purgatory and indulgences that stem from the patristic era, although they are not accepted by the Orthodox.

It is interesting that the Orthodox never developed a requiem liturgy, although that became central in the West. What is most striking in Catholic practice today is that the funeral liturgy truly enshrines the paschal mystery, the death and resurrection of Jesus, the central feature of Christian faith.[51]

NOTES

1. This study is confined to Latin Rite Catholics (officially, the Latin Church *sui juris*). This is the largest branch of the Roman Catholic Church,

and it is the church presumed by most North Americans to be the Roman Catholic or Catholic Church. However, the Roman Catholic Church includes twenty-two eastern churches that follow the distinctive practices of the Alexandrian, Antiochene, Byzantine, Chaldean, and Armenian rites. The practices of the fourteen Byzantine Rite churches are generally identical to Orthodox Churches.

2. Until the time of Constantine, it would be premature to speak of a united church. There were many local variants. Even the largest communities (e.g., Antioch, Alexandria, Rome, and Jerusalem) had different understanding.

3. The Roman Catholic Church is the second largest religious community in the world. Islam is the largest.

4. The Coptic, Syriac, Chalcedon, Ethiopian, Eritrean, and Malankar Orthodox Churches and the Armenian Apostolic and Syrian Church are equally as ancient. These are small churches that do not accept the Chalcedonian formulation of Christology.

5. Some practices of the churches in the Anglican Communion are similar to those of Roman Catholics.

6. Ritual behavior is by its very nature archaic because familiarity helps people cope with the unknown.

7. Resurrection is by definition new bodily life that came after whatever life after death may be. Accounts of Christ's resurrection are at pains to insist on continuity between the historical Jesus and the Risen one; it is never called resuscitation. In Judaism, resurrection was associated with the end of time (Dan 12:1–3.) Identifying the experience of Jesus after his death as resurrection implies a sense that a new and final era had begun. For an explanation of the New Testament resurrection accounts and what early Christians added to first-century Jewish beliefs about resurrection, see N. T. Wright, *Surprised by Hope: Rethinking Heaven, the Resurrection and the Mission of the Church* (New York: Harper One, 2008), 31–74.

8. The Hebrew Scriptures also suggest that death is the nature of the human condition (Gen 2:7; 3:19) because the story of the garden implies that the original couple had access to the tree of life. Jews today recognize that people are sinful but understand death as a natural part of life. (See also Job 10:9, Sirach 41:2–4).

9. Although this story in Genesis 3 has mythological elements, both Orthodox and Catholics continue to adopt the myth uncritically.

10. There are no extant Sadducee writings; it is hard to say whether what others said about them is accurate.

11. Thomas Aquinas called this the beatific vision, understood as the eternal direct experience of God enjoyed by those in heaven.

12. The earliest Christian authors whose works were not included in the New Testament are called the Apostolic Fathers; among the most famous are Clement, Polycarp, Ignatius, Barnabas, Justin Martyr, and Irenaeus; there are many collections of their works. For more details on the understandings of this early era, see Collee McDannell and Bernhard Lang, *Heaven: A History* (New Haven: Yale University Press, 1988), 1–46.

13. Much of the account of the martyrdom of Polycarp is reproduced along with many other related accounts of martyrs in Eusebius' *Ecclesiastical History*. Eusebius (260–339 CE) also wrote *Martyrs of Palestine* in several editions over many years.

14. In Palestine, during the first through third centuries CE, many Jews were first buried in a natural or constructed cave on an open slab to allow the flesh to decay, and a year later, the bones would be placed in a small ossuary and deposited in a cemetery.

15. In Rome, they did not use incense because of its association with emperor worship. When this was no longer an issue, they used incense both to sanctify the body and as a preservative.

16. For many years, Catholics considered a request for cremation renunciation of the faith postmortem. Since the 1960s, the Catholic Church has permitted cremation; however, only in 1997 were funeral Masses with cremains permitted in the United States. The Orthodox have never approved cremation, but they do accept it as a reality in Japan and in some emergency circumstances.

17. For more details, see Richard Rutherford with Tony Barr, *The Death of a Christian: The Order of Christian Funerals* (Collegeville, MN: Liturgical Press, 1990), 6–12.

18. For a detailed discussion, see Jacques Le Goff, *The Birth of Purgatory*, trans. Arthur Goldhammer (Chicago: University of Chicago Press, 1984).

19. In 325 CE, a council of church leaders, called Bishops, was called by the Emperor Constantine to resolve some inconsistencies in the popular understandings of Christian beliefs. This was the first of seven "ecumenical councils" that are accepted by the Catholic and Orthodox Churches. The Catholic Church continued to call Councils to resolve disputed concerns and/or to clarify teachings. The Council of Florence's (1431–1439) principle effort to reunify the Eastern Orthodox Church with the Western Catholic Church was not successful. The Council of Trent was called to respond to the Protestant Reformation in the sixteenth century. It established many reforms that underlie the need for reform yet also established official teachings that countered theological views of the reformers.

20. Current teaching on purgatory is found in *Catechism of the Catholic Church*, 2nd ed. (Vatican City: Libreria Editrice Vaticana, 1997), 269, 1030–32.

21. Both the Catholic and Orthodox Churches have a liturgy of hours, which consists of psalms, prayers, and hymns assigned to different times of the day and distributed to correspond to the church calendar. This practice is commonly called "the office."

22. Paul Bionski, *Medieval Death: Ritual and Representation* (Ithaca, NY: Cornell University Press, 1996), 25.

23. The Catholic Church officially designates saints by "canonizing" individuals it deems to be certain are in heaven. After the Council of Trent, this process took on specific guidelines with a group established in the Vatican for testing the validity of the claim to sanctity. This includes a complete investigation of the life of the potential saint and the requirement of healings

considered miraculous to certify the validity of the claim to sanctity. Those who died as martyrs for the faith are generally assumed to be saints by both Orthodox and Catholics. An Orthodox bishop has the authority to name as a saint those who lived or died in his diocese and whose sanctity is well attested.

24. The reformers advanced differing views both with Catholics and one another. Lutherans speak of the communion of saints as the body of true believers and exclude prayers to if not the memory of Saints, whereas Calvin maintained it was more than a definition of the church but the sharing among believers of the benefits God gives.

25. Although there are many notable examples of paintings of the Dance of Death, that in Berlin portrays the crucifixion in the center, which is unusual. It also includes members of various religious orders and an abbot, a bishop, a cardinal, and a pope, along with representative figures from all levels of society.

26. For a detailed explanation of these texts, see Blinski, 33–47.

27. For a detailed description of these early rites, see Rutherford, 37–54.

28. The Byzantine Rite is believed to draw from that of the Antiochine practice and introduced in the early fifth century in Constantinople as one of the many reforms of St. John Chrysostom.

29. A detailed discussion of early Western rites is found in Eric Palazo, *A History of Liturgical Books from the Beginning to the Thirteenth Century*, trans. Madeleine Beaumont (Collegeville, MN: Liturgical Press, 1998).

30. The *Dies Irae* is attributed to Tommaso di Celano (1200–1255), a Franciscan Friar and the biographer of St. Francis of Assisi. The Latin text is standard. An English translation is found in *Lyrics of the Middle Ages: An Anthology*, ed. James J. Wilhelm (Garland Publishing, 1990). To hear a musical rendering, see http://www.youtube.com/watch?v=Dlr90NLDp-0

31. P. J. Toner, "Extreme Unction," *Catholic Encyclopedia: An International Work of Reference on the Constitution, Doctrine, Discipline, and History of the Catholic Church*, Vol. V, ed. Charles G. Herbermann, Edward A. Pace, Condé B. Pallen, Thomas J. Shahan, and John J. Wynne (New York: Encyclopedia Press, 1913), 726.

32. For further details on the development of funeral rituals of this era, see Rutherford, 54–71.

33. A detailed explanation of medieval understandings is found in Binski, op. cit.

34. For a detailed explanation of Tridentine Funeral Ritual, see Rutherford, 75–112.

35. Catholics are not obligated to believe that some people experience visions or apparitions of Jesus or Mary. The two visions mentioned enjoy an enormous popular following.

36. It is recommended that the dying receive viaticum every day.

37. Harikd Ter Blanche and Colin Murray Parkes, "Christianity," in *Death and Bereavement Across Cultures*, ed. Colin Murray Parkes, Pittu Laungani, and Bill Young (London: Routledge, 1997), 138.

38. *Pastoral Care of the Sick: Rites of Anointing and Viaticum*, Rev. Abridged Ed. (Chicago: Liturgical Training Publications, 2004), 270.

39. There are too many options for the scripture readings and hymns to be included here. The lists are found in the International Commission on English in the Liturgy. *Order of Christian Funerals Approved for Use in the Dioceses of the United States of American by the National Conference of Catholic Bishops and Confirmed by the Apostolic See* (Chicago: Liturgical Training Publications, 1989), 207–95. A few appropriate hymns are listed on 327–30. Most parishes have hymnals that add to these suggestions.

40. International Commission on English in the Liturgy, *Order of Christian Funerals*, 3.

41. A rosary is a circle of beads arranged in groups of ten that are separated by a rope or chain in which a single bead is set and separated in equal length between each interval of ten. Technically, a rosary consists of fifteen groups of ten in a circle with a leading chain or rope extended from the circle that will have one single bead followed by a space, then three beads followed by a space, then another single bead followed by a space and ending with a small crucifix. A shorter version with five decades is more popular; it is called a rosary, but technically it is a chaplet. The number of beads in a rosary corresponds to the number of prayers in the monastic liturgy of hours. The rosary prayer begins with the Apostles' Creed said while holding the crucifix, then holding the single bead that follows calls for recitation of the Lord's Prayer or "Our Father"; the three beads call for a prayer honoring Mary, "Hail Mary," and the final single bead call for a Doxology, a prayer to the Trinity. Then, one begins with the Lord's Prayer on the same bead and proceeds with "Hail Mary" prayers: on each of the ten beads moving to the separated bead, one prays a doxology and the Lord's Prayer before the next decade of beads. There are meditations from the scriptures and traditions of Jesus and Mary assigned to each decade. Traditionally, these were divided into three sections, called the "joyful mysteries" (portioned into episodes from the accounts of the annunciation and birth of Jesus), the "sorrowful mysteries (portioned into episodes from the passion narratives), and the "glorious mysteries" (portioned from the episodes from the account of the resurrection accounts and Catholic traditions concerning Mary's assumption and crowning as Queen of Heaven). These episodes were established in the sixteenth century. Pope John Paul II set up another set of five sequences from the life of Jesus, called the luminous mysteries. The idea is that as one prays the rosary, one meditates on these sequences. *The Scriptural Rosary* (Totowa, NJ: Catholic Book Publishing Company, 2005) assigns Bible verses related to the mysteries before each prayer. These are especially helpful and increasingly popular among Catholics.

42. Ibid., 36.

43. Ibid.

44. Both the holy water and the white pall are baptismal images recalling the baptismal water and the white garment of the baptized.

45. Rubric directive, Ibid., 43.

46. Ibid., 90.

47. Ibid.

48. Ibid., 91.

49. Sincere thanks to the Rev. Michael Oleksa, Ph.D., for his advisement on Orthodox issues.

50. Unfolded, the marks from the folds fall into a cross.

51. Sincere thanks to the Rev. Steven Moore, V.G., for his suggestions regarding Catholic praxis.

CHAPTER 4

Protestantism and Death Rituals

Glenn H. Asquith Jr.

There has always been an important distinction between "religion" and "spirituality." "Spirituality" involves awareness of, and desire for relationship with, the deity as creator and center of one's life and being. Religion seeks to put form to spiritual awareness. The Protestant Reformation itself was about changing ritual for ritual's sake so that religious practice reflected more accurately the actual spiritual expression of the believer. At the beginning of the Reformation, Jan Hus and John Wycliffe sought to put religious practice in the language of the believer to address the mystery and "otherness" of practice. Martin Luther and John Calvin stressed and renewed the biblical understanding of the priesthood of all believers to affirm that believers did not need a human mediator to access and communicate with God. John Wesley affirmed the importance of the individual's "heart" experience as a reliable indicator of the direction and will of God in one's life. Roger Williams, excluded from the Massachusetts Bay Colony because he disagreed with Puritan practice, formed his own community around the Baptist belief of "Soul Freedom"—the view that each individual's experience of God as revealed in scripture is sufficient authority to guide the person's life. The Quakers took this belief a step further by affirming the authority of the "inner light"—the ways in which the individual, emptied of self and human will, would be led by the authority of the Holy Spirit for prophetic and redemptive action in the world.

Death is a spiritual event and experience. With all of the varied Protestant understandings of practice as noted above, it can be seen readily that it is nearly impossible to speak of any practice as normative in the Protestant response to death. For that reason, Protestants probably have been the least "adept" at turning to ritual as a source of comfort and consolation at times of death. As noted in the other chapters in this anthology, other religions have clearly stated rituals and practice that assist the believer, both the bereaved and the dying, in having assurance that the passage of death is going to involve God's presence, blessing, and care.

PROTESTANT MINISTRY TO MOURNERS: A HISTORICAL VIEW

Religious responses to death, including Protestant responses, historically have relied upon theological and faith affirmations at the time of death that were assumed to provide comfort to the believer in a time of loss. Fervent belief in the Resurrection of Jesus Christ and its meaning fueled the early Christian movement and became a central faith affirmation for the believer. In the gospels, the Easter exclamation of the angel to the women at the tomb became the centerpiece and a high moment of Christian festival: "He is not here; for he has been raised" (Matthew 28:6). This leads to Paul's affirmations that nothing, including death, separates us from the love of God (Romans 8:38–39) and that "Death has been swallowed up in victory" for the believer (I Corinthians 15:54).

Before what Lucy Bregman[1] calls the "death awareness movement" of the later twentieth century, these theological affirmations were assumed to provide comfort to mourners, which indeed they did—to a point. Consistent with the scriptural affirmations cited above, our faith claims as a believing community help us to transcend the sting and emptiness of death. In the early twentieth century, the ability to keep a "stiff upper lip" in the face of death and massive loss became a particular virtue of "the greatest generation" who lived through two world wars, especially in the culture of North America and Western Europe.[2] Christianity, and especially Protestantism, in the 1950s thrived in the optimism, emotional rush, and sense of invincibility that followed the end of World War II. As Bregman points out, this sense of invincibility and denial of death were perhaps most poignantly symbolized by the "air raid drills" conducted in public schools, where children somehow got the message that hiding under a wooden desk would help them survive a nuclear attack.[3]

However, this group sense of denial still did not address the full, deep experience of loss by those who mourn. Some misinterpretations of scripture and an overemphasis on the hope of the Resurrection created a culture in Christianity that practically discouraged a deep experience of grieving, even in the midst of hope. As Mitchell and Anderson point out, celebrations of hope and promise in most religious funeral liturgies can discourage awareness and acknowledgment of sadness by neglecting the fact that we are also standing face-to-face with death, including (and especially) our own eventual death. Accurate theological affirmations of hope tend to misplace the pastoral priority for an individual's effective grieving in the midst of loss.[4]

Mitchell and Anderson's point is illustrated by viewing the sermons preached and funeral manuals used by pastors before the death awareness movement. These earlier materials paid good attention to worship and theological understanding, but usually at the expense of attention to the experience of the mourners.

The Star Book for Ministers, by Edward T. Hiscox, was perhaps one of the earliest and most widely used worship manuals for Protestant pastors. It was first published in 1877 and then revised in 1906, 1943, and 1968, just before the death awareness movement. The 1968 version has an interesting editorial note in its preface, citing the differences between *Hiscox's Day* (1877) and *Our Day* (1968). It states that in Hiscox's day, "funerals were commonly held in the homes of the deceased persons," whereas in the present day, "Funeral homes are the more usual locations for funerals, except those held in the church building itself."[5] This shift in the location of funerals indicates a change from a personal, informal setting to a more formal setting for worship, hence the need for a service manual that will help a pastor design a proper service. Also, the "suggestions to ministers" regarding funerals includes the directive that:

> Funeral sermons are used only on rare occasions. A few remarks or brief address, however, are not unsuitable. The mood of these should be affirmative. It is appropriate to recall in these some of the good qualities of the departed, but not in terms of extravagant praise. Faults and sins should not be mentioned. The main theme should be chosen from the Great truths of the Christian faith as a message of consolation and hope to the family and friends present.[6]

In line with that advice, the nine pages of suggested funeral sermon outlines given in the *Star Book* are all exegetical commentary on scripture, designed for "some instruction for those present ...; some of whom seldom attend any other religious services."[7] These include thematic suggestions such as "Providential trials are the discipline which a kind Father sends upon the children of His love" (Hebrews 12:5–6); "God's judgments are right and needed" (Psalm 119:75–76); and "Unreasonable grief in bereavement restrained" (II Samuel 12:23).[8] Even in 1968, the popular *Star Book for Ministers* promoted a ministry to the bereaved that told them to accept death as the will of God and to restrain any "unreasonable grief."

Furthermore, in good Baptist tradition, the *Star Book* makes use of occasions of death and bereavement as opportunities for evangelism for unbelievers and the unsaved. This is "preaching to the mourners" of a different kind than is later suggested in the death awareness movement. It negates and discourages feelings of sadness and loss and instead tells those present to accept the ways of God and get saved before it is too late. Focusing on the feelings of mourners and the life of the deceased would, in fact, detract from what was seen in this era by evangelical Protestants as the primary purpose of the funeral—to point to the universal reality of death and thus prepare those present for their own inevitable end. As such, those attending the funeral were not primarily seen as mourners, but rather as "the future dead."

It is fair to say that the funeral and service manuals of the early twentieth century were responding to the context of their time, which reflected an attempt, especially in Protestantism, to provide more dignity and order to worship in situations that certainly called for it. This is the premise of the *Cokesbury Funeral Manual* of 1932, which arose out of the (now) United Methodist tradition and was used widely by evangelical and mainline pastors of all Protestant traditions. It notes that "Crudeness is out of place in any service of worship, but it is particularly offensive in a service of burial. The purpose of this Manual is to furnish suggestions and material to help the minister to provide beauty and dignity in this most trying task."[9] To this end, funeral sermons are discouraged and are, at best, to be done with great caution. Contrary to the Baptist *Star Book for Ministers*, it does say that funeral sermons should not "use death as an object lesson to reach the unconverted"; instead, they are intended to "comfort and interpret the great facts of life and death."[10] Pastors are strongly warned against the temptation to "make remarks about the dead" because they "must be complimentary remarks," and, once that practice is started, the pastor "will be headed toward much difficulty."[11]

Most of the funeral sermons suggested in the *Cokesbury Funeral Manual* are reflective of the beliefs of orthodox Christianity, although they provide a generally dry theological treatise on the Christian meaning of death without (as is the purpose) really addressing the spiritual and emotional state of the mourners. However, the suggested "Address at the Funeral of a Child," titled "The Transplanted Flower," misses both the theological and the pastoral mark in a serious way. Based on Job 1:21, "The Lord gave, and the Lord hath taken away," it suggests that God took the child away for a purpose—perhaps that "she was too beautiful for this world, so he called her back to him." It asserts that "God has asked for that particular flower, that it may bloom in his own garden. We yield because he has asked that the child be returned to him."[12]

This premature proof-texting of Job's initial response of piety in the face of seemingly meaningless loss misses the richness of the book of Job's portrayal of the divine human dialogue regarding the character and nature of God. The simplistic view of God presented in the above sermon seems very far removed from anything that would be helpful to parents and families in the postmodern world, and yet this view still persists in popular piety, as seen in obituary notices, condolence cards, and funeral poems. Perhaps in the nineteenth and early twentieth centuries, the death of a child was seen less as a theological problem than it is now, and preachers could glibly "defend God" to quell any temptation to question God's will. However, anger and questioning are a normal part of the grief response, and it would more effectively address the needs of mourners to acknowledge and allow the kind of questioning and dialogue with God that is portrayed in Job and in other parts of the Hebrew Bible, including Lament Psalms such as Ps. 22, 69, and 79.

The *Cokesbury Funeral Manual* contains funeral liturgies from several different Protestant traditions. The first is the traditional rite found in the Episcopal *Book of Common Prayer*, 1928 edition. Written in King James language, it has been used widely "in part, or in whole, by many ministers of other communions."[13] It contains traditional scripture readings from the Psalms, I Corinthians 15, Romans 8, and John 14. It also provides sentences and prayers, using scriptural language, for a graveside service, including several benedictions from which to choose.

The scripture passages mentioned above are very frequently used in Protestant services. Psalm 23 is perhaps the best known psalm and is universally used for its comforting words of care and protection by God in the face of death and adversity. I Corinthians 15 is the Apostle Paul's important theological statement about the Resurrection of Jesus Christ, ending with the affirmation that "Death is swallowed up in victory. O death, where is thy sting? O grave, where is thy victory?... Thanks be to God, which giveth us the victory through our Lord Jesus Christ" (I Cor. 15:54b-55, 57 KJV).

Romans 8 is another significant theological affirmation of the Apostle Paul regarding the steadfast love of God that remains despite all human suffering. After pointing readers toward the future glory in the midst of persecution, famine, and peril, it ends with the strong declaration of faith that "in all these things we are more than conquerors through him who loved us. For I am convinced that neither death, nor life, nor angels, nor rulers, nor things present, nor things to come, nor powers, nor height, nor depth, nor anything else in all creation, will be able to separate us from the love of God in Christ Jesus our Lord" (Romans 8:37–39 NRSV).

John 14 is the reassurance of Jesus to his disciples (and all believers) about their future place with him in eternal life. "Let not your heart be troubled: ye believe in God, believe also in me. In my Father's house are many mansions: if it were not so, I would have told you. I go to prepare a place for you. And if I go and prepare a place for you, I will come again, and receive you unto myself; that where I am, there ye may be also" (John 14:1–3 KJV).

This *Manual* also includes the funeral ritual from the Methodist Episcopal Church, South (1926). Its opening sentences and scriptural selections are very similar to the *Book of Common Prayer*, although it also contains selections for the burial of a child (II Samuel 12:16–23 and Mark

10:13–16). This is followed by "a suitable hymn, a sermon, or exhortation, and an extemporary prayer."[14] The suggested rite for the graveside service includes brief sentences in King James scriptural language, the Lord's Prayer, a brief collect, and a benediction.

The third and final service included in the *Manual* is from the Book of Worship for the Reformed Church in the United States (1926), for use by all Reformed and Presbyterian churches and other Protestant clergy to whose tradition it applies. Again, the opening sentences regarding the Resurrection are very similar to the *Book of Common Prayer*. It contains scriptural selections from the Psalms, John 14, Revelation 7, and I Corinthians 15. This is followed by a hymn, a sermon, and one of several written prayers from which to choose. The graveside service is very short, with opening sentences using scriptural quotes about the Resurrection, a written prayer, sentences of committal, and a benediction.

True to its purpose, the *Cokesbury Funeral Manual* provided the Protestant pastor with suitable choices for a dignified, orderly funeral service that articulated basic Christian faith in the Resurrection. Although it paid attention to a variety of circumstances of loss, such as the death of a child, cremation, or burial at sea, it did not allow room for individual expressions of mourning.

MEMORIAL AS RITUAL

It was noted at the beginning of this chapter that Protestants, whose break from the highly liturgical Roman Catholic Church led to a suspicion and shunning of ritual, were left with a deficiency of ritual that provided comfort and assurance of God's presence in the midst of suffering and loss. It was then seen that this deficiency was gradually addressed in the nineteenth and early twentieth centuries with the introduction of Protestant funeral manuals that provided pastors with more orderly ritual for funerals, largely based on the Episcopal *Book of Common Prayer*. However, this turn to faith claims in the midst of orderly worship still failed (mainly by intention) to address the experiences of mourners grieving the loss of an important individual in their life.

One notable exception to this is seen in the funeral practices of the oldest Protestant denomination—the *Unitas Fratrum* (Unity of the Brethren), which eventually became known as the Moravian Church after the persecuted followers of Jan Hus left Moravia and settled in Herrnhut, Germany, on the estate of Lutheran nobleman Count Nicolaus Ludwig von Zinzendorf. Zinzendorf himself was strongly entrenched in the German pietistic tradition, which meant that attention to individuals' experiences with God were of utmost importance in the practice of their faith.

As a result of this, Moravians developed the practice of reading a memoir known as the "*lebenslauf*" at the funerals of members. With the literal

German meaning of "life path," the *lebenslauf* was essentially a brief spiritual journal kept by individuals during their lifetime that highlighted their spiritual experiences and awareness of God's presence in their life. At the time of their death, this record was usually completed by their pastor and used at the funeral as a basis for a memoir. This story was intended primarily as a testimony to God's action in the deceased's life, so that these memoirs not only provided a way to evaluate the life just completed; they were also read as an example to teach others about the Moravian way of life and the spiritual life in general, thus helping to prepare mourners for their own "home-going."[15]

An example of such a biography is found in the following excerpts from the *lebenslauf* of Christopher Elrod, a member of the "English Congregation" Hope in North Carolina.

> The first time, as he remembered that his heart was truly touched by our Saviour, was in a Sermon, delivered by the Rev. Bishop Spangenberg ... in the Year 1789. From that time he grew uneasy, and became concerned for his Souls Salvation, and sought acquaintance with the Brethren ... The Holy Ghost worked powerfully upon his heart, so that he ... turned in faith to our Redeemer and Saviour Jesus Christ, in whom we have Redemption thro' his blood, namely the forgiveness of Sins, and received grace from our Saviour. From that time on he kept in fellowship with the Brethren.... He had a hot and fiery temper, and could often fall heard to others, by his positiveness and absoluteness, and yet he was conscious thereof, and soon made up again, because he loved to live in peace with all Men ... About 7 weeks ago, he began to complain about pain in his Breast, which increased so, that he was obliged to take his bed, and because he grew worse from day to day, soon believed that our Saviour would call him home by occasion of this Sickness.... It was a pleasure to all that visited him, that even in his Fancies, in hot fever, he spoke of nothing save of Jesus' Blood and Wounds, and of the grace our Saviour had done to him. Sometimes he sung English and German Verses intermixt, and in particular his favorite hymn: *How happy that my heart can view, the Lamb in all his bloody hue*, etc., and that Verse: *Unfathomed Wisdom of our King* etc. so that it was evident, that he lived in the faith of the Son of God, who loved and gave himself for us.... As long as he could move his lips he spoke of our Saviour and how good it is to be acquainted with him. On the 29th of Jan. in the Morning at 7 o'clock, being his birthday our Saviour took this faithful Brother home to himself exactly sixty-four years old.[16]

As can be seen from these excerpts from a longer document, the *lebenslauf* was written to show how the pietistic religious practices and devotional life of this eighteenth-century Moravian community were woven into the fabric of daily life. Mention is made of the music of the church, the individual and corporate liturgical life, group confession and prayer (known as "speakings"), and the Moravian view of death as "home-going." As noted earlier, this particularly fit the practice of pietism, where faith and theology were expressed through the witness and experience of an individual life, which was held up as a source of inspiration and instruction for others in their own spiritual development. Through the ritual of memorial, Moravian Protestants were assisted in viewing their own experience while also honoring the individual life of the deceased.

MINISTRY TO MOURNERS IN THE DEATH AWARENESS ERA

Protestant Christianity's response to loss has indeed been influenced by the death awareness movement. Most scholars in behavioral science fields cite the Coconut Grove nightclub fire study of 1942 in Boston as the seminal research that led to the understanding of the grief response of mourners. Conducted by psychiatrist Erich Lindemann, the physical and emotional reactions of 101 patients who survived the fire and the many who lost loved ones in that fire and in hospitals and in the armed services were described.[17] Unfortunately, however, the identifiable stages and reactions to loss were presented as something pathological to be treated, rather than as something normal to be facilitated toward a healing process. In the view of this writer and others, it was not until the assassination of President John F. Kennedy on November 22, 1963, that particular, national attention was paid on a large scale to the reactions of individuals to loss.[18] The vision of a young, vigorous national leader being cut down at the peak of his career and popularity likely signaled the beginning of the end of Western denial of death. This national horror was followed in 1968 by the assassinations of Robert F. Kennedy and Martin Luther King Jr., all in the midst of massive riots, upheaval, and violence surrounding the dual issues of civil rights and the killing of Americans in the very unpopular Vietnam War. The can-do spirit of the greatest generation was replaced with the despair of the Woodstock generation, which developed its own liturgy of love, peace, dropping out, and turning on.

It was in this context that Lindemann's work was rediscovered with the advance of a plethora of other works on death and dying, the bellwether of which was Elizabeth Kübler-Ross's classic, *On Death and Dying*, published in 1969. In this study of dying persons, Kübler-Ross outlined stages of anticipatory grief that were easily translated into stages of grief for the bereaved as well and roughly paralleled Lindemann's stages. With the influence of this movement, religion began to pay attention to the bereaved through the work of pastors and pastoral counselors being trained in this literature at seminaries and in clinical pastoral education programs. Protestantism's emphasis on the experience of the believer made it more open to awareness of the experience of the bereaved, with less dependence on a purely sacramental response to death and loss.

With the help of pastoral theologians such as Kenneth Mitchell and Herbert Anderson, "loss" itself became a more broadly defined phenomenon worthy of religious and pastoral response. As a result, "loss" and "mourning" have become important foci for pastoral theological consideration in the death awareness era. Mitchell and Anderson cite six types of loss that all create and necessitate varying degrees of the same kind of grief work caused by death:[19]

1. Material loss: loss of material objects or familiar surroundings to which one is attached, such as happens in a fire or other disaster when items important to one's identity, like family pictures and heirlooms, are lost. In a religious environment that discourages grieving at times of death, grieving over material objects becomes even more of a challenge. Pastors and religious leaders could still do more to establish rituals of ending for those who have suffered irreversible loss of objects that carry such importance to the being and identity of the person.

2. Relationship loss: the ending of interaction with a particular other human being, not only through death but through divorce, illness, moving, or alienation. Since the death awareness movement, pastors and pastoral counselors have proposed liturgies to recognize the ending of a marriage, with the understanding that such rituals can facilitate healthy grieving in the same way as do funerals. In fact, there is even less "finality" with a divorce because the former spouse is still living, and there may be continued interaction regarding children, and so on. Rituals for divorce seek to address attendant stages of grief, such as guilt, anger, and depression, so that a person who has done the necessary therapeutic work of letting go of the relationship can finally recognize its ending with a liturgical statement in the context of their faith. In 1979, Sam Norman proposed "A Ceremony for the Divorced" designed for each partner that included confessions of anger and guilt; expressions of hurt and grief, acceptance, and gratitude; acknowledgment of forgiveness; and an affirmation by the partner's friends and relatives of the choice for separateness that was made, along with the desire for blessing and newness of life in the journey.[20] As Norman noted, this would obviously not work for all divorced couples or individuals, but it represents an excellent attempt at a ritual ending for a very difficult relationship loss. Likewise, in 1976, a publication of the United Methodist Church affirmed the need for rituals at the time of divorce, noting that, because the church has such a large role in the formation of marriages, so it should also play a significant part in their termination, offering to the couple and to the community a use of religious resources that assists

them in facing grief over a marriage that has died.[21] It proposes a ritual to be incorporated into a service of remarriage, rituals in which
one or both partners participate, and a ritual for the congregation
that includes a litany of hope for the future. The authors conclude
that "the church cannot hesitate to give special attention to this
event in the lives of an increasing number of Christians who are at
the same time seeking to be faithful to the person of their primary
commitment: even Jesus Christ their Lord."[22]

3. Intrapsychic loss: an entirely inward experience, this is the loss of an
   emotionally important image of oneself and the loss of dreams and
   future possibilities. Adolescence is usually our first experience of intrapsychic loss, when we are giving up the relative safety of childhood
   for the uncertainties of puberty and maturity. The aftermath of a
   great achievement for which we have long prepared—the birth of a
   child, holiday or anniversary celebrations, a promotion—can be experienced as intrapsychic loss. Pastoral or religious response to lost
   dreams or major life transitions would assist individuals in acknowledging the effects of these intrapsychic changes.

4. Functional loss: the loss of muscular or neurological functions of the
   body through stroke, paralysis, or amputation. The aging process or
   chronic illnesses bring about gradual functional losses that limit mobil-
   ity, activity, or the ability to work. Erik Erikson depicts the develop-
   mental struggle of old age as "integrity versus despair," where a person
   can graciously move into the functional loss of old age or despair at
   what has been lost.[23] Lewis Sherrill speaks of this stage as one of
   "simplification," in which life is boiled down to basic material and
   physical limits as one ages.[24] Sherrill notes that this transition is made
   easier if one can focus on the spiritual meaning of relationships and
   vocation instead of the acquisition of personal power in its various
   forms. Some form of life review, first proposed by Robert N. Butler,[25]
   can become a ritual response to functional loss, perhaps even in a corporate worship setting. As a person can formally and informally name
   and celebrate the accomplishments of their active life and also intentionally work through the disappointments and losses, the result is a
   sense of integrity, peace, and thanksgiving for the gifts of one's life.

5. Role loss: the loss of a specific social role or one's accustomed place
   in a social network. Obvious examples of this would include "empty
   nest," when parents no longer have day-to-day responsibilities as
   parents, and retirement, when the social and economic structure and
   attendant personal power in a workplace has ended. Less obvious
   examples, which can also cause a sense of loss, might include promotion, when one must get used to new responsibilities and a new social
   group, and marriage, adjustment of children in a blended family, leaving the security and enjoyment of school through graduation, or
   returning to school at midcareer after having a place of power and

authority. Protestant rituals such as marriage ceremonies, baptism or dedication of infants, and funerals already occur at times of role transition. Perhaps these rituals could be expanded to celebrate and consecrate other changes such as promotions, empty nest, and graduation.

6. Systemic loss: simply stated, this is the loss of an important social system to which one belongs. Systemic loss is experienced at the closing of a company because of bankruptcy. Jobs are lost, the surrounding community experiences economic decline, with the loss of other businesses that served that company, and a "way of life" is radically changed. A major change in an organization, because of new leadership or new procedures, is experienced by longer term members as systemic loss. A church that has lost a pastor or other major leaders because of sexual misconduct or other major crises experiences systemic loss. After 9/11, the United States experienced systemic loss though radical changes in security procedures in many sectors of society, major economic losses, and the anxiety of being at war as a nation.

Protestant religious practice could certainly improve in its response to systemic loss. After 9/11, there were many prayer services, prayer vigils, and memorial services for those lost that continue on each anniversary of 9/11. These are indeed helpful events that, among other things, address our corporate sense of systemic loss. However, more specific liturgies that help mourners name and grieve the effects of economic loss, leadership loss, or loss of security in the midst of radical change would also be helpful rituals in these occasions.

"DIFFICULT" MEMORIALS AND FUNERALS

In addition to national tragedies such as 9/11, Protestant pastors are regularly called upon to respond to large-scale deaths and losses from natural disasters (tornadoes, floods, hurricanes) and mine disasters, fires, school shootings, and commercial transportation accidents. A disaster of any kind creates a number of public dynamics. One is the division between "the affected" and the "unaffected." The "unaffected" may not have empathy or understanding of what "the affected" have experienced and yet either want to claim some ownership in it or may be quick to provide "answers" or judgments as to why the event happened, which causes further alienation and division between the two groups.

On the other hand, the "affected" quickly form a tight community of suffering that has the quality of family relationships as they gather to console one another and strategize a response to the disaster or losses. This is regularly seen, for example, among families of those trapped in a mine, the community affected by a natural disaster, families of war dead, or families of those lost in a commercial plane crash.

Protestant ministry in these situations requires sensitivity to the mourning experience of both groups. For the "affected," there often needs to be a ritual presence with those waiting to hear official news of the status of their loved ones, through the use of public prayer, scripture reading, storytelling, and liturgies. As remains are removed from a disaster scene, the opportunity to view any such remains frequently also calls for a ritual presence. In some cases, such as war, explosions, fires, or plane crashes, there may not be any remains to view or to have present at a funeral service. Nevertheless, especially in such occasions, it is extremely important to have some kind of memorial or funeral ritual that provides mourners the opportunity to eulogize, remember, and say goodbye to loved ones within the liturgical context of their faith.

In 1993 and 1994, this author was invited by the Moravian Church in Nicaragua to provide ministry to Miskito residents on the east coast of that country, many of whom had suffered multiple losses in the civil war between Sandinista and Contra fighters from 1981 to 1988. Some had lost entire villages; others had lost one or more family members, most of whose remains had never been recovered. Symptoms of unresolved grief and posttraumatic stress disorder were very common among religious leaders and the general population of Miskito towns and villages. The author and an accompanying group of seminarians provided a pastoral presence in churches and schools where, in the context of worship, Bible study, and psychodrama, stories of loss were shared, and mutual support was received.

The highlight of that ministry was a trilingual memorial service held for over three hundred members of several different ethnic groups who had all suffered war losses. At the conclusion of the service, relatives of the dead placed flower petals in a hole dug in the ground in front of the Moravian Church headquarters, while the names of their loved ones were being read. A tree was then planted in the hole, which became a living memorial to the dead. For most or all of the participants, the service and ritual burial served as the only funeral rite they had been able to attend in the years after the war; fear from continued surveillance by government officials had prevented such events of memorial and remembrance.[26]

It should be noted that the "unaffected" in a public disaster also need to participate in some ritual remembrance of those lost in the disaster because of their need to feel some "ownership" in the event and to express their care for the bereaved in a recognized, structured way. Larry Kent Graham, a pastoral counselor and pastoral theologian who was among the many religious leaders who responded to the Colombine High School shootings in Littleton, Colorado, in 1999, notes the importance of the many ways that the "unaffected" in the community responded to assist the bereaved and traumatized:

I shall never forget the way the churches in the Columbine area of Littleton provided safe space and a place to pray, cry, support, and reorient a terrified and shattered community. On a larger scale, there were numerous civic-sponsored events in which persons could come together to support one another and to lament and memorialize losses with which we were all struggling. The public presence of religious leaders and the open availability of their sacred spaces became indispensable....[27]

A large-scale response to multiple losses in a disaster also raises the question of what type of service should be held for persons who may or may not be part of any faith tradition. Can religious leaders use traditional funeral rites on such occasions? The answer may lie in situations such as the Columbine tragedy cited above. It has always been affirmed that funerals and memorial services are "for the living."[28] With that in mind, pastoral leaders consider the context and situation of the mourners. If they are a diverse, multifaith group, including those who are part of no faith group, some religious symbolism and commentary are generally still appropriate as long as the various sensibilities of those present are considered. Death, especially sudden and traumatic death, causes most persons to at least ponder the existence of a higher power in the face of such a threat to one's own existence. Some also ponder the possibilities of life after death and the fate of the deceased. A ritual response that honors the dead while also responding to the needs of the living for some sense of community in which to lament, grieve, and reach for hope is always appropriate.

LIFE STORY AS EULOGY AND CELEBRATION

Each life has a story, and telling that story can be powerful and healing for mourners who are searching for meaning and comfort in the midst of death. The telling of the story leads to a hermeneutic, an interpretation of the story, and thus one affirmation of the meaning of that particular life story. In a Christian or religious context, this hermeneutic leads, in part, to an understanding of how God has worked in that person's life. This narrative of the self adds to general knowledge about the nature of God, which thus confirms or adds to others' experiences. Each person's story can contain its own inherent truth about God's action in the world.

Before the death awareness movement, some traditions in Protestant Christianity struggled with including any form of "personal details" in the funeral service. In 1953, Charles Wallis observed that "the use of an obituary in the funeral service is almost extinct in many quarters." Wallis went on to say that this omission is regrettable because there is little in life details themselves that are objectionable; the problem has been when funeral preachers abuse the practice by making statements that are "more laudatory than factual, more fictional than truthful."[29] Wallis recommended that such profuse statements could be avoided by including one of two forms of the obituary: a brief statement of facts about the person (birth, family, education, affiliations, honors, etc.) or a brief "tribute" prepared in advance of the funeral by members of the deceased's church or community and read by the pastor, noting that person's contributions to the community.[30]

The primary meaning of eulogy (from the Greek for "speaking well") is "tribute" or "praise." Protestant funeral practice may benefit from a broader definition of what it means to "speak well" of the deceased. Instead of an overstated beatification of the deceased that anyone who knows him or her well knows is not the "whole story," "speaking well" can also simply be the telling of real stories of events, values, and relational characteristics that are remembered by the deceased's family and community. Such stories honor the real meaning of that life to the bereaved. Told in the context of the community's faith, such stories become a celebration of the life that was lived and open the pathway for thanksgiving for that life.

An excellent example of a pastoral way to address the spiritual situation of mourning is the 1985 publication of Robert Hughes, *A Trumpet in Darkness: Preaching to Mourners*. The premise made by Hughes is that interpreting the word of God in an empathic and understanding way can sound a trumpet of hope to those in the midst of the deep darkness of death. Instead of "defending God" or attempting to explain what feels meaningless at the time of a funeral with the use of theological statements, Hughes outlines ways to prepare a funeral sermon that take into account the particular situation of death faced by the mourners and the feelings they are likely to be experiencing. The funeral is then designed to name, facilitate, and address the process of mourning in a way that utilizes faith to bring hope by understanding morning from a spiritual perspective.

Hughes seeks to address the reality of death by retelling the story of death as the mourners have experienced it in light of the Christ story. People gather with the pastor and with visitors at the funeral home to retell their death story. Hughes seeks to make the funeral sermon a mutual storytelling process that "begins in the parlor and continues in the pulpit."[31] Assisting mourners to name their story of death in light of the biblical and theological story is a true ministry to mourners in that it starts with their own experience and addresses faith in light of that experience. An example is Hughes's comments about death by suicide, which causes serious theological questions in many traditions and funerals for "unbelievers." In such situations, he believes that advice given to pastors before the death awareness movement about not saying specific things about the deceased is actually sound if such comments are intended to "preach the dead into heaven or hell." The basic message of the Gospel can be preached without wounding the bereaved with judgments or by insensitive use of the occasions for evangelism.

In telling the story of the dead person, pastors can affirm the individual's place in the lives of the survivors and point honestly to the joys and benefits of those relationships. The truth of the good news is simply preached, but judgments are left up to God. The good news is that Jesus died for the preacher, the deceased, and the mourners, and "the reality of the Redeemer's pain and suffering will connect with the experience of all sufferers who believe."[32] Protestant preaching from a theology of the cross "acknowledges that suffering is part of the essence of God," that God can take on the suffering of the world without deviating from God's purpose of love. The theology of the cross "assists mourners to face the reality of death even as it sounds the trumpet of hope."[33]

Kenn Filkins unfolds his discoveries of the necessity and power of stories in the midst of the darkness of grief. On one occasion, he was called upon to lead a funeral service at the untimely death of a young husband and father of two grade-school children who had fallen to his death, along with three others, in a tragic construction accident. Filkins had never met the man, but he learned that he was a popular person, a volunteer firefighter, and very active in community affairs. He intuited that the large numbers of people from every segment of the community who would attend the funeral would be there because of what this man meant to them. In his attempts to learn the details of this meaning, he was responded to warmly by family and friends alike, who packed an auditorium the next day for the funeral. Knowing that an impersonal "canned message" would not speak to these mourners, Filkins began sharing the anecdotes he had learned the day before.

> During the stories, I saw the recognition in the audience—they remembered too. Fred's elderly neighbor's eyes brightened as she remembered how he helped her with a flat tire. Firefighters nodded as they recalled how Fred fought fires with them. Aunts and Uncles smiled as they recollected Fred playing with his two children. Each had *their* story to tell about Fred. Their hearts opened, healing had begun.[34]

Filkins tells another example of a funeral for his wife's grandfather. Family members asked if he wished to give the funeral, but he declined, believing he was too close to the situation and also desiring to be comforted himself. The funeral director enlisted a pastor who led a four-minute service, mentioned the grandfather's name only once in passing, and read a "canned" prayer. The family was left feeling very empty, stunned, and cheated. In their shock, they gravitated toward the casket, feeling the need to "do something." Then, as they stood with their arms intertwined in front of the casket, Filkins reports that:

I spoke of Grandpa and what he meant to me. I mentioned the white-tailed deer he shot—illegally—out his kitchen window while drinking his morning coffee. I commented that he lied about his age to enter the military and to serve in World War I. In China during the war, he fought "our guys" with boxing gloves in a ring. Grandpa also held dozens of patents for his inventions and he had travelled all over America collecting stones for his Rock Shop. In tears I recalled how he had given me some of his tools. "Every man should have tools," he had said. I acknowledged that I had the tools, but still could not use them. Then I spoke of our pain and loss, then of Jesus, who could heal our grief and give hope. I closed with prayer and we left for the funeral dinner.[35]

Filkins notes that no one pretended that his grandfather was perfect; they knew his faults but loved him anyway. Telling the story of life and death reminds the survivors of their life with the deceased. Filkins affirms that, at times, the quality of a person's life can itself proclaim the Gospel, so that the "sermon" becomes the eulogy itself. At other times, depending on the situation, a eulogy/sermon format serves the needs of the mourners by celebrating a life and then comforting with the hope of the Gospel.[36]

This life story approach works equally well for both funeral and memorial services. In the Protestant traditions, a funeral service is held shortly after the death of the person, usually with the remains of the deceased present. A memorial service might be held sometime after the death of the individual, often in a location for persons who could not attend the funeral. Memorial services are also held in the case of cremation, when remains are not present. Before the death awareness movement, Protestants were largely opposed to cremation, but this has now become more universally accepted as an option for disposal of remains, especially in cases of traumatic or difficult death. Likewise, memorial services after burial or dispersal of ashes are generally well accepted in Protestantism. In fact, the rhythm of celebrating life after a burial frequently is a more hopeful and inspiring event than the reverse order experienced at funeral services.

In contemporary times, the Moravian *lebenslauf* remains as a powerful, effective, and healing method of telling the life story of the deceased at a funeral or memorial service, in such a way that it proclaims the good news of the comfort of God's presence in the lives of the mourners. A recent example in the life of this author was the memoir given at a memorial service for a beloved Moravian pastor, colleague, and friend who had suddenly died after a heart attack. The large Moravian church was filled with mourners in deep grief over the sudden and unexpected loss of this man, who had recently relocated to another country with his wife and young daughter. The memoir (*lebenslauf*) was written by the deceased three years before his death and then concluded by family members and read by one of the presiding pastors, who had been a close family friend. Altogether, this statement allowed the mourners to celebrate the life that was lost in a very personal way because some part of the statement connected with the personal experience of each person present in a particular way. As an example of how the *lebenslauf* speaks of God's presence in the individual's life, this particular memoir cited the scriptural text given to the deceased at the time of his confirmation of faith and how that text was borne out in all of the subsequent places and circumstances of his ministry.

At the conclusion of the service, a hymn of praise was sung in a robust, joyous fashion in affirmation that this colleague and friend was now "in the more immediate presence of the Savior." Verse 2 of the hymn, "Sing Hallelujah, Praise the Lord," which had special meaning to the deceased, also affirmed the faith of the mourners:

> There we to all eternity shall join th'angelic lays
> and sing in perfect harmony to God our Savior's praise,
> he has redeemed us by his blood,
> and made us kings and priests to God,
> for us, for us, the Lamb was slain! Praise ye the Lord! Amen.[37]

POSTFUNERAL MINISTRY TO MOURNERS

In Protestant traditions, and in Western culture in general, there is no official "mourning period" in which bereaved persons and communities have a structure for mourning. Pastoral care and counseling professionals have long recognized the importance of anniversaries, especially the anniversary of the death, in facilitating the grief process. Pastoral and congregational attention to grieving persons on such anniversaries, including the deceased's birthday, wedding anniversaries, and holidays, is good practice in the religious response to mourning.

Protestant churches that follow the liturgical church year are more likely to have a structured postfuneral follow-up. Occasions such as All Saints' Day are a natural opportunity to recognize congregational members and friends who have died in the past year. A practice in some United Methodist churches on All Saints' Sunday is to read the names of the deceased in the morning worship while family members come forward to light a candle at the altar. In one United Church of Christ congregation, those in attendance at the All Saints' Day service file out to the church's cemetery after the service for ritual remembrance of the dead.

The Moravian Easter dawn service has long been a prime occasion for ritual remembrance of the deceased in the context of the celebration of the Resurrection of Jesus Christ. Such services are held, beginning just before sunrise on Easter morning, in Moravian cemeteries accompanied by brass bands and with the reading of the Easter Dawn Liturgy as an affirmation of faith. Perhaps one of the most significant aspects of this rite for families of the deceased is the preparation that takes place in the cemetery on the Saturday before the service. At the God's Acre cemetery in Winston-Salem, North Carolina, hundreds of families diligently prepare graves on the day before the service by cleaning and polishing the flat stones and placing flowers. These activities alone become an important ritual of remembrance for mourners.

The naming and dedication of memorial gifts is another important occasion for postfuneral remembrance in Protestant congregations. Memorial gifts frequently reflect the values and activities of the deceased while living and, thus, become a continual reminder of that person's legacy in congregational life. One congregation had established a college scholarship fund in memory of a young man tragically killed in an auto accident. Each annual disbursement of the funds to a recipient was recognized in Sunday worship by a close friend of the deceased, who was also a member of the congregation. This annual remembrance continued to facilitate the mourning process for family, friends, and the congregation.

CONCLUSION

LeRoy Aden, a professor emeritus of pastoral theology, points out that the religious and even pastoral literature on grief that has been used in training generations of pastors primarily presents death as a psychological struggle with feelings. Aden asserts that ministry to mourners would be more effective and relevant to their experience if clergy viewed grief instead as a spiritual struggle with faith.[38] Indeed, as Hughes so articulately stated, the feelings of grief must be considered when preparing for ministry to mourners. However, if that ministry is seen as primarily dealing with a spiritual struggle, Protestant responses in the face of death would be less likely to "miss the mark."

When faith encounters death, what we believed were "ultimate answers" are undermined, and the weaknesses of our faith are exposed.[39] Like Job, however, death and loss also have the potential of deepening our faith by bringing us into a new assurance of God's presence in the midst of suffering. In the face of his catastrophic loss, Job nevertheless proclaimed, "I know that my Redeemer lives." (Job 19:25a) Ministry to mourners, given with a listening, empathic ear to individual stories of death, will create a climate for the mourner to take a deeper leap of faith and make that proclamation.

NOTES

1. Lucy Bregman, *Beyond Silence and Denial: Death and Dying Reconsidered* (Louisville, KY: Westminster John Knox Press, 1999).

2. Tom Brokaw, *The Greatest Generation* (New York: Random House, 1998).

3. Bregman, 6.

4. Kenneth Mitchell and Herbert Anderson, *All our Losses, All our Griefs: Resources for Pastoral Care* (Philadelphia: Westminster Press, 1983), 142.

5. Edward T. Hiscox, *The Star Book for Ministers*, Rev. Ed. (Valley Forge, PA: Judson Press, 1968), i.

6. Ibid., 18.

7. Ibid., 185.

8. Ibid., 190–91.

9. William H. Leach, ed., *The Cokesbury Funeral Manual* (New York: Abingdon-Cokesbury Press, 1932), 7.

10. Ibid., 25.

11. Ibid., 25–26.

12. Ibid., 128.

13. Ibid., 31.

14. Ibid., 57.

15. More detail on the structure and use of these biographies is found in Beverly Prior Smaby, *The Transformation of Moravian Bethlehem: From Communal Mission to Family Economy* (Philadelphia: University of Pennsylvania Press, 1988), 126. See also Glenn H. Asquith Jr., "The Lebenslauf as a Source of Theological Understanding," *Transatlantic Moravian Dialogue–Correspondence (TMDK)* 7 (1995): 53–62.

16. "The Burial Entry of Christopher Elrod, 1721–1785," transcribed from Hope Register A, Moravian Archives, Winston-Salem, NC.

17. Erich Lindemann, "Symptomatology and Management of Acute Grief," *American Journal of Psychiatry* 101 (1944): 141–48.

18. Several large national samples were surveyed in the weeks after Kennedy's assassination, documenting physical and emotional symptoms of grief similar to those reported by Lindemann.

19. Mitchell and Anderson, 36–46.

20. Sam R. Norman, "A Ceremony for the Divorced," *Journal of Pastoral Care* 33 (1979): 62–63.

21. *Ritual in a New Day: An Invitation* (Nashville, TN: Abingdon, 1976).

22. Ibid., 95.

23. Erik Erikson, "Identity and the Life Cycle," in *Psychological Issues 1:1, Monograph 1* (New York: International Universities Press, 1959), 120.

24. Lewis Joseph Sherrill, *The Struggle of the Soul* (New York: Macmillan, 1951).

25. Robert N. Butler, "The Life Review: An Interpretation of Reminiscence in the Aged," *Psychiatry* 26 (1963): 65–76.

26. Glenn H. Asquith Jr., "Disaster Recovery in a Cross-Cultural Setting: A Nicaragua Experience," in *International Pastoral Care Network for Social Responsibility Newsletter* (1994–1995), 20–23. cf. Glenn H. Asquith Jr., "Seminarians Bring Healing and Renew Faith In Nicaragua," *Moravian College Magazine* 43 (1994): 12.

27. Larry Kent Graham, "Pastoral Theology and Catastrophic Disaster," *The Journal of Pastoral Theology* 16 (2006): 7.

28. See Earl A. Grollman, *Concerning Death: A Practical Guide for the Living* (Boston, MA: Beacon Press, 1974).

29. Charles L. Wallis, ed., *The Funeral Encyclopedia: A Source Book* (New York: Harper & Row, 1953), 40.

30. Ibid.

31. Robert Hughes, *A Trumpet in Darkness: Preaching to Mourners* (Philadelphia: Fortress Press, 1985), 22.

32. Ibid., 46.

33. Ibid., 49–50.

34. Kenn Filkins, *Comfort Those Who Mourn: How to Preach Personalized Funeral Messages* (Joplin, MO: College Press Publishing Co., 1992), 17–18.

35. Ibid., 20.

36. Ibid., 21–22.

37. *Moravian Book of Worship* (Bethlehem, PA: Interprovincial Board of Publications and Communications, Moravian Church in North America, 1995), 543. Used with permission.

38. LeRoy H. Aden, *In Life and Death: The Shaping of Faith* (Minneapolis, MN: Augsburg Fortress, 2005), vi.

39. Ibid., 20–21.

CHAPTER 5

African and African-American Traditions in America

Tonya D. Armstrong

Persons of African descent in America, and indeed throughout the Diaspora, are deeply familiar with death. The traumatizing experiences of capture and the Middle Passage, the sheer brutality of chattel slavery, the aggressions of the Jim Crow era, bloodshed of the civil rights movement, documented medical neglect, significantly higher morbidity and mortality rates, and deeply entrenched community, gang, and domestic violence that continue to the present all constitute real peril in the collective African-American[1] consciousness. The fragility of life and the ubiquitous threat of death across gender, religion, geographic, and even social location simultaneously result from and contribute to a unique history and complex trajectory across multiple facets of the African-American experience. This chapter will explore how an African worldview, parlayed through practices and retentions, infused with five centuries of experience in the New World, has contributed to the particular attitudes and practices surrounding death and dying adopted by African-Americans in the twenty-first century.

DEATH AS A REAL CULTURAL PHENOMENON

Whether conscious or subconscious, death is a consistent theme in African-American life. Moreover, terrorism has been closely linked to death in many aspects of the African-American experience for centuries. Even before the first captured Africans reached the shores of the New World, they were exposed to countless deaths attributable to "that peculiar institution" of chattel slavery. Africans died as a result of their involvement in warfare associated with the Atlantic slave trade, in small pens often devoid of sufficient food and water as they awaited embarkation on slave ships; during the Middle Passage on crowded, disease-ridden ships; and after crossing the Atlantic, while awaiting shipment to their final destinations.[2] During slavery, slaveholders often used violence, even murder, as a means of discouraging escape and increasing the compliance of slaves with plantation culture. After Emancipation, the social behavior of persons of African descent was controlled through deadly practices such as beatings and lynching during the Jim Crow era.

Such events by no means ended with Jim Crow, nor did they exclude children. In fact, some of the most egregious displays of racial hatred involving children were pivotal in catalyzing the civil rights movement. The heinous murder of fourteen-year-old Emmett Till in Money, Mississippi, purportedly in response to his alleged flirtation with a white female grocery clerk, made international headlines in 1955. Still others were deeply affected by the bombing by Ku Klux Klan (KKK) members of the Sixteenth Street Baptist Church in Birmingham, Alabama, which resulted in the deaths of four black girls attending Sunday School. In the post-civil rights era, homicides have disproportionately affected African-Americans. The Atlanta child murders, in which twenty-nine black persons (mostly child and adolescent males) were killed between 1979 and 1981, ushered in a sense of vulnerability for yet another generation of children. Widely publicized murders of African-Americans, such as the 1998 dragging death of James Byrd Jr., in Jasper, Texas, or the 1999 shooting (by forty-one bullets) of unarmed Guinean immigrant Amadou Diallo in New York City, stand in stark contrast to white, mainstream notions that America has transcended racial violence. For every publicized murder, there are countless community deaths (including but not limited to "black-on-black" crime) that have all but numbed the African-American psyche. Furthermore, the suicide rate among blacks has risen exponentially since 1950.[3]

Perhaps less dramatic but even more prevalent are deaths that result from health disparities (for a much fuller discussion of these issues, see Richard Payne's chapter). Not only death, but the very process of dying, is often racialized. New cases of HIV/AIDS are diagnosed at a significantly disproportionate rate in African-American communities, and although the current generation of those diagnosed benefits from increased survival rates, the disease still significantly affects quantity and quality of life. In other leading causes of death (e.g., heart disease, diabetes, cancer, and stroke), African-Americans suffer disproportionately from and die earlier from these illnesses. Even the beginning of life is unduly threatened.[4] Medical experimentation on the reproductive viability of female slaves, decades of forced sterilization or contraceptive use, greater proportions of unsafe abortions, and insidiously high infant mortality rates to the present despite significant technological advancements all constitute threat to African-Americans who are "the least of these."

How do African-Americans respond to the pervasiveness of death and dying? Responses range from suspicion, even distrust, of the white establishment, to acceptance and transcendence. Some African-Americans have internalized a broader cultural message that there is relatively low value placed on their lives, recalling, for example, how that value was quantified for political purposes as three fifths of a person in the late eighteenth century. Contemporary academic literature and popular culture, for example, are replete with references to low self-esteem among blacks. Other African-Americans externalize blame for their mistreatment throughout the life course. The Tuskegee Syphilis Study serves as an unfortunate yet apt illustration of this perspective. Conducted from 1932 to 1972, lead investigators for the study withheld penicillin from black men diagnosed with syphilis, even after it became a standard treatment for syphilis in 1943. This discovery demonstrated to many African-Americans a blatant disregard for their health status and has likely contributed to the ongoing distrust of the medical establishment, both for clinical and research purposes.[5]

Religion presents a salient prism for meaning-making for many African-Americans, the vast majority of whom identify as Christian. For many, death represents an escape from the troubles of the world and a hope for a better existence in the next world. Death secured the freedom that was ever-elusive for black slaves and restores the humanity and dignity that many contemporary African-Americans find elusive in the present life. Religion provides the theological, scriptural, sacramental, liturgical, pastoral, and spiritual tools to transcend the disappointing, sometimes bitter realities of African-American life, particularly at the end of life.

Although blacks have been in America for nearly four hundred years, it is generally agreed that there exists an ongoing connection between African-American life and African influences. To what degree might we surmise that contemporary African-American responses to death and dying are attributable to cosmological and ritualistic inheritances from their ancestors traced back to what they affectionately call "the Motherland"? It is that question to which we now turn.

AFRICAN WORLDVIEW

To more fully appreciate the influence of African traditions at the end of life on Americans and on African-Americans in particular, it is important to examine the African worldview. Because the continent of Africa reveals significant diversity across countries, tribes, languages, and customs, any attempts to speak of an African worldview (singular) will, to varying degrees, misrepresent the distinctive nature of Africa's cultures. For the purpose of identifying common themes, however, this chapter will focus on similarities in worldviews and practices and will mention particularities where appropriate.

There are several important elements of the African worldview. One prominent theme is the centrality of *communality*, which is summed up in the aphorism, "I am because we are, and since we are, therefore I am." Accordingly, the *kinship group* is highly significant, displaying great cohesiveness.[6] Additionally, Africans exhibit a *holistic approach to life*. There are no dichotomies between sacred and secular; the spiritual realm pervades all facets of life. Moreover, *equality in the relationship between the human and God* allows the perfect qualities of God to be viewed as attainable.[7] Unlike the Western, primarily linear, conception of time, the *African perspective of time is cyclical*, repetitive, and lacks the notion of eternity. Time is an event that is not pursued but a resource that is utilized as it comes.[8] Religion is typically *pluralistic*, with tolerance for other religious traditions.[9]

From these elements of the African worldview emanate particular African notions about death. First, Africans widely hold the belief that the dead are not really dead; rather, they enter another plane of existence in the spiritual world, resulting in an ever-growing kinship group. Thus, life and death are cyclical rather than dual.[10] Additionally, beyond its inevitability, death is viewed as destiny. Moreover, although a Christian awareness of death is driven by rationality, an African awareness of death is motivated by maintaining the natural connection between the human and natural worlds. Charlton McIlwain notes that within the African worldview, there is a preparation for, even a longing for death:

> [P]reparation, in the African cosmos, is not motivated primarily out of the individual's need or desire for reward in the afterlife. Rather, motivation stems from the desire to prepare oneself for a smooth transition—one that neither upsets the natural balance between the human and natural world nor between the individual and his or her ancestors. To put it succinctly, the meaning of death extended beyond the individual.[11]

Even in death, the African maintains and promotes a sense of communality.

AFRICAN DEATH RITUALS

Quite naturally, worldview contributes significantly to what is valued and how that value is expressed. It follows, then, that common elements in African religious experience include the importance of ancestors, multiple deities, myths, medicine, divination, sacred kingship, rituals, and festivals.[12] There exist myths about the origin of the world, of various institutions, and of the myriad facets of human activity, including death.[13] For example, African myths generally suggest that death robbed God's creatures of paradise, signaled a separation from God, and ushered in trials and tribulations.[14] Although myths vary by ethnic group and have different supernatural entities beyond the Supreme Being, they are almost always demonstrated through ritual, which allows the tangible expression of the relationship between human and divine. Priests, diviners, herbalists, sacred kings, and chiefs are all religious functionaries. These intermediaries orchestrate major events such as hunting, war, weather, the elements, and death. Death is most commonly understood in the African context to be caused by sorcery, spirits, or a curse. In addition to learning the physical cause(s) of death, many persons seek the mystical causes of death.

A Mande proverb succinctly states, "It takes more than death to make an ancestor." Some rites of passage are only performed for initiated elders who have acquired much, made their contributions to society, and had many descendants. Death rituals typically correspond to the honor ascribed to the deceased. How one dies has implications for the communal understanding of the quality of the deceased's life. Dying in old age from natural causes, for example, is considered a good death. Dying from war, other brutal causes, or as a child is considered a bad death. The servants of ancestors, and of royalty in particular, are often buried with their masters, because it is thought that the servants will continue to provide needed assistance in the spiritual world.[15] Slaves and outsiders, on the other hand, are excluded from the society of ancestors.[16]

Historian John Hope Franklin describes the African funeral as "the climax of life."[17] Inasmuch as Africans believe that how they treat their dead will affect their quality of life, final rites are of utmost importance. Consequently, extensive and expensive death rituals are commonly accepted as the "sacred obligations of the survivors."[18] Such elaborate funeral rites acknowledge the ongoing, symbiotic relationship between the living and the dead. The rites pay homage to the dead and remind them of their duty to help the living through troubled times.[19]

Moreover, the cohesiveness of the African family is demonstrated by the extent of death ceremonies and customs. The detail and specificity of arrangements reveal how significant the deceased was to the community and remind the community of the cyclical nature of life.[20] For instance, the size, significance, and length of a funeral depends on the importance of the deceased. The funeral formally marks the separation between the living and the dead. Rites include weeping and wailing, mourning the death of the person, memorializing the deceased's positive contributions to society, and reminding the community that the person lives on in the next world. Different tribes, depending on whether they are matrilineal or patrilineal, memorialize the dead using various rituals.

There exist both open and secret societies across the African continent, a significant role of which is to provide financial and practical support for bereaved families. Upon the death of an impoverished member, the orga-nization gathers collections to pay for burial expenses and to support the deceased's family members. At the funeral, the organization is represented with a banner and an organizational drum.

Music, specifically choral lamentations, dirges, and drum music, figure prominently throughout African death rituals, particularly in the proces-sion. The procession often includes a statue, a physical representation of the deceased, allowing him to metaphorically dance at his own funeral. The choral lamentation, typically customary chants or funeral songs sung by wailing women as they walk through the streets, honors the widow. These first songs acknowledge the widow's grief while also announcing her new status to the community. Funeral dirges are poems of lamentation of-ten improvised by the mourners. Its main themes include references to the deceased and to the ancestors, references to the domicile of the deceased and ancestors, transmissions of messages to the other side, and reflections on the passing of another acquaintance of the singer. Dirges provide the flexibility to allow the singer to express her own grief while honoring and praising the deceased. They also permit the cathartic release of grief for all mourners. Dirge singers accompany the body to the burial place; some walk in front of the coffin, whereas others walk behind it. The entomb-ment marks the third musical event—drum music accompanied by singing and dancing. The body is typically buried the same or the following day in the family's burial place, the backyard of one of the homes in the village, or at the original place of birth.

Not only sacred remembering of the deceased, but also harmonious liv-ing leads to blessings from the ancestors. One powerful mechanism for attaining these blessings is the covenant. Covenants are negotiated between the living and the dead to secure resources and protection from evil spirits.[21] Covenants between the living and ancestors are facilitated by libations and sacrifices. Libations are offerings that initiate contact with the ancestors through the use of fresh water, millet flour mixed with water, and millet beer (or palm wine).[22] Contact with the ancestors culminates in the offering of a bloody sacrifice. Another aspect of ritual that facilitates contact with the ancestors is the erection and use of the shrine. Historian Benjamin Ray describes shrines as channels of communication between the human and the spiritual worlds and the focus of ritual activity.[23] In harmony with water, soil, air, or fire, shrines may range from a natural set-ting (e.g., a tree) to a large building. Such personal shrines allow for more frequent contact with the ancestors.

Feasting after the rites is both to comfort the bereaved and to thank those who assisted with the rites. One or two days of fasting may precede the feast. Stopping work for a few days is also customary. Some shave their heads as a symbol for the separation of the deceased and smear themselves with white clay, refrain from washing their bodies for a period, and/or sacrifice bulls or goats. "By doing these things people are able to come to terms with the agonies, sorrows and disruptions caused by death. By ritualizing death, people dance it away, drive it away, and renew their own life after it has taken away one of their members."[24]

McIlwain, in his characterization of African death rituals, identified four major themes. First, such rituals always occur within a familial context. Depending on kinship structures, roles for assuming responsibilities around the ritual event are preestablished and clearly delineated. Second, the type of burial accorded the deceased is determined by numerous social distinctions including tribe, gender, social status, the number of offspring, the gender of offspring, social status of spouses, and one's hierarchical position in the family tree. Third, there are particular methods for preparing the corpse for final disposal. Decapitation, mummification, and washing or chalking all carry meaning within ethnic groups. The place of burial could be under the house, in an earthen grave, or in a canoe that would carry the body downstream. Animal or human sacrifice is sometimes present in the death ritual. Finally, death rituals are ultimately always public, although the broader community may only be invited to participate in the "second burial," similar in some respects to a memorial service, which was in earlier times held twenty-eight days after the first burial but might be conducted 6 weeks to one year after the death.

BELIEFS ABOUT THE AFTERLIFE

The hereafter[25] is imagined to be similar in many ways to the current world. In many African imaginations, the dead remain in their neighborhoods and are still a part of the family for up to four or five generations. This conception of continual ancestral presence underscores the importance of keeping alive the memory of the deceased. Unlike other religions such as Christianity that emphasize a physical, otherworldly place as the locus for noncorporeal continuation, Mbiti observes "... [O]n the whole African Religion has neither heaven nor hell, and neither rewards nor punishment for people in the hereafter."[26] Even after the spirit leaves the body, it retains its former personality. People may encounter the living dead through visions, dreams, spiritual possessions, or certain illnesses. In these latter two categories, a diviner or medicine man is sought to investigate the reason for the encounter. In many cases, family members leave food and drink for the dead. The dead are also recalled during family ceremonies and rituals, particularly those involving children. In some African cultures, the living dead are named in prayer so that they may serve as intercessors.

Perhaps because ancestors are seen as part of the community and kinship groups, they are venerated. Many outside of the African worldview, however, seem to have a misconception of "ancestor worship." African religions are often marginalized or summarily dismissed because the so-called worship of ancestors is viewed as simplistic or idolatrous, particularly to those from a monotheistic context. Yet Mbiti notes:

> Through rituals, dreams, visions, possessions and names, [ancestors] are recalled and respected. This does not and cannot mean that they are worshipped. The departed are considered to be still alive, and people show by these practices that they recognize their presence. In this way, African Religion is being realistic; since nobody wants to be forgotten by his family immediately after dying.[27]

Acknowledging the whole family, dead and surviving, points to the importance of balance between the visible and invisible worlds.

PARTICULAR TRIBAL DEATH RITUALS

Based primarily in Nigeria, the Yoruba "believe that the dead travel to a sphere above and join with their ancestors. In death, the dead merely transform from a lower state of being to a higher one, yet, through this transference, the invisible dead gain power over the living."[28] The dead must be appeased by an appropriate funeral and burial to avoid havoc and to gain their blessings and protection from the Orishas (i.e., the deities representing God).

In Akan social life, the celebration of the funeral is a significant social event with codes for expected behavior. Rather than displaying a solemn occasion, the funeral has more of a festive atmosphere. Final rites include music and dancing with appropriate commentary from observers, laughing and joking by guests, the pouring of libations, the firing of guns, and the giving of money to the family to help cover expenses. Males and females are responsible for different roles during the death ritual. Women generally provide the vocal music, although men sing dirges for a deceased hunter. Also, men are responsible for playing drum music for dancing.

The practice of voodoo, especially among the Fon, the Yoruba, and the Ewe, features another African perspective on life and death. Voodoo, or *vodun* in the Fon language of Benin and Togo, refers to "an invisible force, terrible and mysterious, which meddles in human affairs any time."[29] The voodoo can be gods, spirits, or sacred objects that protect the village, the family, and kinship ties. One special feature of *vodun* is the *egun-gun*, or the cult of the dead, which brings families and tribes together in large gatherings, festivals, funerals, and other celebrations that guarantee the continuance of religious traditions.[30]

Within voodoo practices, the family remove the dead spirits (*Gede*) from their home by waking (watching over) the body for several days. On the eve of the burial, community members gather for entertainment (e.g., playing cards), tea and coffee, and sharing stories of the deceased until the funeral the next morning.[31] The goals of the vigil are to lighten experiences of grief of the survivors and to heal the community's grief. It is not uncommon for the living to ask favors of the dead, given their proximity to the *lwa*, or angels. After the burial, family members are obligated to remain at the gravesite for a short period, to make at least annual visitations to the cemetery, and to observe special holidays for the dead. After all, those who practice voodoo believe in the balance between the living and the dead; one cannot live without the other.[32]

Many of these African death rituals existed for centuries before the advent of the Atlantic slave trade and have undoubtedly influenced attitudes and practices of generations of African-Americans. To what extent have these rituals been retained? What is unique about African-American death rituals, and why? We will begin exploring these answers by examining the lives and experiences of the first generations of Africans in America.

SLAVERY

The African worldview continued to exert its power in the lives and psyches of Africans in America. Such influence was observed in attitudes and practices of daily life, not the least of which included death. The experience of slavery, then, presented multiple occasions for encountering the threat of death, death itself, and death rituals.

The Middle Passage describes collectively the journeys and the experiences of millions of captured Africans from the coast of West Africa to the New World. Overall, it is estimated that between eleven million and fifteen million slaves were exported from Africa across the three centuries of the American slave trade.[33] The severe overcrowding, inhumane conditions, and resultant rampant disease were likely responsible for millions of African lives lost during the colonial slave trade. Their bodies were often tossed overboard into the Atlantic Ocean, which was seen as a particularly inhumane burial. Slaves who survived the Middle Passage were traumatized not only by the experience itself but also by the sheer loss of human life during each reprehensible voyage. Even as fellow voyagers may have represented different tribes, the experiences of loss in the context of shared communal perspectives likely exacerbated their grief.

As slaves reached their ultimate destinations, plantation life was the typical experience for most slaves and carried with it many threats to life. These threats were both internal, such as poor health stemming from harsh working conditions and vulnerability to disease, and external, such as severe punishment for disobedience. Once a slave died, the community might be notified through the firing of a gun twice in close succession. In the absence of embalming practices, immediate burial was required to protect the body from animals.[34] During colonial times, the wake was referred to as "sitting up."[35] Much like their African forebears, family and friends would "sit up" with the body the evening after the death. As was the custom then, family members themselves were charged with taking measurements of the body and crafting a coffin.[36]

A slave might be buried the same day or the next day, with or without a formal death ritual ceremony. Without a funeral to memorialize their loved ones, slaves were left to merely grieve as they labored. If there was a funeral, the ability to attend a funeral was determined by the slaveholder. Slaves preferred night funerals because it allowed their friends from neighboring farms to attend and because the funeral event would not be disrupted by work. The funeral usually included singing, praying, and a short sermon, typically provided by a white preacher. Occasionally, slaves would be permitted to preside publicly over their own funerals as an acknowledgment from slaveholders that to deny the humanity of the deceased slave was to come precariously close to inciting a slave revolt. Granting such permission, then, was as much about pragmatism as it was about pity for the slaves.

Similar to the African practice of firing guns, gun(s) would fire toward the north, south, east, and west at the burial, which sometimes occurred at the graveyard on the slaveholder's property. According to some accounts of the earlier period of slavery, the corpse was sometimes placed directly in the earthen grave along with extra clothes and food and drink for the journey that lay ahead. It was customary for the grave to be dug from east to west and the decedent's head to be turned to the left at burial and facing east.[37] Those attending the ceremony were cautioned not to step on the new dirt around the grave, lest they fall sick. The bereaved family would then return to their slave quarters, scatter medicine around the house to ward off any illness, and build a new fire. Life quickly returned to the realities of slave labor.

NEW ORLEANS

Although slaves who survived the Middle Passage arrived at various ports across what has come to be known as the Americas and the Caribbean, slaves who arrived in New Orleans created a particularly vibrant culture around death ritual practices. Commonalities in ethnic heritage, similar religious influences, and unique resources make New Orleans an ideal geographic and cultural location for the study of African-American experiences with death and dying.

In terms of ethnic heritage, slaves in New Orleans frequently were imported from West African regions that held some customs and social, religious, and linguistic cultural values in common. Preferring slaves who were skilled agrarians, resistant to disease, and able to withstand the swampy regions of southern Louisiana, the French began in 1719 to select humans from Senegal, Senegambia (i.e., the geographical regions between the Senegal and Gambia rivers), and the Windward Coast. Between 1726 and 1731, regions from which Africans were captured included Kongo, Angola, the Gold Coast, and the Slave Coast. Today, these regions correspond to Senegal, Mali, Gambia, Guinea, Guinea-Bissau, Sierra Leone, Mauritania, and Cape Verde. Noting that the majority of the African slaves coming into New Orleans were either from Senegambia or descendants of Senegambian captives from the French Caribbean, Ardencie Hall observed that Africans living in southern Louisiana reestablished their connections with Africa with the advent of each new ship.[38]

Although later importations of Africans originated from other geographic areas of African's western coastline, this early and sizeable Senegambian presence provided a stable foundation into which other African cultures were eventually blended. The West Africans were often taken to Haiti for a period where they could be "seasoned," that is, inured to the realities of slavery. Two thirds of slaves, according to historian Gwendolyn Midlo Hall, came from a relatively homogeneous culture of Senegambia, thereby limiting in New Orleans the cultural fragmentation that characterized other aspects of the African slave trade. In the 1730s, Africans outnumbered Europeans two to one in the southern half of Louisiana.[39] To be sure, Europeans maintained control over the lives of Africans, yet the numerical domination of the latter suggests the likelihood of pervasive cultural influence.

In Louisiana, slaves were forced to practice Catholicism, the religion of their slaveholders and oppressors. Catholicism, like most other religions practiced in the New World, was used to justify and sustain the slave trade for centuries. Oppressors apparently believed that they could save the souls of their slaves by converting them to Christianity. The Black Codes, created by Louis XIII in 1635, institutionalized this practice: "All slaves who come to our islands will be baptized and instructed in the Catholic, Apostolic and Roman religions. The Governors will give the necessary orders for the baptism and instruction of the slaves within a suitable period."[40] Religion, in many cases, was used to remind slaves of their duty to obey their masters, with the hopes of thereby producing a more docile servant. Religion also ostensibly helped slaveholders to assuage their consciences of moral wrongdoing, although many seemed oblivious to their own moral obligations invoked in the same Scriptural passages (e.g., Ephesians 6:5–9, Colossians 3:22–4:1) that they quoted to their slaves.

Catholicism offered not only theological support but also liturgical resources for honoring the dead. "The influence of Catholicism with its emphasis upon the observance of certain religious forms, especially the proper burial of the dead, was the greatest. The practice of visiting the burial grounds, and the erection of elaborate graves, in the old cemeteries of the city are evidence of the influence of Catholicism."[41] Nonetheless, many "converts" continued to practice their African religion even as they adopted Christian practices and beliefs, which fits with the more tolerant, pluralistic worldview commonly observed in Africans. Witness, for example, the interplay between Catholicism and voodoo. Fitting with an African worldview, voodoo did not perceive death as a punishment from God or nature, but "a re-generational source for the society and the deceased."[42] Appropriate to the New World emphasis on Catholicism, the funeral mass became the major contribution to voodoo and remained that way even after Emancipation.

Similar in many ways to open and secret societies in Africa, benevolent societies had proliferated in every community and parish in Louisiana by the late eighteenth century and endured well into the twentieth century, indicating their influence on its members and the broader community. It is estimated that three hundred to six hundred groups were established in New Orleans, and many were outgrowths of both Catholic and Protestant churches, whereas others grew out of free black and Creole communities. Some were based on occupation, whereas others were based on friendship, class, color, gender, and/or age distinctions. Members paid dues, which insured them an appropriate burial, an important means of security for many blacks. Beyond sponsoring sophisticated wakes and funerals, benevolent societies provided opportunities for social intercourse through recreational activities, parties, and political meetings. These societies are also credited with offering visitation, a form of pastoral care, because visits were required by the organization's constitution and often administered by the relief committee. Those members who were seriously ill were visited in pairs, who would sit with the sick person each night. Depending on the chronicity of the illness, sitting would sometimes rotate to other members of the organization. These benevolent societies offered care that was communal (in that it fostered social networks) and relatively holistic (in that it sought to address the multiple challenges of its members).

NEW ORLEANS JAZZ FUNERALS

The New Orleans jazz funeral is a unique cultural phenomenon originating with the slaves of that region. Some speculate that the jazz funeral originated in response to the slave rebellions of 1795 in New Orleans. Slaveholders and governmental authorities reportedly responded to this rebellion by brutally executing the slaves who led the rebellion and displaying their bodies in the city square. Slaves developed the jazz funeral as a form of protest against the blatant public disrespect of their community leaders. Through its elaborateness, emotional expressiveness, and festive celebration, the jazz funeral helped to restore the dignity of the slave.

Challenges that were somewhat unique to the region contributed to the refinement of the jazz funeral as an art form. For example, New Orleans revealed the highest death rate among blacks in the South during the 1800s, partly because of outbreaks of yellow fever and cholera during the late 1870s and early 1880s. Hurricanes and flooding further contributed to the uncertainty of life in that region. With a fairly high death rate, black residents in New Orleans needed a method for including the entire community in the grieving process *and* in the celebration of sustained life. Enter the jazz funeral.

The New Orleans jazz funeral is comprised of two parts. The first ceremony constitutes the funeral proper, with somber demeanor and respectful stillness. The funeral procession winds it way to the place of burial as community members fall in line with the family and the band. From the institution of the jazz funeral, street parade bands corresponded to West African parade traditions because they were less rigid than military marching bands and allowed for the improvisation of both music and movement. Ragtime and early jazz music played by brass bands were incorporated into the funeral event.

The second ceremony begins after the body is buried. The grand marshal of the band instructs the mournful procession to "cut loose" the body, after which the band picks up the tempo of the music. The mood of the crowd significantly brightens as festive singing and dancing ensue. Survivors transition from mourning the loss of the deceased to celebrating life itself and the afterlife of the deceased.[43]

CONTEMPORARY AFRICAN-AMERICAN RITUALS

Notwithstanding the particularities of New Orleans blacks during the colonial period, African-American communities demonstrate diversity in end-of-life rituals. Such diversity may be attributed to religious, socioeconomic, geographic, and community variations. Nonetheless, there are commonalities that exist in these rituals. This section reviews several primarily Protestant Christian death rituals, from end-of-life vigils to aftercare for bereaved families. Readers will note a number of continuities with the African worldview and practices, while observing a number of discontinuities, as well.

In anticipation of the imminent death of a loved one, many African-Americans organize vigils whereby family and fictive kin attend to the needs of the dying person around the clock. During these final hours or days, there may be spontaneous or informal prayer services at the bedside that include prayers, singing, and stories about, for, or even by the dying person. African-American psychiatrist and theologian James Carter has observed that African-Americans want loved ones to die at home surrounded by family and friends.[44] However, in the event that a loved one's final moments are spent in a hospital, African-Americans are reluctant to give permission to discontinue mechanical life supports. Similar to the beliefs of most Africans, dying is regarded as being in the hands of God. On the other hand, African-Americans typically have relatively few formal resources from which to draw at the end of life. Hospice awareness and utilization are significantly lower,[45] and faith communities are less likely to have organized care teams and support ministries.

PREPARATION FOR FINAL RITES

Once death has occurred, African-Americans may use a variety of terms to describe it. Carter notes that "passed on," "at rest," and "gone to their reward" are all used interchangeably with "died."[46] Discourse around the "transition" of the dead is also popular in some African-American circles. Although some suggest that euphemistic use of these phrases is a means for creating distance or avoidance with the reality of death, others argue that these terms reflect the African worldview that emphasizes the continuity between life and death. Carter further notes that African-Americans tend to readily disclose to children the occurrence of death,[47] perhaps as part of a necessary socialization process for helping their young grow accustomed to the harsh realities of life.

Whether an African-American dies at home, in the hospital, or at a hospice facility, the next step in the death ritual involves making the "first call."[48] The family or very close friend must contact the mortuary or, more precisely, the mortician or funeral director. It is not primarily the professional service itself but the relationship with the professional funeral director that is pivotal to the family in grief. Because of the historical precedent of black undertakers being the only recourse for black decedents and their families, many African-Americans continue to pursue funeral arrangements through black funeral directors. There are several reasons that this alliance endures. First, not only is the black funeral director frequently well-integrated into community life but also is frequently an active member in a local black church, further cementing his/her credibility. Church membership increases greatly the likelihood that the funeral director already has established a relationship with families before the experience of death and implies that the funeral director will attentively serve the needs and desires of the family. Moreover, the black funeral director is often sought for aesthetic reasons because he/she generally has greater familiarity with African-American hair styling and cosmetic sensibilities compared with nonblacks. Finally, although numbers are decreasing, many black funeral homes are both black- and family-owned, which is attractive to many African-Americans striving for economic empowerment of their communities.

Once the body is retrieved by the mortician, the family must set about the tasks of making arrangements for the death ritual event. First, the family must decide the nature of the ritual. Most African-Americans will opt for a funeral service in a church. Many families will call the pastor very early after learning of the death, not only to inform the pastor of their loss and to secure his/her pastoral support but also to secure the space and to reserve a time on the church calendar. Regardless of whether the decedent was involved in the life of the church, there is frequently a close family member who successfully negotiates for the funeral to be held in a local church.[49] Although rates of cremation among whites have increased steadily over the last few decades, rates of cremation among blacks hover at around 10 percent and show fewer indications of increasing.[50] "Secular"[51] memorial services are relatively rare.

Second, the funeral service program must be prepared. Because aesthetics are important, African-American funeral programs often feature the image of the decedent. This image may be recent or from an earlier part of the decedent's life and presents a dignified or cheerful view of the decedent. Close family members are typically charged with the practical arrangements of writing the obituary, which will typically be included in the program. Beyond the writing and publishing of the obituary, family members must consult with the pastor and mortician about the order of the service. Often, the delegation or execution of these tasks primarily fall not necessarily to the next of kin, but to the individual regarded by the rest of the family as the most powerful, perhaps by virtue of his/her accomplishments, financial or social resources, or influence within the family.

In his content analysis of five hundred newspaper obituaries selected from geographically diverse areas of the United States, McIlwain posited that African-American families, churches, and funeral homes are more significantly connected than in many white contexts. He noted that 59 percent of African-Americans mentioned a church in the obituary, whereas only 31 percent of whites did the same. Ninety-four percent mentioned a funeral home, compared with 67 percent of whites. Finally, the name of the church's pastor was mentioned 83 percent of the time by African-Americans, whereas 6 percent of whites mentioned the pastor's name. Obituaries for deceased African-Americans also tended to be significantly longer, with 66 percent exceeding fifty words, compared with 20 percent for whites. These public announcements are not primarily about notification, given that 97 percent of obituaries in black newspapers were after the funeral event, whereas 85 percent of those in white newspapers were before the event. Rather, the data suggest that such announcements aimed to properly memorialize the decedent.[52] McIlwain concludes that although persons from all ethnic groups clearly express love and mourning for their loved one, African-Americans may be more likely to take more time to reflect on the death of a loved one and its related meaning for the family. Varying orientations to time may help to account for these racial differences in obituary content and length.

Making financial arrangements for the final death ritual event is another responsibility that regularly creates an especially difficult burden for many black families. For many African-Americans, there is the deep desire to preserve as much as possible the dignity and respect of the deceased, particularly in light of the larger context where respect has not always been accorded readily in the broader society. At the same time, there are sometimes grim economic realities that militate against the ability of the family to ably provide their preferred mode of respectful expression through the funeral service. Although benevolent societies historically have played a major role in the financial support of bereaved families, in many respects their functions have been replaced by those of insurance companies.[53] Even so, many African-Americans do not have sufficient insurance to cover the costs of the funeral, which reflects both the impact of poverty and a history of racial exploitation by the broader insurance industry (e.g., through the sale of race-based policies that were more expensive than policies offered whites). Lower-income African-Americans, for example, are more likely to own burial insurance rather than life insurance policies.[54] The need for flexibility in financing the disposal of the body underscores again the importance of the family's relationship with the funeral director. Black funeral directors may be more likely to extend credit to families, particularly when there is a history of having provided funeral arrangements for a previous decedent and the further implicit understanding that those services will be needed again in the future.[55]

Whether or not the obituary has been published promptly in the newspaper, word of mouth travels quickly to deliver news of the death and information on "who's got the body."[56] The response of community members is vital to both preparation for the funeral and to the healing process, and many African-Americans receive support from various networks. Fictive kin, neighbors, friends, and associates from job, civic, fraternal, and sororal organizations will often phone the family to express condolences, send sympathy cards, visit, and prepare food for the bereaved family. Depending on the involvement of the bereaved family members in the faith community, the "church family" may become even more engaged in important tasks such as running errands, performing household chores, and providing financial support. Fellow members of church auxiliaries or ministries may pray with the family and serve as honorary pallbearers or floral bearers during the funeral. Unlike societal arrangement in several African cultures, family members and close friends are not necessarily assigned roles (explicitly or implicitly) to perform after the death of a family members; nevertheless, some will avail themselves to provide whatever support may be needed.

The death of a family member sometimes provides the occasion for the (re-)emergence of challenging family dynamics. Familial issues such as secrets (e.g., the patriarch of the family secretly sired a child out of wedlock who now wants to attend the funeral), suppressed sibling (or other) rivalries, and other long-standing resentments are typically confronted as the family makes preparations for final rites. Working on tasks and spending concentrated time together under the burden of grief can contribute to further strife in discordant relationships. Even more devastating is the decedent who has become, for any number of reasons, isolated from his/her family and consequently has few, if any, persons to make preparations for or to attend last rites. Within African-American communities, incarceration, protracted substance abuse, homelessness, and HIV/AIDS are all life experiences (sometimes co-occurring) that have created significant frustration, suffering, and distance within families. Although these life circumstances occur across ethnic and racial groups, their disproportionately high occurrence among African-Americans can create greater strife for these families.

Although the wake historically has been held the evening before the funeral, some note a recent trend toward holding the wake during the one-hour period before the funeral. The family is escorted to the site of the service by the funeral home associates, typically in a caravan of limousines sufficient to transport immediate family members. Family members are usually seated according to their biological affinity with the deceased. Spouses, children, parents, siblings, aunts, uncles, and cousins sit most closely to the body during the ceremony. Longer term, unmarried, and heterosexual partners are often acknowledged the same rites as spouses; given the slower acceptance of homosexuality within African-American communities, gay or lesbian partners are much more likely to be disenfranchised. Fictive kin may be afforded the rights of biological family members, typically at the discretion of the most powerful next-of-kin relative.

During the wake, members of the community are invited to visit informally with the family, often at the church or funeral parlor. Guests are instructed to sign the guest book (if they had not already signed it during a home visit). Next, they are invited to view the body, which is historically placed in a half-opened casket. Mourners may pass by the body fairly quickly or linger for a while, generally depending on the depth of the shared relationship. They may have an opportunity to greet family members personally, often sharing affectionate gestures and words of comfort. There is usually a period during the wake when members of the broader community are given the opportunity to share reflections about the deceased, some of which are injected with humor. Moreover, depending on the civic involvement of the deceased, there may be an organization (e.g., Order of the Eastern Star, Masons, fraternity, or sorority) that offers final rites for a five- to fifteen-minute period. Although these rites are sometimes incorporated into the funeral proper, some churches dispute this placement on theological grounds and encourage the performance of these rites during the wake.

AFRICAN-AMERICAN FUNERALS

The funeral itself is the prototypical culmination of the death ritual for most African-Americans. It may be delayed for several days to allow family to arrive from distant locales. For many African-Americans, consistent with the African emphasis on the cohesion of the kinship group, attending the funeral of a relative, even one who is relatively distant in terms of the bloodline, is a given. The funeral is recognized as the final opportunity to pay last respects to the dead, to gather with family to mourn the loss, and to celebrate together the continuity of life with the living. The occasion is at once a homecoming for loved ones and a home-going for the deceased. Themes of home-going recur through scripture, music, and eulogy.

The stereotypical African-American funeral is one characterized by overt expressions of boisterous emotionality. As with most stereotypes, there is an element of accuracy to this characterization. Importantly, there are a number of factors that contribute to intense grief more commonly in African-Americans compared with their white counterparts. First, sudden death is more common among African-Americans, particularly stemming from homicide and controversial exchanges with law enforcement agents. Even when death is not sudden, many deaths of African-Americans raise questions of social justice. Environmental threats (e.g., lead poisoning in substandard housing, community landfills), occupational hazards (e.g., jobs that require greater exposure to biohazardous materials), and decreased access to quality health care all contribute to a shorter life expectancy among African-Americans. Thus, there exists the tension between a more traditional African worldview that dying is in the hands of God and implicit observation of the sometimes preventable cause(s) of death.

Weeping, wailing, passing out, or fainting may occur at various points during the funeral, particularly by family members upon viewing the body. Various explanations have been proposed for such shows of emotion. Some suggest that emotional expressiveness plays an important role in cathartic release of pent-up grief; others posit that it demonstrates a need for social support[57]; still others point to emotionality as an indication of how profoundly the deceased was loved. Some data on African-American mourners suggest a positive correlation between emotional expressiveness immediately after the death and less incapacitating grief several months later compared with white controls.[58] Beyond the stereotypes, however, is perhaps a waning of emotionality, some of which has been explained as a sign of assimilation into the mainstream white culture. With greater urbanization, increased educational achievement, and socioeconomic ascendance, particularly during the second half of the twentieth century, African-Americans may be less likely to demonstrate emotion at funerals. Still, even subdued emotionality is likely to be remarkable for cultural outsiders.

If the wake does not take place immediately before the funeral, the family procession begins the formal funeral. Others in attendance respectfully stand during this procession. Often, the pastor or pastoral officiant reads scripture during this time. Common scriptural passages include "I am the resurrection and the life; if any man believes in me, though he were dead, yet shall he live,"[59] or:

> All our days pass away under your wrath;
> we finish our years with a moan.
> The length of our days is seventy years—
> or eighty, if we have the strength;
> yet their span is but trouble and sorrow,
> for they quickly pass, and we fly away.
> Who knows the power of your anger?
> For your wrath is as great as the fear that is due you.
> Teach us to number our days aright,
> that we may gain a heart of wisdom.[60]

Because many African-American Christians have a high view of scripture, these passages comfort and ground listeners through the crisis of bereavement. Just as in other liturgical forms, music figures prominently in African-American funerals. Typically, there is an opening hymn that captures the spirit of celebration and the joy of home-going for the deceased. Hymns commonly used include "Blessed Assurance," "I'll Fly Away," or "We Will Understand It Better By and By." Within the black church tradition, spirituals and gospel music have long been crucial for infusing hope. It stands to reason, then, that these songs are vitally woven throughout the service. Hope is stirred simultaneously for the deceased to find rest and for the survivors who seek rest from their troubles as manifested in these lyrics:

> Soon-a will be done with the troubles of the world
> The troubles of the world, the troubles of the world
> Soon-a will be done with the troubles of the world
> Going home to live with God.[61]

Other songs such as "My Soul's Been Anchored in the Lord," "His Eye Is on the Sparrow," "I Won't Complain," "Goin' Up Yonder," and "Precious Lord, Take My Hand," often rendered by soloists, are usually highly stylized, may involve call and response between the singer(s) and mourners, and may model and encourage movement, thereby engaging the active participation of mourners. The central significance of music and movement are reflective of many African-American worship experiences and show a vital connection to African funeral practices.

Other elements of the funeral service include the reading of scripture, usually from both Old and New Testaments; the reading of the obituary[62]; the public acknowledgement by a church representative or family friend of cards, flowers, and other caring expressions. Often, just a few cards are read during the service, with the remainder to be acknowledged by a note of thanks from the family at a later date.

Another practice common to African-American funerals is the public reading of resolutions. In this context, a resolution is a statement provided by church, ministry, or auxiliary organization detailing the deceased's relationship to the organization, her duties and responsibilities, length of membership, and special accomplishments on behalf of the organization. The resolution regularly ends with a remark about how the resolution will be archived (in addition to the customary practice of giving the family a copy). This ritual highlights the worthiness of the deceased for the next life.

At this point in the service, close family and friends are often given a few minutes to share reflections about or memories of the deceased. These stories often incorporate humor surrounding family experiences or some aspect of the deceased's personality. Family members often discuss what they will miss about the deceased or provide a word of encouragement to other mourners about what the deceased would have wanted for the funeral, or even for how the living will go on with their lives. McIlwain describes such "speaking for the deceased" as a common theme in African-American funerals. Arguably, this practice is yet another acknowledgement of the noncorporeal continuance of the deceased. Just as some traditional African funeral processions allow the deceased to "dance at his own funeral," this current practice allows the African-American decedent to speak at his own funeral.

The apogee of the funeral is the eulogy. Consistent with the theme of home-going, the eulogist must uplift those gathered with a message of hope for a better future for the deceased. The preacher, often the pastor of the deceased and/or of the powerful next-of-kin, emphasizes the character and good qualities of the deceased, perhaps with some embellishment. It is not uncommon for the eulogist to paint the most positive image possible, often leaving mourners with the memory of the decedent in mythic proportions. Although this practice is ostensibly intended to comfort the family with the notion that their loved one experienced a life well-lived, such a mischaracterization of the deceased sometimes promotes tension in a family well-acquainted with, perhaps even divided around, a more realistic view of the person. Eulogists, for their part, seem to reason, implicitly or explicitly, that no human can judge the relationship that the deceased had with her Maker before death.

This significant point perhaps demonstrates a point of discontinuity with African influence. Although much of African religion does not focus on a morally informed destination after death, many African-Americans acknowledge a preoccupation with a loved one's final resting place. This discontinuity has likely occurred as many African-Americans have assumed traditional Christian beliefs about heaven and hell. In the consciousness of the contemporary African-American, how one has lived has tremendous repercussions for how one spends eternity, which can either be a source of great comfort or grave consternation for surviving loved ones.

After the eulogy, there may be a song from the choir followed by directions from the funeral home director regarding the logistics of the recession and the interment. In some Pentecostal traditions, there is a second viewing of the body. Otherwise, other mourners stand as the family follows the casket to the hearse. The family returns to their limousine(s) and are typically accompanied by local governmental escorts to the final resting place, typically the cemetery. At the graveside, there is typically a brief service of prayer, provision of a resource such as a hymnal or Bible to the family, and acknowledgement by the preacher or funeral home director that the body returns to the earth "ashes to ashes, dust to dust." Family members may elect to place a flower or other object on the casket. Occasionally, family will remain to witness the lowering of the casket into the ground; more commonly, the family adjourns the ceremony after the final words of the officiant.

The family and close friends reunite for the repast, the meal that is served after the funeral. It is typically held in a church fellowship hall, although it may also take place in a community setting or at the home of a family member. The food, often prepared by the church kitchen or social committee and friends of the family, is provided for several reasons: it provides comfort to the mourners in their grief; and it provides much-needed sustenance for those who have traveled and may be preparing for their return home, especially in days past when travelers relied primarily on automobiles, buses, or trains. The food also provides an expression of gratitude for the officiants and close friends.

By the end of the repast, the crowd begins to disperse. Most travelers return home, and local family and community members attempt to resume the "normal" routines of life. It is precisely at this time and in the months to come, however, that the human need for support climaxes. What supports are typically available for African-Americans experiencing grief, and how effective are they? Are there any religious resources available, and to what extent are they provided and utilized? Reflection around these important questions follows.

Pastoral Care

From a Christian theological perspective, every believer is instructed to "Carry each other's burdens, and in this way you will fulfill the law of Christ."[63] The burden of grief is often one of the most onerous that we face in life, yet is one that is most often neglected. Among African-Americans, as with most Americans, the pastoral care available to bereaved family and friends dissipates fairly quickly. Pastoral visits, once a community norm, now fade as pastors struggle with greater numbers of congregants and often become preoccupied with the next crisis in the church family. Some faith communities have begun to develop pastoral or congregational care

ministries that have a specific charge to support bereaved persons over a longer period of time, some for one year or longer. Informal support may be provided by church and/or community members. Anecdotal accounts speak to
the power of these informal supports;[64] nonetheless, such support may occur
arbitrarily and varies greatly in its quality and effectiveness. Many African-
Americans may find themselves lost in the clash of cultures: mainstream
culture emphasizes an individualistic outlook, whereas African cultures
emphasize the importance of communality. Commenting on the discrepancy
she perceived between African and African-American cultures at the end of
life, a Nigerian caregiver living in the southeastern United States observed
a policy she labeled as "Don't ask, don't tell, don't give."[65] Compared with
her communal experiences in Nigeria, where rituals of public mourning last
for months, she noted that many African-Americans tend to demonstrate a
spirit of independence in the context of receiving care.

Although this story is anecdotal, it does begin to illustrate the disruptions in living out communalistic impulses in the United States. Not only
is it less likely that the current generations of African-Americans extend
community support to the grieving, but it is also less likely that grieving
African-Americans will articulate their needs or receive help. Contemporary practices of mourning are pervasive within African-American culture,
if one takes the time to observe them. Death murals, tattoos, jewelry and
other trinkets, and T-shirts ("Gone but not forgotten") all memorialize the
dead, often with vivid images of the deceased. However, it is less clear
the extent to which those memorials are focused on the deceased to the
neglect of the survivors. Because of the frequency, intensity, and duration
of grief they often experience, African-Americans can scarcely afford the
cost of such independence.

Because of the relative frequency of loss, the virtual absence of aftercare
likely results in greater functional impairment over time. Because even the
most generous bereavement policies in corporate settings allow only two
weeks off, many persons find themselves returning to work before they
have had a chance to sit with their grief. Their time off is frequently consumed by legal and fiduciary concerns related to the decedent's estate.
Moreover, such benefits are at best only available for immediate family
members; those mourning the death of extended or fictive kin are rarely
permitted bereavement leave at all. Persons who return to work after the
loss of a close family member are more likely to miss more days of work,
experience negative health consequences, and exhibit symptoms of complicated grief.[66]

Despite experiences of minimal bereavement support, ongoing contact
with the deceased is practiced by many African-Americans. Paul Rosenblatt
and Beverly Wallace interviewed several African-Americans in grief and
learned that contact was pursued through cemetery visits, in thoughts of
and language around reunion in heaven, and through an awareness of the

enduring presence of the deceased. In some instances, this presence was desirable because it gave the bereaved person a sense of help and protection. In other instances, the presence was perceived as unwelcome, particularly if the bereaved person had experienced a contentious relationship with the deceased. Experiences of the dead rarely enter public discourse, yet they are consistent with the African worldview that recognizes the deep connection between the living and the dead.

Beyond human needs for presence and practical supports in bereavement, mourning persons often need existential and spiritual support. Because African-Americans as a whole are religious and spiritual in their outlook, religious and spiritual questions often arise in the context of bereavement. In his work on African-American notions of death, social worker Hosea L. Perry notes, "For the religious, illness, recovery, or death are all viewed as reflections of God's plans."[67] Holy scripture and Christian doctrine are replete with narratives of suffering and death as normative for the Christian journey. Many theological interpretations offered by pastors, preachers, and Christian educational materials honor these experiences. Even as African-Americans hold this belief, there is a tension around social justice issues, particularly as they relate to preventable deaths. Relatively infrequent opportunities for discourse around death in general and sudden, preventable deaths in particular, many of which result in disenfranchised grief, may reinforce notions of the acceptability of death. Further, rare opportunities for discourse may contribute to a paucity of critical thinking around patterns of death that might otherwise call for advocacy and other forms of community action. Leaders in Christian communities, and religious communities in general, can encourage dialogue around death by explicitly addressing the topic and/or sharing narratives during teaching and sermonic moments. Leaders and laypersons alike can resist the invisibility of grief and offer resources to the bereaved. The ministry of presence, or accompanying the bereaved "through the valley of death," is a gift that knows no ethnic or racial boundaries.

CONCLUSION

"God of our weary years, God of our silent tears, Thou who hast brought us thus far on the way...."[68] For most African-Americans, the same God who ruled in the motherland is the same God who has sustained us through time and space and is present at the end of life and beyond. There are several timeless themes that unite Africans and African-Americans. The centrality of community and its importance in celebrating final rites and providing compassionate care endure. The cohesiveness of the kinship group, or extended family, helps families bear under the pain of grief. The emphasis on the elaborate funeral continues, with less emphasis on adhering to a prearranged time frame. Music, movement, and dynamic eulogizing restore hope for the living and for the dead. A deep belief in the continuation of life in another realm means that death is not so much avoided as it is anticipated.

On the other hand, several points of discontinuity exist. Emotional expressiveness may be tempered, as are many rituals around public mourning that might identify survivors as candidates for compassionate concern and care. Individualistic tendencies of contemporary African-Americans may militate against a thoroughgoing communality that benefits others and self. Christianity, in particular, has offered views of heaven and hell, and the morally prescribed paths thereto, that rub against the grain of more pluralistic African religions. Diverse opinions within African-American Christianity may be more likely to surface in questioning whether dying is solely determined by God's hand or whether humans play a role in stemming the tide of preventable deaths. Nevertheless, African-Americans as a whole agree, "Shadowed beneath thy hand, may we forever stand, true to our God, true to our native land."[69]

NOTES

1. The terms "African-American" and "black" are used interchangeably in this text. Although these terms carry nuanced meanings that are beyond the scope of this work, the majority of persons of African descent in America identify as one or the other.

2. Gwendolyn Midlo Hall, *Slavery and African Ethnicities in the Americas: Restoring the Links* (Chapel Hill: The University of North Carolina Press, 2005), 10.

3. Alvin Poussaint and Amy Alexander, *Lay My Burden Down: Unraveling Suicide and the Mental Health Crisis among African Americans* (Boston: Beacon Press, 2000).

4. See, for example, Dorothy Roberts, *Killing the Black Body: Race, Reproduction, and the Meaning of Liberty* (New York: Pantheon, 1997).

5. Tonya Armstrong et al., "Attitudes of African Americans Toward Participation In Medical Research," in *Journal of Applied Social Psychology* 29 (1999): 552–74.

6. John Hope Franklin and Alfred Moss, *From Slavery to Freedom: A History of African Americans*, 8th ed., (New York: Alfred A. Knopf, 2000), 25.

7. Dominique Zahan, "Some Reflections on African Spirituality," in *African Spirituality: Forms, Meanings, and Expressions*, ed. Jacob Olupona (New York: The Crossroad Publishing Company, 2000), 4.

8. Jacob Olupona, "Preface," *African Spirituality: Forms, Meanings, and Expressions*, ed. Jacob Olupona (New York: The Crossroad Publishing Company, 2000), xviii.

9. Olupona notes, however, that as many Africans identify with the exclusivist claims of Christian and Islamic fundamentalist groups, significant conflict, violence, and suspicion have increased.

10. Charlton McIlwain, *Death in Black and White: Death, Ritual and Family Ecology* (Cresskill, NJ: Hampton Press, 2003), 27.

11. Ibid., 28.

12. Olupona, xvii.

13. Ibid., xvi.

14. John Mbiti, *Introduction to African Religion* (London: Heinemann, 1975), 111.

15. Ogbu Kalu, "Ancestral Spirituality and Society in Africa," *African Spirituality: Forms, Meanings, and Expressions*, ed. Jacob K. Olupona (New York: The Crossroad Publishing Company, 2000), 56.

16. Zahan, 11.

17. Franklin and Moss, 26.

18. Ibid., 26.

19. Ardencie Hall, *New Orleans Jazz Funerals: Transition to the Ancestors*, unpublished dissertation manuscript, 31.

20. McIlwain, 30.

21. Kalu, 56.

22. Zahan, 13.

23. Benjamin Ray, "African Shrines as Channels of Communication," *African Spirituality: Forms, Meanings, and Expressions*, ed. Jacob K. Olupona (New York: The Crossroad Publishing Company, 2000), 26.

24. Mbiti, 116.

25. I have retained Mbiti's use of the term "hereafter" in this section. Although many African-Americans, and Americans in general, use the term "afterlife" or "eternal life," the very juxtaposition of the words "here" and "after" corroborate my arguments regarding the cyclical pattern of life and the presence of the ancestors in the African worldview.

26. Mbiti, 117.

27. Ibid., 125.

28. Hall, 31.

29. Ibid., 47.

30. Ibid., 48.

31. Ibid., 56.

32. Ibid., 59.

33. Ibid., 17.

34. Hosea Perry, "Mourning and Funeral Customs of African Americans," in *Ethnic Variations in Dying, Death, and Grief: Diversity in Universality*, ed. Donald P. Irish, Kathleen F. Lundquist, and Vivian J. Nelsen (Washington, DC: Taylor & Francis, 1993), 56.

35. James Carter, *Death and Dying among African Americans: Cultural Characteristics and Coping Tidbits* (New York: Vantage Press, 2001), 7.

36. Eventually, because the work was undesirable, black undertakers emerged as those who would care for and dispose of black and, often, white bodies, and lead the procession to the graveyard. Given the scarcity of jobs for blacks after emancipation and the high mortality rate of blacks, undertaking became a much sought-after "profession," the positive community reputation of which arguably continues to the present.

37. Based on an interpretation of Christian Scripture, the dead will rise again facing east.

38. A. Hall, 41.

39. Ibid., 69.

40. Metraux, as quoted in A. Hall, 51.

41. Walker, as quoted in A. Hall, 76.

42. A. Hall, 55–56.

43. Ibid., 6.

44. Carter, 7.

45. National Hospice and Palliative Care Organization, "African American Outreach Guide," http://www.caringinfo.org/userfiles/File/aa_outreach_guide/African_American_Outreach_Guide_FINAL.pdf.

46. Carter, 25.

47. Carter, 26.

48. Karla Holloway, *Passed On: African American Mourning Stories* (Durham, NC: Duke University Press, 2002), 9.

49. Although a minority of African American pastors may resist conducting the funeral for a nonmember on theological grounds, the majority of pastors will support the family for social and practical purposes.

50. Angelo Henderson, "Death Watch? Black Funeral Homes Fear a Gloomy Future as Big Chains Move In," *Wall Street Journal*, July 18, 1997.

51. I place the term "secular" in quotes to denote the general African worldview that avoids dichotomizing "sacred" and "secular." In this view, even a death ritual event devoid of ostensible religious references would still be viewed as necessarily spiritual.

52. McIlwain, 99–101.

53. For example, the North Carolina Mutual Life Insurance Company is the oldest and largest black-owned insurance company in the United States.

54. Erik Eckholm, "Burial Insurance, at $2 Week, Survives Skeptics," *New York Times*, December 3, 2006.

55. Nellie T. Jones, interview by author, Durham, NC, December 27, 2008.

56. Holloway.

57. Paul Rosenblatt and Beverly R. Wallace, *African American Grief* (New York: Taylor & Francis Group, 2005), 39.

58. See McIlwain op cit.

59. John 11:25, KJV.

60. Psalm 90: 9–12, KJV.

61. "Soon-a Will Be Done," alternatively, "Soon I Will Be Done," traditional spiritual.

62. Although the literacy rate among blacks has risen exponentially since slavery, the continued practice of reading the obituary aloud underscores the centrality of the perjuring oral tradition among African Americans.

63. Galatians 6:2, New International Version (NIV).

64. Rosenblatt and Wallace, 145–52.

65. Monica Nneji, comment during Circles of Care presentation, December 5, 2008.

66. Katherine Shear et al., "Treatment of Complicated Grief," *JAMA* 293 (2005).

67. Hosea Perry, "Mourning and Funeral Customs of African Americans," in *Ethnic Variations in Dying, Death, and Grief: Diversity in Universality*, ed. Donald P. Irish, Kathleen F. Lundquist, and Vivian J. Nelsen (Washington, DC: Taylor & Francis, 1993), 63.

68. Lyrics from the beginning of verse 3, "Lift Ev'ry Voice and Sing," by James Weldon Johnson, 1900.

69. Lyrics from the end of verse 3, "Lift Ev'ry Voice and Sing," by James Weldon Johnson, 1900.

CHAPTER 6

When Death Occurs: Islamic Rituals and Practices in the United States[1]

Gisela Webb

ISLAMIC RELIGIOUS STRUCTURES

Islam is one of the major world religions, with over a billion Muslims across the globe. Its historical beginnings were in seventh-century Arabia, with the life and experiences of Muhammad, the Prophet of Islam. Within two centuries after the Prophet's death, Islam had become a major religious and political force in the world, extending from (today's) Spain to Afghanistan and well into regions of Africa and Southeast Asia. Islam is the second largest religion in the world; within a decade, it will be the second largest religion in the United States. Islam came to North America with African slaves (who generally could not practice it openly), with immigrants from the many regions where Islam has flourished (the Middle East, South and Southeast Asia, Africa, Turkey), and through American converts (African, Anglo, Latin, and other Americans). Presently, there are approximately five million Muslims in the United States, although this number is subject to much dispute.

The religious structures that guide all areas of life in the Islamic community—globally and locally—including matters of death and burial—are: 1) the Qur'an, the sacred book of Islam; and 2) the *sunna* and *hadiths*, the living example and sayings of Muhammad, Prophet of Islam (d. 632 CE); and the shariah, or Islamic law, the codes of what is allowed and not allowed in Islam, which are derived from the Qu'ran and hadith. These sources have been transmitted in written and oral forms since the time of the Prophet, interpreted by Muslim scholars and pious teachers of Islam, such as al-Ghazzali, and are still learned and practiced in Muslim communities around the world. This unity of traditional sources of knowledge accounts for the shared practices surrounding death in Islamic communities across the globe. There are also local—often pre-Islamic—cultural practices that account for some differences in mourning and grieving among Muslims. Finally, it should be said that as the Islamic community has grown in the United States, a few accommodations have been made in Muslim burial practices to conform to U.S. legal requirements for funerals; yet, the traditional requirements and practices of Muslim beliefs and practices regarding death prevail.

This chapter will focus on beliefs and practices regarding death, burial, and beyond shared by Muslims in the United States. It will include two sections: a summary of major teachings from the Qur'an and the Prophet on what happens at death, and a discussion of how those teachings are reflected in the way in which Muslim funerals are conducted in the United States. The latter will be based primarily on the example of a particular mosque community in the United States, the Bawa Muhaiyaddeen Fellowship and Mosque in Philadelphia.

TRADITIONAL BELIEFS AND LAWS

The traditional accounts of the life of Muhammad—contained in the collections of *hadiths* (sayings) and traditional biographies of the Prophet—present Muhammad as a prayerful and sensitive person who had been orphaned at an early age, raised by his uncle 'Abu Talib within the traditions of the pre-Islamic Arabian tribal custom, and married to a widow and business woman named Khadijah, who supported him as he began his prophetic career. In 610 CE, Muhammad began to experience "revelations" (*wahy*)—both aural and visionary—that continued over a twenty-year period until his death in 632 CE. The core of the revelations criticized two major components of Meccan society: the worship of multiple gods and the plight of the needy, as the Meccan leadership gained wealth not only through trade routes that passed through Mecca, but with the ancient pilgrimage site—the Kaaba—situated in Mecca, which housed the idols of many deities the Arabians worshiped. In those twenty years, Muhammad experienced both rebuke and attack from the Meccan elites. He made the historic *hijra*, or emigration to Medina—establishing the first Islamic community (and the beginning of the Islamic calendar). He returned to Mecca, reclaiming the Kaaba, emptying it of idols, and reestablishing it as a symbol of submission to Allah, "the God." The revelations of Muhammad were experienced in a number of types of situations—some during prayer and meditation, some in times of community opposition and persecution for his teachings, and some in response to evolving social, political, and religious demands as the Islamic community grew.

The revelations were memorized, written down, and collected by his followers and, according to tradition, put in the order prescribed by Muhammad. This collection of recitations/discourses, which consists of 114 chapters (*suras*), constitutes the Qur'an, the sacred text of Islam. For Muslims, the Qur'an has the status of "Word of God"—comparable with the status of the Torah for Orthodox Jews or Christ (as *logos*) for Christians. The words and sounds of the Qur'an are experienced by Muslims not only as sources of religious knowledge but of grace (*barakah*) and inspiration (*ilham*).

For Muslims, the Qur'an also contains the divine law, that is, principles and mandates for belief and practice in everyday life. The shariah (Islamic law) holds the same importance that Jewish law holds for Jews (particularly Orthodox Jews). All areas of life—from how one prays to what one eats, to how one is buried—are seen in the light of law and traditions taught by the Prophet of Islam. The major duties are known as the Five Pillars and are incumbent on all Muslims:

1. *Recitation of the Shahadah* (the "witnessing"). Muslims must recite the two-part creedal statement, "*La ilaha illa Allah, Muhammadun rasul Allah*," meaning that there is no god but Allah (*the* God) and that Muhammad is the final prophet of God. In reciting this, one also affirms the belief in the previous revelations, holy books, and prophets (including Abraham, Moses, and Jesus), the belief in angels, *jinn* (beings "created from fire"), and a final dispensation of divine justice—with consignment to heaven or hell—of all persons at the end time.
2. *Salat* (liturgical prayer). Muslims are to pray five times daily (morning, noon, afternoon, evening, night) facing Mecca in this ritual of unity, submission, and remembrance of Allah.
3. *Zakat* (the "poor tax"). As a symbol of "purifying" one's wealth and one's commitment to help the poor, the Muslims promise a portion of their wealth to the needy.
4. *Sawm*. During the lunar month of *Ramadan*, Muslims (in good health) are required to fast from food, liquid, and negative thoughts from sunrise to sundown as a means of engendering compassion for the poor and inner reflection and discipline.
5. *Hajj*. Muslims are to make the pilgrimage to Mecca at least once in their life as a symbol of submission to God at the site that is the center of the universal Islamic community. It is worth noting that during the pilgrimage, everyone is required to wear the *ihram*, the white shroud-like garment, as a symbol of the unity and equality of humankind and the death shroud and preparedness for death.

The Qur'anic verses are described as "descending" from the common source of all knowledge and wisdom available to human beings—the *umm al-kitab*—literally, the "mother (or archetype) of the book," or "word" of

God, which has been transmitted from the beginning of time through the prophets. The Qur'an warns individuals and communities of their heedlessness and forgetfulness of the divine command to care for those in need, and it criticizes their habitual return to idolatry. It makes particular criticism of the "reversion" of the Arabs from an earlier monotheism—belief in one God—to polytheism (belief in multiple gods), calling upon the idol worshipers in Mecca to restore the original function of the pilgrimage site of the "Ka'ba," which, according to Islamic tradition, was built by Abraham and Ishmael as a symbol of rejection of idolatry and submission to the one God, Allah.

The Qur'an refers to the times of trial, rejection, and persecution experienced by all the prophets and the guidance, wisdom, and hope given by God that sustained them. The Qur'anic stories of the Hebrew prophets (and other Arabian prophets not named in the Bible) do not include the full Biblical narrative (except for the story of Joseph and "the Potiphar") but function as summaries and examples of deeds of the ongoing legacy of God's mercy and revelation. Jews and Christians are described as *"ahl al-kitab"* "people of the book," that is, prior historical groups that had received authentic revelations. The Qur'an criticizes certain aspects of Jewish and Christian religion (political opposition to Muhammad posed by some of the Jewish tribes, the divinity and sonship of Jesus, the "trinity" of God), but it affirms others (the authenticity of all the Hebrew prophets—including Jesus and John the Baptist, the miraculous birth of Jesus to Virgin Mary, the role of Gabriel in revelation, the status of Jesus as "prophet," "word," and "spirit" of God, and the role of Jesus at the end time).

In terms of the organization of the written corpus of the Qur'an (the *mushaf*), the earlier revelations received by the Prophet are found at the end of the Qur'an. They tend to be short, highly evocative, and "hymnal" in character. Many of them describe the cataclysmic "end time." The later *suras* received by Muhammad are lengthier and more directed to legal, economic, and social issues in the emerging Muslim community. Many of these verses can be found in the beginning of the *mushaf*, after the opening *sura*, the *Fatihah*. In contrast to the prevailing ethos of the pre-Islamic Arabians, where ultimate loyalty belonged to the tribe, where fate, time, and destiny unalterably determined the course of one's life, the Qur'an affirmed that life had purpose; that events in human history and individuals are in the hands of a merciful and just God; and that death is not the end, but rather a passage to new and eternal existence. Moreover, the Qur'an puts extraordinary emphasis on the binding relationship between faith (*iman*) and practice, or righteous deeds (*a'mal al-salihat*)—with many specific references to caring for parents, relatives, orphans, the needy, the wayfarers (*sura* 2:215)—promising rewards for those who heed the message of the prophets and calamitous results in this world and the next for those who do not.

ON DEATH AND DYING IN ISLAM

There are sections and themes in the Qur'an that have special importance for the beliefs and rituals associated with death. These are the passages about creation, revelation, and the end of the world. Creation
themes speak of an original time or state of unity with God, referred to
as the "day of the covenant" (*al-yawm al-mithaq*), which human beings
seek to regain. The revelatory experiences of the prophet Muhammad,
particularly Muhammad's "Night Journey" (*sura* 17, Isra'), would come to
represent an interior, spiritual state of "returning" to God—in this life.
The "states and stations" of Muhammad's journey would become a model
for the spiritual life of the devout and for the "*barzakh*" (interim) experience between one's physical death and one's consignment at death to
paradise or to hell. The *barzakh* (interim) also refers to the interim
between individual death and cosmic death. Finally, the many visually
and orally powerful Qur'anic verses about the day of the Resurrection (*al-
yawm al-qiyamah*)—when the cosmos itself reverses in a cataclysmic annihilation (*fana'*) and returns to its origin—led to speculation about the
kind of experience and knowledge this would mean for the individual at
the end time. It also led to discussion of an interior spiritual experience
of "death before death," in which the individual could see with clarity
"the truth of oneself" in the annihilation of the *nafs*/self that separates
one from God.

I make a cautionary note about interpretations of Islamic texts, particularly the Qur'an and sayings of Muhammad. As is the case with Judaism,
Islam has no central authority who pronounces official doctrine. Nevertheless, there are interpreters and traditions (theological, juridical, mysti-
cal/sufi) that became accepted as "orthodox," or at least of lasting
influence, in Muslim communities. These are the traditions and interpretations to which I refer. For example, in terms of figures that represent
the mainstream of Islamic thought, the figure of Abu Hamid al-Ghazali
(d. 1111) is considered "orthodox." Not only was he prolific, but he functioned as an interpreter in several of the traditional Islamic sciences: theology, philosophy, law, and mysticism (*tasawwuf*). He is considered by
Muslims to be a "reconciler" between theological extremes, taking a
"middle way" approach to such issues as whether and when one ought to
read the Qur'an literally or symbolically. Ghazzali's manual on what happens to the soul at death—*al-Durra al-Fakhira* (*The Precious Pearl*), with
its vivid description of experience awaiting the dead "in the tomb" and
on the "day of Resurrection" (*al-yawm al-qiyama*), reflects a lasting heritage in Islamic views on what happens at death. Abdul Qadir al-Jilani (d.
1166 AH) represents a major line of transmission of Muslim piety and suf-
ism (mysticism).

CREATION THEMES RELATED TO DEATH AND DYING

The Qur'an speaks of human beings—male and female—as being created from God's one *nafs* (or "soul"). God asks Adam to "name" things. Adam could, whereas the angels could not (*sura* 2:30), which Muslims read (and elaborated in theology and poetry) as a demonstration of the human capacity for creative knowledge. God "pulled from the loins of Adam" the souls of all future generations of human beings and asked them, "Am I not your Lord?" (*sura* 7:172) The souls of all human beings answered "yes," and this testifying to God's sovereignty was interpreted as indicating that human beings have within themselves the reality of a "preexistent," "natural" state of "*islam*," submission to God, which human beings perennially forget. This primordial affirmation of unity with God—testified to in their knowledge of, and submission to, their Lord—is called the "day of the covenant," *al-yawm al-mithaq*, and it would become a model or goal of life itself: a "return" to that state of unity with God. In the Qur'an, Adam and Eve disobey God in the Garden, but they repent and are forgiven; thus, Islam does not teach a cosmic rupture in the relationship between humans and God, as expressed in the Christian doctrine of original sin. For Muslims, Adam's sin is an example of the tendency—or stage—in the human soul called the *nafs ammarah*, the "soul that commands evil." The Qur'an and its commentators also speak of the aspect—or stage—in the human soul that is at peace with God, the *nafs al-mutma'inna*, and other "loci" in the human being for intimate knowledge and certitude of God—*qalb* (*heart*) and *'aql* (*intellect*).

The Qur'anic language of an innate, primordial, "forgotten" experience of man's primordial confession of God's lordship (*rububiyyah*) would be interpreted by theologians and mystics of Islam as signifying the possibility for all generations to actualize that state of union with God. The mystical interpreters, such as Ghazzali, would describe both the spiritual path in this life and in the hereafter as a gradual discarding of the veils of the human soul—the passions and inclinations of the body and those associated with ignorance and self-centeredness. The extent to which one is able to remember and live that primordial covenant with God *during one's life* is seen as determining one's experience at death.

THE PROPHETIC EXPERIENCES OF MUHAMMAD

The Qur'anic verses describing two of Muhammad's paradigmatic experiences—the descent (*anzala*) of the Qur'an to Muhammad and the ascension (*isra'*) or Night Journey of Muhammad—provide models for deepened experience of "*islam*" in this world and for the experience that the soul will have in the interim period (*barzakh*) between the death and the end time. The Qur'an makes a brief reference of a night journey of the Prophet in which he traveled from "the sacred mosque to the farthest mosque," a journey from Mecca to Jerusalem. By the ninth century, many versions of this story have come in the form of *hadiths*, which vary in version and degree of detail—describing the awakening of the Prophet by Gabriel (in some versions accompanied by the angel Mika'il), who leads Muhammad on a night's journey from Mecca to Jerusalem, then through the heavens described in Ptolemaic astronomy to the gates of paradise, and finally to the throne of God. Muhammad's journey always includes the vision of hell and the "appropriate" punishment experienced by sinners who have committed various kinds of evils and a vision of the paradisal garden. The guide angel of Muhammad acts as interpreter of the visions to which the Prophet is witness. At each stage of the journey, Muhammad is blinded by the light, and Gabriel, in many versions, is comforter and advisor, interceding with God so that Muhammad is granted a new vision. Gabriel is not allowed to go all the way to the throne of God, signifying the theological understanding that the human creature has "higher" status than the angel. This refers to the role of the human being as *khalifah*, vice-regent, of God, the possessor (potentially) of all the names and qualities of God, and in various other traditions, that humans have higher status than the angels because they partake of both spirit and matter, body and emotions.

By the ninth century, this Mi'raj literature of Muhammad's individual night journey had developed side by side—and in a sense become fused with—Muslim eschatological literature. What the angel reveals to Muhammad in his journey becomes the prototype of the experience of the soul upon "physical" death; the angel functions as both part of the hierarchy of being and revealer/interpreter of that hierarchy. By the third Islamic century, the theologian and mystic Bistami (d. 874) begins to use the Qur'anic term *fana'*—the "annihilation" of all things in God at the end time—as a reference to the spiritual pilgrim's own *mi'raj* (journey) experience: the various stations and stages of inner transformation and attainment to the presence of God . . . within *this* life.

ESCHATOLOGY: BARZAKH AND AL-YAWM AL-QIYAMA

Parallel to the development of *mi'raj/isra'* literature are traditions that detail and interpret the process of death, the structure of heaven, and the day of Resurrection; that is, eschatological, end-time themes. Descriptions of death found in manuals on death and dying, such as Ghazali's al-*Durra al-fakhira* and the *Kitab ahwal al-qiyama*, still dominate belief and practice in popular Islamic piety. Although if one asks the question of whether the events depicted in these texts are "literal" or "symbolic," the consensus is that they happen "in some real sense." Perhaps the question as posed this way is simply foreign to the way most traditional Muslims think. We must remember that the Qur'anic discussions on death and resurrection are aspects of the theme of the nature of divine justice. The "symmetry of the heavens" in Islam refers to the idea that there is a perfection of justice and accountability in the universe; there are "natural" consequences to human deeds—both good and evil—and there is ultimately no evasion from acknowledging and experiencing the configuration of one's *din* (faith). So, these concerns about justice outweigh the need for exact decisions about the "symbolic" status of the imagery used in Muslim eschatology.

The Qur'an makes numerous references to the categories of the "here" (*al-dunya*), the world in which human beings live for an appointed period of time (*ajal musamma*), which is known only to God, and the hereafter (*al-akhira*), which human beings enter at death.

> "He it is who has created you out of clay, and then decreed a term [for you]—a term known [only] to him ..." (6:2) ... "when the end of the term approaches, they can neither delay it by a single moment, nor hasten it." (10:49)[2]

The terms *dunya* and *akhira* refer to both time and space and to two moral alternatives. The Qur'an warns those who seek the *dunya* at the expense of the *akhira*:

> "To the one who desires a harvest in the life to come (akhira) we shall grant an increase in his harvest; whereas the one who desires [but] a harvest in this world (dunya), we [may] give something thereof—[but]he will have no share in [the blessings of] the life to come (akhira)." (42:20)

The Qur'an describes an intermediary stage between the *dunya* and *akhira*: the *barzakh*, which is understood by Muslims as a period in the grave, and much discussion in theology and in the traditional manuals on dying have focused on the nature of the experience (and the nature of the "experiencer") in the grave/*barzakh*.

> "[As for those who do not believe in the life to come, they go on denying] until, when death approaches anyone of them, he prays: O my Lord Sustainer! Let me return [to life] so that I may act righteously in whatever I have failed. Nay it is indeed but a [meaningless] word he utters; for behind those [who leave this world] there is a barzakh until the day when all will be raised from the dead." (23:99)

Traditional creeds mention the questioning of the soul upon death by the angels Nakir and Munkar and the punishments of the grave (*adhab al-qabr*).[3] The works of Abu Hamid al-Ghazali's *al-Durra al-fakhira* (*The Precious Pearl*) and the *Kitab ahwal al-qiyama* represent the prevalence of traditions and manuals on death, still used today, that inspire commitment, hope, and fear by describing experiences undergone by the deceased at the time of death. All of these deal with the theme of ultimate individual accountability before God. God, through the angels, orders the time of the individual's death. We see the theme of the recording angels removing the soul/spirit from the body, with differing degrees of ease, shock, or pain depending on the quality of faithfulness of the person in life. In some narratives, these recording angels allow the deceased a glimpse of the gates of paradise. Once the person is in the grave and buried, he or she is asked by the angel, "Who is your Lord?" "What is your din?" "Who is your prophet?" and questions about the Qur'an, prayer, and right action. The descriptions of the fate of the soul after death parallel the *mi'raj* imagery, the overarching theme being the soul's immediate tastes of the fruits of their religious duties as it ascends on a journey—as in *mi'raj* literature—with Gabriel acting as guide and interpreter for the soul as it ascends through the successive heavens.

The faithful soul's journey is through the (Ptolemaic) cosmological heavens to the "throne of mercy." The impious soul is described as trying to attempt the journey in the company of the angel Daqya'il but is thwarted as Daqya'il flings the soul back into the body even as the corpse is being washed. Another element in the eschatological manuals, related to Zoroastrian themes, are narratives describing the visitation of persons by beauty or ugliness—personifications of the good or bad deeds of dead persons while on earth.

The question of who (or what) experiences the events of the *barzakh* has been debated in Islam. Is it truly the same person who lived? The soul? Some other nonmaterial essence? However, the majority of Muslims regard the "experience of the tomb" as a conscious experience of the deceased in the grave. Of course, the literature is also seen as a way of speaking about an inevitable reckoning of our life's works, that even as we die, the ease or hardship of the transition "takes the shape" of our life's deeds. Some commentators interpret this time in the grave and its punishments as a kind of purgation of sins, a means of divine mercy for the person whose deeds do not merit "eternal" punishment. Some suggest that all people have some deeds that need purgation. Another interpretation is that it warns the living and, finally, that it serves as a bridge, a symbol of continuity between this life and the next, between our actions on earth and the final dispensation of justice.[4]

The Qur'an speaks in vivid language of the signs of the arrival of the day of Resurrection (*al-yaum al-qiyama*), and the [final] hour (*al-sa 'ah*). Ultimately, the end time is no less than a cataclysmic, transformative reversal of the world and our individual selves.

> When the sun is shrouded in darkness
> And when the stars lose their light
> And when the mountains are made to vanish

And when the she-camel being with young, about to give birth, is left
unattended
And when all beasts are gathered together and when the seas boil over
And when all human beings are coupled with their deeds
And when the girl child that was buried alive is made to ask for what crime
she was killed
And when the heaven is laid bare
And when the blazing fire is brought into view
[on that day] every human being will come to know what he/she has prepared
for him/herself. (81:1–14)

The hour is announced by the sound of a trumpet (usually associated with
the angel Israfil), with human degeneracy and cosmic disintegration signal-
ing the end of the world—and with that disintegration, only the unity of
God will remain.[5] Other "signs of the hour" include references to an "anti-
Christ" figure, al-Dajjal; the creatures Yajuj and Majuj (Gog and Magog); the
eschatological mahdi, a savior figure sometimes equated with Jesus and sometimes a separate figure; and the (second) coming of 'Isa/Jesus (based on
4:158–159); the reckoning (hisab) or weighing of each person's deeds on a
scale (mizan); and the individuals' crossing a bridge (sirat) over hell.

Ultimately, all perish but Allah.

"There is no Deity save Him; Everything is bound to perish, save his
[eternal] Self. With Him rests all judgment; and unto Him shall you be
brought back." (28.88)

Commentaries on the Resurrection/hour experience suggest several
implications of the language. First, as with the barzakh/grave experience,
the notion of individual accountability is paramount. Moreover, the traditions emphasize the conscious recognition/awareness of the configuration
of the din, the life of faith, during one's earthly existence (dunya), and the
angel is the constant companion/agent/cognitive intermediary in the death
process. The imagery of the hour (al sa 'ah), however, seems to emphasize
the moment when every human being is shaken to the foundations in a
unique and unprecedented self-awareness of his/her deeds. "We have rent
your veil so your sight today is keen" (sura 50:22). Modernist interpreter
Fazlur Rahman suggests that it is indeed the quality of transparency of the
heart that the Qur'an intends the human being to achieve. The events of
both the barzakh and the events of the hour point to the inevitable transparency of oneself to oneself and to God.[6] The mystical interpreters took up
the discussion of the day of Resurrection, focusing on "the day when the
earth shall be transmuted into something else and the heavens as well ..."
(sura 14:48). As in the case of Christianity, these eschatological themes
occasionally became linked to political upheavals and transitions, but
overall, their primary references have been to the themes of individual and
cosmic death and resurrection.

WHEN DEATH OCCURS: FUNERAL, BURIAL, AND DEATH RITUALS

The religious structures that guide all areas of life in the Islamic community, including matters of death and burial, are based on the teachings of the Qur'an and the *sunna*, the example and teachings of the Prophet of Islam, which have been transmitted in oral and written forms through the many cultural zones of the Islamic world. One sees common elements of death and funeral practices in Islamic communities from the Middle East to Southeast Asia to the United States. The theological themes we have just examined shape the universal practices and understandings.

It is true that there are local and unique customs in parts of the Islamic world, permitting a variety of mourning and postdeath practices. For example, the Indonesian ritual of selamatan is the "religious meal" held by family and friends of the deceased at particular intervals after the death, to both honor and pray for the deceased at the transition of death and to restore balance and peace in the household. However, this discussion of what Muslims in America do when dying and death occur will focus on the burial rituals and practices of one community that reflects the diversity of Muslims in the United States, the Bawa Muhaiyaddeen Fellowship and Mosque. This mosque has membership of Muslims from many regions and cultures around the world, and Bawa is recognized for his teachings in Islamic spirituality and his adherence to traditional Islamic law (the Hanifi rite) in matters of Islamic mosque rituals and practices.

Bawa Muhaiyaddeen was a Sufi *shaykh* (teacher) from Sri Lanka who came to the United States in the 1970s and founded a community (the "fellowship" and mosque) in Philadelphia (with branches elsewhere). Bawa died in 1986, but the community continues his work and teachings. Bawa's directive was that all mosque activities and teachings conform to traditional Islamic forms of rituals based on the Qur'an and the example of Muhammad so that Muslims from anywhere in the world would feel comfortable. These include the daily five-times prayer (*salat*), the Friday congregational prayers, Ramadan activities (including prayers, cooking for evening "breaking fast"), and *dhikrs* (Sufi rituals of "remembrance" of God). Bawa instructed the community to purchase land outside of Philadelphia for farming, holding retreats and community activities, and for creating a cemetery (with proper municipal zoning) for the community's needs. A year after the death of Bawa Muhaiyaddeen, the fellowship built a mazar, or structure for a Sufi saint's burial site, over the grave where Bawa Muhaiyaddeen is buried. This is the first of its kind in the United States. The mazar offers some comfort and protection from the elements for those visitors who come to offer prayers of thanks to God for sending wise sheikhs as teachers. As with the Philadelphia mosque, visitors include Muslims (and non-Muslims), both local and global.

As we look at the rituals and practices associated with death and dying in this community, we see that there are local governmental laws and requirements for funerals that must be met, and there are specific religious requirements for Muslim funerals. Bawa mandated that all public laws be observed *and* that the funeral procedures—the activities of preparing the body for burial, preparing the grave, the burial, the prayers and rituals associated with the funeral—all conform with traditional Islamic practices (of the "orthodox" Hanifi rite). Moreover, one sees that at all stages, the burial practices are meant as a kind of preparation and support for the soul's inevitable encounter in the grave with "the reality" of their life's deeds and intentions, which are experienced at death, a foundational belief based on the Qur'an and *hadith*. As we have seen, the Qur'an speaks of "the day of the covenant" (*al-yaum al-mithaq*), when in primordial time (before creation), the souls of all human beings testified their unity with God. The devout Muslim hopes to remember—in life, and at death—that unity with their Lord. The Qur'an speaks of Muhammad's "night journey" and the calamitous end time experience (*al-yawm al-Qiyamah*) as events that symbolize the clarity—and pain or joy—that one experiences in seeing and understanding the meaning of their actions. These beliefs and hopes influence how the rituals of body preparation and burial are performed by this community.

The activities and practices that begin with the death of a Muslim community member *in the United States* are many and specific and must be coordinated and supervised by a licensed funeral director. Muslims are to be buried within twenty-four hours of the death (or as near to that limit as possible). When death occurs, the Muslim ritual preparation of the body must begin, but there are also particular U.S. and local legal and municipal requirements that must be met. Legal requirements include gathering information from family, acquiring a death certificate, registering the death with the civic authorities, and obtaining a burial permit. These legal requirements must be completed before burial can take place. In Muslim communities that do not have their own cemeteries (and many do not), burials may be done in any cemetery that has a Muslim section within it that conforms to the proper positioning of the grave facing the Qiblah (facing Mecca), and these requirements may be met in Jewish, Christian, or other nondenominational cemeteries that allow burial of nonembalmed or casketed persons. Increasing numbers of funeral homes in the United States now accommodate the needs of the Muslim families for the ritual washing of the body of the deceased Muslim.

Within the mosque communities in the United States, there is often a funeral committee. The Bawa Muhaiyaddeen community has its own cemetery and burial committee, whose members were trained in the specific actions and prayers that commence with death (taught by the *shaykh*). The duties of completing and filing the death certificate and registering the death before a burial can take place are the responsibility of the licensed funeral director. The preparations of the deceased that must happen before the burial, washing and preparing the body, are generally done by cemetery committee personnel. When others are asked to assist, this is considered an honor for them, not an unpleasant burden.

Correct practice and an attitude of tenderness and care are requirements of preparation of the body of the deceased. The body and soul of the person are to be cared for—properly and lovingly—by community members whose duty is to assist in the transition from this life to the realm of the hereafter. Moreover, Bawa maintained that the community's instructions for burial are consistent with the *sunna* (example) of Prophet Muhammad and that Muslims should emulate the Prophet's qualities and practices. Burial instructions in this community include directives and guidance on personal attitudes and intentions regarding death and on the practices of shrouding and burial of the body. Our quotes and paraphrasing on funeral directives are primarily from *Burials, Instructions and Guidelines: The Policies and Procedures for the Bawa Muhaiyaddeen Fellowship.*

With respect to one's attitude toward death, the living should show the person who has died great compassion and respect: one "should pay ten times the respect to a dead body than we pay to a body when that body was alive." To some degree, the question of how much residual consciousness remains with the person's body—a question traditional Muslims pondered—seems to influence this guidance. "A dead body should be treated like a delicate, tender flower. While alive, the body may have suffered and been beaten so much; thus, when dead, it should be treated with great gentleness and care. The nails and the whole body must be cleaned softly, just like washing a flower. While this is being done, the appropriate prayers must be said."[7]

Bawa commented on the oddity of the expense of burials in the Western countries. In sharp contrast, in Muslim countries, there is no charge for the burial or the coffin, no burial expense, and everyone unites to bury the person. Although this may no longer be the case everywhere, it is the kind of critique voiced frequently by those who remember the practices and attitudes of religiously based cultures. Funerals are important occasions in traditional Muslim communities; one must attend and pay their respects to the dead; if one knows of someone unable to afford a funeral, one should inquire and take care of the arrangements to help give a person a good burial. Why should people's minds be on money and expenses, when the real issues are the transition of the deceased from here to the hereafter?

Caring for the body (before burial) includes washing it an odd number of times (three, five, seven) and giving a full ablution (*ghusl*) as if the person were going to prayer. Men prepare men for burials, and women prepare women. The body is shrouded. Casketing is discouraged, and cremation is forbidden. The traditional funeral prayer, the "Janazzah," is said over the body. Men carry the body after Janazzah and from the hearse to the grave. The grave is prepared with a lower chamber designed to hold the remains. When the body is placed in the lower chamber, wooden slats are place over this chamber "so the earth does not fall on the corpse; so it does not press down on the body, and so the grave will last for thirty or forty years...."[8] Once again, this practice seems to presume a kind of residual awareness on the part of the deceased or at least a continued awareness of the body's "personhood." The grave is filled with earth, and during all times and procedures, those present recite the Kalimah: "There is no god but Allah and Muhammad is the Messenger of God." The atmosphere at the burial site should have composure, peace, tenderness, and compassion. In this community, the grave is filled with earth, and small stones are placed as a cover of the burial mound. Wooden slats are stood upright at each end of the mound, symbolizing the scale that weighs the balance of the deeds in one's life.

After the grave is filled, the call to prayer, the *adhan*, is made. Islamic teaching is that this is the time when we are questioned by the angels, Munkar and Nakir. The answers are to be inscribed in the heart of the Muslim during life so that one is ready for the questioning "in the grave." The deceased is asked to wake up to answer a number of questions:

1. Who is your God? Who is your Lord? ("My God is Allah.")
2. Who is your Prophet? ("Muhammad.")
3. What is your ancestry? ("I belong to the family/tribe of Abraham.")
4. Whose son are you? Whose child are you? ("I am the son/child of Adam.")
5. Which is your Qiblah (the direction you face for prayers)? ("The Ka'bah is my Qiblah; I face the Ka'bah for prayer.")
6. Who is your Imam, the one who leads you in prayer? ("The Qur'an is my Imam. Truth is my Imam.")
7. To which group do you belong? Who are your relatives, your companions? ("We are Muslims, the Mu'mins ... the ones ... who accept God in purity.")

Among Bawa's discussions of what constitutes the good, he speaks of justice and respect among religions and races: "Judgment is in God's hands alone, and understanding truth includes overcoming religious and racial difference.... The soul remains in the body until this questioning is finished.... If one understands this truth, then he will give up his religious differences and racial differences. He will give up all of these differences and focus on that point of God."[9]

Bawa Muhaiyaddeen, speaking to his American audiences, compared the experience at death, where our "sight is made keen," with (movie) reels that show us our entire life history without missing a point; we cannot speak but only see and hear the good and bad actions of our life. We know all we have done. This perspective, and the questions themselves, reveal how attention to the fate of the soul and its relation to God at and after death continue as the focus of the funeral events. The bereaved are to remember how they, too, will be interrogated after their deaths, a more ultimate concern than their current but temporary situation as those who have suffered a loss.

In the evening after the burial, members of the community are invited to come to the mosque to recite in congregation the Qur'anic chapter, *Ya Sin*, the subject matter of which expresses the essence of one's final self-understanding of one's life, purpose, and ends, namely a return to the unity of God.

> "Is it not He Who created the heavens and the earth able to create the like thereof?" Yea, indeed! For He is the Creator Supreme, of skill and knowledge (infinite)! (36:81)
> "Verily, when He intends a thing, His Command is "be," and it is." (36:82)
> "So glory to Him in Whose hands is the dominion of all things: and to Him will ye be all brought back." (36:83)[10]

The *Ya Sin* is also recited in a prayer service forty days after, and then a year after, the death of a fellow Muslim. Muslims are discouraged from "excessive" grieving and mourning practices, particularly local cultural traditions in parts of the Islamic world such as wailing, tearing one's clothes, or beating one's chest. However, there is a large place for hospitality and charitable activities from members of the community in the days, weeks and months after the funeral; these include visits, paying respect to the family of the deceased, and cooking and bringing them food.

Muslims constitute one of the largest religious communities in the United States and in the world. Muslims in the United States—who represent the wide cultural and ethnic diversity of the global community of Islam—have found it necessary and possible to follow their most fundamental traditions in Islamic law and spirituality as they deal with death, dying, burial, and bereavement. This contemporary reality is a reflection of the historic continuity and transmission of Islamic teachings and practices associated with death and dying—and life itself.

NOTES

1. This chapter is in part based on an essay by the author, "Death and Dying in Islam: 'This Day Your Sight Is Made Keen,'" in *Death and Dying in World Religions*, ed. Lucy Bregman (Boston: Pearson Custom Publishing, 2004).
2. Asad translation of Qur'an (*The Message of the Qur'an*).

3. Jane Smith and Yvonne Haddad, The *Islamic Understanding of Death and Resurrection*, 35ff.

4. Ibid., 48ff.

5. Ibid., 71ff.

6. See Fazlur Rahman, *Major Themes in the Quran* (Chicago: University of Chicago Press, 1980, 2008).

7. Muhammad Raheem Bawa Muhaiyaddeen, *Burials: Instructions and Guidelines, Policies and Procedures for the Bawa Muhaiyaddeen Fellowship* (Philadelphia).

8. Ibid.

9. Ibid.

10. Yusuf Ali translation of Qur'an (*The Holy Qur'an*).

CHAPTER 7

Grieving Tradition in a New Land: Hindu Death and Dying Rituals in America

Kyoko Murata

Traditionally, Hinduism values a "controlled death," that is to say, being able to choose the time to die or, rather, the time to leave the physical body. In other words, death should be a voluntary relinquishment of life, a controlled evacuation of the body.[1] Most Hindus would like to live long enough to see their sons and daughters marry, to see their grandchildren born, to take care of all unfinished business, and to be surrounded with loved one at the time of death. Because Hindus believe in reincarnation, it is not the physical body that is important, but rather the *atman* (soul). To facilitate the journey that the *atman* takes to the next life, the *atman* needs to be released from the physical body.[2] The *atman* may be reborn in another life through reincarnation. The goal is for the *atman* to be released from *samsara* (the endless cycle of rebirth). Thus, death provides the opportunity for one to attain *moksha* (release from *samsara*) and is treated very seriously. In addition, some people claim that cremation of the physical body is an act of self-sacrifice to Agni, the god of fire. Therefore, death is one of the most important life cycle events in Hindu life.

Hinduism is native to India and is comprised of various multiple perspectives on the nature of divinity and reality such as monotheism, polytheism, monism, and dualism. Some scholars argue that the origin of Hinduism can be traced back to the ancient Indus Valley Civilization, which dates from 2500 BCE to 1500 BCE. Both the Indus Valley Civilization and the Aryan culture contributed to the rise of Hinduism after Aryans moved from central Asia through the northern plain of India around 1500 BCE.[3] Although the term "Hindu" was used by Persians and Greeks since the first millennium BCE as a name for the people who lived east of the Indus River, more recently, the term was designated by British scholars during the British colonization of India with more precise religious meaning.[4] Because of the diverse and complex forms of Hinduism that have developed over the centuries reflecting regional, language, cultural, societal, and caste differences, it is almost impossible to provide a set list of beliefs and practices that apply to all Hindus. There may be times when certain views seem contradictory within Hinduism. However, this wide variety is seen as complementary to the perspectives of other Hindus rather than contradictory. As Hindus started to migrate to other countries throughout the world, the values of the countries to which Indians immigrated started to have an effect on traditional Hindu values. This chapter will examine how Hindus have incorporated some aspects of American values and practices into their traditions when performing death and dying rituals.

Hindus have been living in the United States since around 1893, when Swami Vivekananda, on his first visit to the United States from India,[5] gave a dynamic speech at the World Parliament of Religions in Chicago. He described Hinduism, specifically Vedanta, as a form of Hinduism that is concerned with self-realization, by addressing his listeners as "sisters and brothers of America" instead of "ladies and gentlemen." In the following year, he toured the country and established the Vedanta Society in New York, the first Hindu organization in America. Most American Hindus at the time were from the Punjabi region of India, working as farmers in the Western states of America. Many were not literate in English.[6] They bought farmland by pooling the money they had earned. Later, small numbers of well-educated professionals such as physicians, engineers, businessmen, and professors began to immigrate to the United States under the "special skills" provision of the immigration law. The Immigration Act of 1965 dramatically increased the national annual quota of Asian immigrants from one hundred to twenty thousand, which allowed many Indians to immigrate to the United States, the majority of whom were Hindus. The pre-1965 immigrants were usually well-educated and very fluent in English. The post-1965 Hindu immigrants are very diverse because they come from various regions of India. These post-1965 Hindu immigrants initially settled in major metropolitan cities such as New York, Chicago, San Jose, Los Angeles/Long Beach, Washington, D.C., Houston, and Atlanta. Gradually, the number of Hindus increased in other metropolitan cities. Since the 1970s, American Hindus have constructed Hindu temples that are in accordance with traditional Hindu architecture. Examples of these temples include the Vaisnava Sri Venkateswara Temple in Penn Hills, a suburb of Pittsburgh, built in 1976; New York Ganesha Temple built in Queens in 1977; the Rama Temple in Lemont and the Chicago Balaji Temple in Aurora, both built in 1986 in the suburbs of Chicago; and the Hindu Temple of Atlanta (Venkateswara) in Riverdale, a suburb of Atlanta, built in 1991.

Although these urban temples reflect traditional Indian architecture, the community activities in these temples include adaptations and innovations that portray contemporary life in America. Many temples in the United States originally were dedicated to Lord Venkateshwara or Balaji, a south Indian form of the deity Vishnu. As time passed, many of these temples started to construct additional buildings to house other major deities, such as Shiva, in an effort to address the increasingly diverse community's religious needs. In addition, these temples became not only places of worship but also places to socialize and to educate children in traditional Hindu beliefs, Indian and regional languages, and culture. In this way, these temples have become multipurpose centers for Hindus. For example, in one major Atlanta temple, an educational building was constructed to house Sunday school classes for children. An auditorium was built in the basement of the temple building to accommodate celebratory events. A large kitchen and dining area capable of providing meals to hundreds of people were added so that devotees who travel long distances can have traditional Hindu vegetarian meals during their visits to the temple. Moreover, many Hindu priests who were raised and trained in India and who perform the temple regular *arti* (worship with display of camphor flames waved before deities) and *puja* (worship including offering to a deity) do not speak fluent English. As a result, the laypeople, who actually work or go to school in mainstream American society, act as public relations representatives, often explaining rituals and Hindu philosophy to visitors. Also, laypeople conduct the administrative work of local temples. These temples, with the exception of a few employees such as the temple priests, temple cook, office manager, and some maintenance crew workers, are run by volunteer members.[7]

Although the temples are important to Hindu community life, the importance of home should also be mentioned here because the home is central to Hindu religious life in India. For Hindus in India and the United States, the home has certain sacrality. Daily activities such as cooking and eating express religious devotion. In addition, most of the religious life takes place at home rather than in temples. Hindu homes usually have a shrine for deities, who are treated with respect. *Puja* is performed at home. Finally, most life cycle events, including weddings, naming ceremonies, and sacred thread ceremonies,[8] occur at home. As Hindus immigrate to the United States, the place of these rituals shifts from home to the temple.

Since the change in the 1965 immigration law, the American Hindu population has increased rapidly. Families have expanded by marriage, birth, and immigration, with more Hindu immigrants arriving in the United States every day. The number of rituals, such as wedding and naming ceremonies, performed on the temple premise increased as well. More public spaces were needed to accommodate these rituals. Because of the rise in Hindu population and the desire to maintain traditional practices, Hindus had to figure out how to deal with death as Hindu communities in America. The rest of this chapter focuses on describing how the Hindu death practices have changed.

TRADITIONAL DEATH RITUALS

The traditional Hindu approach to death and dying is based on three basic beliefs.[9] First, the *atman* is considered to be immortal; although the material body eventually ceases to exist, the *atman* lives on. The physical body is compared with an old piece of clothing in the story of the *Bhaga-vad Gita*.[10] Second, through the process of reincarnation, the *atman* comes back to this world in different physical forms, which include human and nonhuman forms, e.g. animals. The ultimate goal of Hindus is to attain *moksha*, liberation from *samsara*. Hindus may only be released from *samsara* in human physical form. The third basic concept is *karma,* which is equivalent to "action." The *karma* a person accumulates during her lifetime determines the physical form in which she will be reborn. In Hinduism, each person has *dharma* (duty) to fulfill. *Dharma* differs depending on one's caste, life stage, and gender. For example, the *dharma* of a twelve-year-old boy who is in school is to study, whereas the *dharma* of a forty-year-old man is to provide a good living for his family, including his wife, his children, and his parents. One accumulates good *karma* by fulfilling his *dharma*. At death, the *atman* leaves the body and will either reincarnate or obtain *moksha*. Because Hindus speak different languages and are also from different castes, different regions, and different socioeconomic backgrounds, there are many variations in the death and dying rituals they perform. One thing that is central, however, is the practice of cremating the body rather than burying it.[11]

The paradigmatic death and dying ritual is the traditional ritual for an old man from a *Brahmin* caste.[12] Traditionally, this man would die at home, surrounded by his children, grandchildren, and extended family members. Families do not hide death from young children because they believe that death is a part of life, so his room would be filled with people bidding him farewell. Some people chant mantras. A few drops of Ganges water and a *tulsi* leaf are placed in his mouth. He would be placed on the floor to be closer to the mother earth. Once he passed away, women would wail, and men would fall silent.

Women in the household, including the widow, daughters, and daughters-in-law, take care of the domestic arrangements. They take a cleansing bath and change into funeral attire, usually white saris. All the fires in the house including the kitchen are extinguished, and no cooking is allowed in the house until after the thirteen-day mourning period has passed. Instead, cooks are hired to feed the family members and also the people who visit to pay condolences. The widow of the deceased wipes away the traditional red dot on her forehead and breaks the bangles from her arms to signify her change in status from married to widowed. She is no longer in charge of domestic chores. All the extended family members and community members gather at home. The sons wash the body of the deceased man and wrap the body with white muslin cloth. No embalming is performed. The body is placed on a bier, a flat frame made of bamboo. As male family members slowly carry the deceased to the cremation ground, people chant *Ram Ram, Satya hai, Sat naam, Satya hai* (God is truth, in God is truth), and women bid farewell to the deceased because they usually do not follow the funeral procession to the cremation ground.

Once at the cremation ground, the funeral attendant checks the death certificate issued by the town office and prepares the funeral pyre. A funeral priest recites some prayers, which are repeated by the eldest son. He sprinkles the body with sacred water from the Ganges, pours *ghee* (clarified butter) on the body, and lights the funeral pyre, which is his duty as the eldest son. His father is no longer the head of the household; the eldest son has replaced him in this role. After the funeral pyre is lit, everybody leaves, with the exception of close family members. After eight to ten hours, they collect the ashes into an urn or a jar. They go to a nearby river, perform the ash-spreading ceremony, and disperse the ashes. Upon returning from the cremation ground, they take a ritual bath, change into a fresh set of white clothing, and recite a brief prayer.

For the next twelve days, a priest visits the family each morning to perform a prayer session. The family members sit around and reminisce about the deceased and make offerings of *pindas* (rice balls) to their forefathers to make sure that the deceased reaches their realm. Neighbors and friends stop by to offer condolences to the family. The priest comes back in the evening to give a sermon. On the thirteenth day, several priests perform the last ceremony to mark the end of the mourning period and to signify that the deceased has reached the realm of the dead. The priests and all the guests who came to the ceremony are then fed a vegetarian meal.

AMERICAN HINDU DEATH AND DYING RITUALS

In America, Hindus who want to observe traditional death ritual have often made changes reflecting their adaptation to American culture and local regulations. To illustrate the various ways in which Hindus have adapted to America, two examples will be provided that occurred in Atlanta within a month of each other at the same funeral home.[13] In both examples, the deceased men had ties to the Gujarat State in India. However, both men followed two different forms of Hinduism, Shakta and Swaminarayan. This is significant because the funeral ceremony is conducted differently depending on where the deceased was born and raised and the form of Hinduism he or she followed.

The Case of Mr. Patel

Seventy-five-year-old Mr. Patel, who worked at a Wendy's drive-through for over twenty years and later at a Wal-Mart, died at a hospital in Atlanta. He was originally from the Gujarat region of India. He was a member of Shree Shakti Mandir in Lake City, Georgia, which is located just southeast of Atlanta, although he lived in Norcross, a city just north-east of Atlanta. He developed a multisystem failure that required him to be hospitalized and placed on life support. His family did not want him to continue suffering, so they decided to take him off of life support when it became clear that he was going to die soon. With his wife and daughter present, he died peacefully.

His body was taken to a funeral home immediately after the death certificate was issued. Mr. Patel's distant relatives from India suggested bringing Mr. Patel's body home to perform a *puja*. His close family members in Atlanta decided not to perform the traditional *puja* because they wanted his grandchildren to remember him as someone with whom they used to play. If they held the traditional *puja*, the grandchildren would see the dead body and that is how they would remember him. In addition, the family did their best to bring Mr. Patel's son from India to Atlanta for the funeral. The family postponed the funeral rite for a week, in the hopes that he would be able to come. However, his travel visa was not granted in time, so ultimately the family had to perform the funeral in Atlanta without his presence.

The deceased's wife and daughter[14] were not permitted to cook at home, according to tradition. Therefore, his relatives brought simple and basic comfort foods, such as *khichdi* (yellow rice), *dhai* (yogurt), and *suki bhaji nu shak* (potato boiled and sautéed with spices). The family was allowed to boil water to serve tea to people who dropped by to offer condolences. His photograph, which had been taken at the photo studio in a local Wal-Mart where he worked, was decorated with a garland of flowers and displayed on a small table. A *divo* (a candle with *ghee*) was lit and remained lit until after his cremation. Men sat in one room, talking occasionally, but mostly watching TV. Women sat in another room, singing devotional songs that would help the deceased move on to the next life, praying, or chatting about what happened at the funerals of other relatives in the past. Older women, including the widow, wore white or light-colored saris because the color white is traditionally associated with death and mourning. During this time, Mr. Patel's body was kept at the funeral home.

On the day of the funeral, which took place a week after he passed away, the family took a coconut, *ghee*, and lots of flower petals to the funeral home. The funeral ceremony was held in the chapel of the funeral home. The deceased, dressed in a brown suit, was placed in a plain white coffin that was lined with a white sheet. All the women sat on the left side of the chapel, and all the men sat on the right side, facing the altar where the body was placed. Most people wore white saris or white clothing to the funeral, and the ceremony was conducted entirely in Gujarati. After everybody was seated, a priest once affiliated with the local Hindu temple that Mr. Patel attended recited some prayers and a sermon to the effect that it was Mr. Patel's time to die. Then, the son-in-law, standing in for the eldest son, took a coconut with a flower on top, walked clockwise around the body, and put the coconut between the deceased's feet. He then sprinkled *ghee* onto the body.

The deceased's daughter and friends of the deceased gave eulogies. Then, immediate family members took flower petals in their right hand and walked around the body clockwise to drop the flower petals on the body. Then everybody, row by row, stood up and did the same. At this point, all the women, including the widow and the daughter, went outside. Male family members took the body in the coffin to the crematorium in the basement of the funeral home. The rest of the immediate family members went to a separate room with a window that viewed the crematorium so that they could see the body being inserted into the chamber. Interestingly, a computer with a webcam utilizing wireless Internet was set up so that the eldest son in India could watch the funeral and the people who gathered for the funeral could see him. It was very important for the eldest son to be able to witness his father's funeral because the funeral is considered the most important life cycle sacrament.

A few days after the funeral, the family sponsored a prayer ceremony in memory of Mr. Patel. A priest from Shree Shakti Mandir performed the ceremony to officially end the mourning period. The family paid Shree Shakti Mandir to prepare a traditional Gujarati meal for those people who had come to the ceremony. A few weeks later, his wife took his ashes back to India and spread them in the Ganges with the eldest son who could not attend the funeral.

Case B

In a very different situation, a twenty-three-year-old man, whose nickname was Neal, died in a car accident on a Saturday night in January of 2008. Neal was born and raised in Atlanta, but his parents were from Gujarat. He was a devout Swaminarayan, a sect in Hinduism that is very popular in Gujarat, and he regularly attended the Bochasanwasi Akshar Purushottam Sanstha (BAPS) Swaminarayan Temple in Clarkston, a suburb of Atlanta.[15] Neal recently had become engaged to a woman who was in India through a traditional marriage arrangement process. Family and friends gathered at his house to mourn his death immediately after he passed away. His funeral date was set for a week later at a local funeral home. During that time, his body was kept at the funeral home.

On the day of his funeral, Neal's close friends made giant posters with his photos for display and for people to write comments on in front of the chapel of the funeral home. Several swamis performed rituals in the chapel to make sure that the young man's soul would not turn into a ghost because he died very young. During this ceremony, women were not allowed inside the chapel. After the swamis left, the chapel was open to everyone. Women sat on the right side, and men sat on the left side facing the altar. Neal's immediate family occupied the front row. The chapel was full of people, including Neal's family and his non-Hindu managers and coworkers from the retail store where he had worked. The priest gave a sermon for Neal, stating that because he was only twenty-three years old, it was not really his time to die. In a particularly American twist, Neal's sister-in-law acted as a master of ceremony, a role which does not appear in a traditional Hindu funeral. Four of his cousins and three of his friends offered eulogies. One of his best friends, who attempted to read a prepared eulogy, became overwhelmed with emotion and could not say a word. It was too much to see his friend lying in the coffin. Later, an eleven-year-old cousin who was in training to be a priest at BAPS Swaminarayan Temple sang a devotional song.

Neal's brother and father took a coconut with a flower on top, walked around the body clockwise, and then put the coconut between the deceased's feet. They also sprinkled *ghee* and put flower petals on the body. Next, row by row, all the men rose and put flower petals on the body, followed by the women. After that, the men took Neal's body down to the crematorium and placed his body into the crematorium chamber. Then, his brother pushed the button to start the process of cremation. His funeral was conducted almost entirely in English. At this funeral, most Indians wore white, but some wore black, just as non-Indians did.

A few days after the funeral, the family sponsored a prayer ceremony in memory of Neal. The family had arranged with the BAPS Swaminarayan Temple to prepare a traditional Gujarati meal for those who had come to the prayer ceremony. Then, his family took his ashes to their home. After consulting with one of his mother's relatives, Neal's family decided to spread the ashes in Atlanta where Neal was born and raised, instead of in India.[16]

DIFFERENCES BETWEEN INDIA AND THE UNITED STATES

For Hindus in India, death is a family affair that includes even children because most people die at home. In contrast, when Hindus immigrate to the United States, increasingly, death moves from the familiar surroundings of home to an unfamiliar hospital room. This is because of several factors. One is family structure. Many American Hindu families do not have anyone who can stay at home all day to take care of a sick or aging person. Unlike their Indian counterparts, American Hindus live in a nuclear family structure, without extended family, and in many households, both husbands and wives work full time. In addition, American society encourages family members to provide professional medical care when someone is suffering, which is usually the case when someone is dying. Some American Hindus feel compelled to take a dying family member to the hospital. This may be because of the fact that in the United States, if someone dies at home, an authorized professional such as a doctor, hospice nurse, police, fire department employee, or coroner has to pronounce death for the death certificate to be issued. In India, many village officials would take the word of the family member and issue a death certificate. Some American Hindus utilize hospice programs that allow the dying person to stay at home; however, very few do because the hospice program is not a part of Indian tradition.[17] In this sense, it is interesting to note that many Hindus have already adopted an American attitude toward death after only a few decades of living in America.

Family members often want to be with the loved one at the moment of death. However, there is a limit to the number of visitors permitted in most American hospital rooms; in India, hospitals allow as many people as possible.[18] Hospitals in the United States that are sensitive to the needs of Hindu communities sometimes make accommodations so that family members and friends can stay without interfering with other patients.[19] In addition, in the United States, some family members may not be present for a loved one's death because they live far away. In that case, community members often take on the role of the extended family members. Some American Hindus acknowledge the inevitability of not being able to spend the last moment with their loved one if the patient is in the intensive care unit or emergency room. "Who gets to see the person breathe last? A machine probably.... So you are strapped in [the] ICU to a machine that goes blip, blip and boom. And the nurse telephones you telling you that your loved one is no longer there."[20] Depending on the care a patient receives in the hospital, close family members may or may not be able to be with the dying person at the last moment.

When there is no hope for recovery, Hindus in the United States seem to accept the inevitably of death relatively easily. Instead of intervening by feeding a patient through a tube or administering medicine intravenously just to prolong life by a day or two, family members often prefer to allow the person to die without trying extraordinary measures.[21] When families realize that death is inevitable, Hindus handle the moment of death in a variety of ways. Some people consider it crucial to perform a ritual such as *puja* or to administer holy water. Others consider being present with the dying person more important than performing any particular ritual. In any case, family and friends prefer to make the dying person as comfortable as possible rather than prolonging life. Some Hindus consider it problematic if one is "well-fed" at the time of death through a feeding tube because the vital breath struggles to leave the well-nourished and strong body.[22]

Despite the adaptations that have to be made, some traditions persist. Many put a spoonful of water from the Ganges River, which is considered to be holy, into the dying person's mouth.[23] A basil-like *tulsi* leaf, which is considered to be a holy plant, may be placed in the mouth as well.[24] Some chant the name of deities such as Ram so that the deity is carried in the dying person's consciousness into the next life. Others chant passages from the *Gayatri Mantra*[25] or the *Bhagavad Gita*. Some people place a lamp using *ghee* near the dying person's head.[26]

Traditionally, Hindus place the body right before the moment of death. It is understood that by being closer to earth, it is easier for the breath to escape. Some people believe that if you die on the bed, you die as an evil spirit.[27] Also, Hindus traditionally turn the body so that the feet face south, which is the direction of *Yama*, the god associated with death. However, in the United States, Hindus cannot place the dying family member on the floor because of hospital regulations, and they cannot turn the dying person's body. In some cases, the family may call for a temple priest to perform the last rite because hospitals do not have Hindu "chaplains" on staff. Once the patient passes away, and the physician pronounces the death, the body is taken to the morgue by the hospital personnel. In the United States, family members cannot take the body home from the morgue in their car as they do in India. Instead, a professional undertaker must transport the body to a funeral home.

In India, before the body arrives home, the family members start preparing for the rituals by collecting necessary items used in the cremation ritual. Many Hindus bathe themselves and change into white clothing to indicate that they are in mourning. The family members take care of the body by washing or bathing it, dressing it in white cloth, and laying it on the floor, feet facing south. Then, they wait for extended family members to arrive so that they can conduct the funeral rite, which traditionally begins within twenty-four hours of death. Hindus in India cremate the body immediately, mainly for two reasons. One is a spiritual reason; they believe that cremating the body facilitates the soul's journey to the kingdom of *Yama*. The other is a hygienic reason because the climate of India does not allow the body to be kept for a long period of time. Usually, people in the community stop by to pay their respects to the deceased, and there is a constant stream of people coming in and out of the house. Professional wailers may be hired to mourn.

In India, the deceased's family also extinguishes the central household fire that is essential to the household chores including cooking, and they hire a group of cooks who will prepare food outside of the family's house for the members of the immediate and extended family and guests. In the United States, the deceased's immediate family usually does not cook from the time the death occurs until the end of the mourning period.[28] Instead, they cater from regional Indian restaurants to provide meals, or close family members and temple community members bring food to the deceased's family.[29] The food is usually very simple, such as vegetarian meals of rice, vegetables, and sometimes yogurt.

In the United States, the body usually remains in the funeral home unless the family member decides to perform a *puja* at home. The body is not embalmed because Hindus do not believe in beautifying the deceased as prescribed in the *Garuda Purana*. However, the body is kept cold by refrigeration to avoid deterioration.[30] This is a new process for Hindus in the United States. Some family members prefer to send the deceased's body back to India so that proper rituals can be performed. In this case, the body needs to be embalmed, not to beautify it but in accordance with international shipping regulation to preserve the body for transport. A deceased's passport, a death certificate, and an embalming certificate must be presented to the consulate or embassy to receive the authorization to send the body back to India. Some funeral homes allow close family members to bathe, anoint with sandalwood paste, and dress the body, by furnishing a special room or allowing these activities in the embalming room.[31] Other people prefer to have the undertakers "prepare" the body if they choose to have a viewing, which mainly involves washing the body, putting on clothes, and placing the body in the coffin. Some people, especially the second generation, seem to appreciate the fact that they do not have to deal with the dead body because they have never observed the traditional ritual themselves, and they do not know what to do.

Use of a coffin is something new to Hindus. In India, Hindus do not use coffins. When they have to transport a body to the cremation ground, they place the body on a chair or a flat frame made of bamboo called a bier to publicly display the death. In the United States, when the body is transported from the hospital to the funeral home or to the crematorium, a plain white van or hearse is used so that the body is concealed from the public. If a family chooses to have a direct cremation, a coffin made out of cardboard or fiberboard is required. If the family decides to have a viewing in the funeral home, they are required to place the body in a very simple coffin.

Although the concept of a "viewing" is not completely foreign to Hindus in India because the dead body is laid out in the home of the deceased so that family and community members can pay their respects, the practice of *dressing* the body for a viewing is not an established custom for Hindus. In India, Hindus wrap the body with a white cloth, whether the deceased is a man or a woman, with one exception.[32] A married woman who dies before her husband is considered very auspicious, so she is dressed as if she were a bride with a red embroidered silk sari.[33] In the United States, Hindus tend to dress a man in a Western suit, and a woman in a sari. If a family chooses to have a viewing in the United States, the need for refrigerating the body arises. Also, because family members may be scattered throughout the United States, the local family would have to wait for them to arrive to carry out the death ritual. If this is the case, refrigerating the body would be necessary as well.

In India, once enough family members have gathered to be able to perform the death ritual, the body is placed on a bier and carried out of the house by close male family members. The procession heads to a cremation ground. Usually, only men are permitted on the cremation ground. Once the funeral procession reaches the cremation ground, pall bearers place the body on a funeral pyre made of wood, preferably sandalwood if they can afford it. The funeral pyre is prepared by the *Dom* (cremation ground attendant), who is traditionally from the lowest caste. *Ghee* is poured over the body, and sacred water, such as water from the Ganges River, is sprinkled on the body for ritual purification purposes. The *Dom* prepares "sacred fire," which is said to have been burning from the beginning of time. When the body is ready to be cremated, usually the eldest son circumambulates the body with the sacred fire and lights the funeral pyre. This ceremony is called *Antyeshti*.

There are several things to be noted. First, the ceremony of *Antyeshti* is the cultural equivalent of a graveside ceremony, that is to say, it is the ceremonial disposition of the body. Second, a priest may or may not preside over this ritual in India. If the death ritual takes place in a city such as Banaras, the sacred city in India for Hindus, then priests called *Mahabrahmins* perform the ritual. These priests are of a different caste from the temple priests (traditionally from the *Brahmin* caste) who attend to the regular temple *puja* and *arti* and other life cycle rituals. The need for a different priest arises because the dead body is generally considered to be impure, and temple priests from the *Brahmin* caste do not touch anything impure. However, in the United States, many temple priests are often called to perform funeral rites. Because the funeral usually occurs at some place other than the temple, U.S. priests have learned new skills and taken on new roles. For example, some priests have learned to drive to get to funeral sites, which is not common in India. Sometimes, the priest has to travel a great distance because the family may easily live fifty miles away from the temple location; in India, people traditionally live within walking distance of a temple. As a result, priests in the United States not only have to interact with devotees and the general public, but they also have to be able to speak some English to explain the ritual.

It is important to note that temple priests in the United States have a far greater range of responsibilities than most priests in India,[34] but they never take on quite the wider spectrum of roles that Christian clergy do. Hindu priests remain primarily "religious ritual specialists" who know how to conduct certain rituals including the recitation of mantras. They visit the homes of religious community members to perform last rites if they are called. However, unlike American pastors, they do not make "pastoral visits" to the homes of the bereaved after the traditional mourning period is over to console the family or offer support in the time of grief, unless they are asked by the family to lead the commemorative rituals at their home. They do not help coordinate communication with relatives back in India. Their basic role is to deliver the rituals with precision, as they are trained to do. Also, very few Hindu priests participate on local interfaith boards or represent its religious community on various civic occasions; these roles are filled by lay leaders, who are very active in American temple life.

In the United States, a Hindu funeral is often held at the chapel of a funeral home or a crematorium. However, this is not a traditional practice for Indian Hindus. Moreover, Western funerals often include a eulogy to praise the life of and to memorialize the deceased. Hindus do not traditionally practice memorialization. However, increasingly, many U.S. Hindus have started to adopt this practice by calling it "*karma*," the same word that signifies the consequences of one's action throughout his life. They have chosen this word instead of "eulogy" because the person making a speech is talking about the consequences of the deceased's actions. In addition, the person making the speech is accumulating good *karma* by performing the eulogy. Therefore, a question such as "who does *karma* for this body today?" may be asked before the funeral. During the funeral, mantras may be chanted by a priest. Traditional Hindu hymns are sung, and prayers are said. Some families prefer to have a recording or an actual recitation of the *Bhagavad Gita* during the ceremony. In India, women usually do not attend any funeral rite. However, in the United States, many women attend the funeral or the service right before the cremation in the crematorium.

Once the funeral is over, the body is taken to the crematorium by the funeral home personnel, and the cremation is carried out by the crematorium operator. Many Hindus prefer funeral homes with an attended crematorium when available so they do not have to transport the body to a different location. In this case, male family members and friends carry the body in a coffin to the crematorium, which is usually located in the basement of the building. In India, *Doms* prepare the funeral pyre with logs. In the United States, Hindus deal with only a crematorium operator. If allowed, male family members help the crematorium operator place the body into the chamber. Usually, the eldest son pushes the button to ignite the furnace just as he would light the funeral pyre in India, fulfilling his duty as the eldest son. If the eldest son is not available, another male relative pushes the button. In some instances, a daughter may push the button.

Traditionally in India, the skull of the deceased is cracked open with a stick during cremation to facilitate the release of the soul. Recently, even in India, this practice has been replaced with breaking a clay pot. In the United States, this ritual is not performed at all. The eldest son who torches the funeral pyre and performs the ritual for his father takes on the role of head of the household at this point. Some Hindus may choose not to have a "funeral" in a funeral home chapel. Instead, they may choose direct cremation. This may involve a very brief ceremony right before the body is inserted into the cremation chamber.

In India, if the cremation site is located beside a river, the ashes are swept into the river. Alternatively, the family may collect the ashes in a pot and take the ashes to the Ganges, the closest river, or to the ocean. In the United States, once the body is cremated, the ashes are collected by a crematorium attendant, and a family member picks up the container with ashes. Many American Hindus, especially the first generation or their family members, ask to have their ashes brought back to India and immersed in a river, such as the Ganges River or Yamuna River. In this case, a family member takes the ashes to India, or the family may ask a friend who is returning to India to spread the ashes. This desire to have the ashes transported to India has lead to the establishment of a company, the Sacred Rites of the Ganges, which transports ashes to India, conducts *Asthi Visarjam* ceremonies on the bank of the River Ganges in Banaras, and sends videotapes of the ceremony back to family members in the United States. In contrast, some American Hindus who have experienced professional success, raised a family, or spent most of their lives in the United States, increasingly choose to spread the ashes in the United States because of their strong ties with a local hometown.

In India, a mourning period follows right after *Antyeshti* for ten to twelve days depending on a variety of factors. This period is called *śrāddha*. This is the final stage during which the surviving family bids farewell to the deceased, who is understood to be going into the realm of the ancestors. Family members sit around the house, talking fondly of the deceased, and inviting priests to come to the house to recite prayers and give sermons. The mourning period is usually observed in the house where the deceased used to reside. However, for practical reasons, some may observe the mourning period in their own homes, especially if the funeral has taken place at a distant location or city.

It is traditional and socially acceptable to observe a long mourning period, which usually lasts ten to twelve days in India. In the United States, because most workplaces have a set number of days an employee can take for compassionate leave, this is not usually possible. Therefore, many Hindus in the United States adapt their observances, shortening everything including the mourning period. During the mourning period, family members hold prayer services in the deceased's home every day in the morning and receive visitors who come to offer condolences and to comfort the survivors. Even with a shorter mourning period, a temple priest may visit the house to perform the traditional prayer session in the morning at the family's request. Hindus believe the soul of the deceased still remains in the vicinity of the family for a period of time, and family members perform certain acts to convince the soul to leave the earth and go on to the realm of the ancestors. The departed soul is believed to travel through the realm of ghosts and spirits (*pretaloka*) to the realm of ancestors (*pitrloka*). To encourage this, family members pray, chant mantras, sing *bhajans* (devotional songs), offer rice balls called *pindas*, and reminisce about the deceased.

To mark the end of the mourning period, *puja* is performed. Several priests conduct the ceremony, and then the family offers food to priests who can symbolically pass food to the soul because it has a long journey ahead to reach *pitrloka*, the realm of the ancestors. The family also offers food to those who come to mourn the loss of the deceased. This is usually done in a home in India. However, in the United States, this ritual is mostly done in a temple because many temples these days are equipped with an industrial kitchen that can handle cooking for a large number of people. As Hindus started to establish communities in the United States, changes occurred in the observance of many life cycle events from home to temple. Although the funeral ritual never takes place on temple property, the end-of-mourning period ceremony often takes place there. In this sense, the role of Hindu temples has been Americanized or Westernized.

After the end-of-mourning period ceremony, family members go back to work, but some continue to pray in the morning and evening in front of their domestic shrine throughout the prescribed *śrāddha* period. Some people donate clothes that used to belong to the deceased as a good gesture to those who cannot afford to buy clothes. Many follow the monthly and annual commemorative rites at home, which seem to take the minds of survivors off of loss by going through the motion of ritual. Also, all the rituals during *śrāddha* period are intended to help the bereaved grieve, and it is socially acceptable to express grief freely during this period. As Vasuda Narayanan[35] expresses, "Rituals give us a way of cathartically dealing with our grief. Every one of the rituals within the Hindu ceremonies is a reality check to help us confront our grief, interact with it, accept it and keep going on—both in life and spiritually."[36] What gives solace to American Hindus is the notion that the deceased's *atman* either is reincarnated or attains *moksha*. Some people believe that the time of death was determined by God.[37] During this difficult time, many people recite the thousand names of Vishnu or read the *Bhagavad Gita* or the *Ramayana*.[38] In an extended family situation, as in India, private extended grief may have been less of an issue because the other family members who have gone through bereavement can share their experience.[39] However, in the United States, where many families are living in nuclear family situations, they rely on friends within their Hindu communities to look after each other, just as extended family members would do. At Sri Siva Vishnu Temple in Lanham, Maryland, a suburb of Washington, D.C., there has been formalized in the *Mitra Mandala* (Circle of Friends), an organized community outreach effort that provides assistance to those dealing with loss even if the devotees do not have close friends within the community.[40]

The experience of adjustment and recovery from bereavement depends on many factors, such as the individual's personality and the level of social support.[41] However, some suggest that there is some correlation between perceptions of good/bad death and the experience of adjustment and recovery. If the death was a good death, where the deceased was elderly and had seen his or her children get married and the birth of his or her grandchildren, the survivors are more likely to accept the death easily and be able to go on with their lives. However, if the death was a bad death, also called "untimely death," where the deceased was young, the survivors seem to have more difficulty adjusting back to normal life.[42]

IMPURITY ISSUES

Hindu practices and rituals center on issues of purity/impurity. Traditionally in India, a dead body is considered "impure." Moreover, anything that has to do with the funeral rites are considered to be impure as well.[43] In India, *Doms* who attend the funeral pyre usually are from the lower caste. In addition, there is a separate subcaste of priests who perform death rituals in some regions. However, some priests in the United States feel that they are obligated to perform the funeral rite for the dead, especially when the deceased was a devotee of the temple. To resolve the problem of impurities, the temple priests, who customarily never used to perform death rituals in India but perform the funeral rites in the United States, conduct a cleansing ritual. For example, at Hindu Temple of Atlanta in Riverdale, Georgia, if a temple priest performs a funeral ritual, when he returns to his residence, he takes a bath, performs a *puja* at his residence, and is excused from all his regular temple duties until the next morning. After that, he is free to perform his regular temple duties. Concerns about purity/impurity may help to explain why there has been no Hindu-owned funeral home in the United States.[44] First, the dead body was considered impure, and anybody who deals with the funeral rites is usually from a lower caste. Second, there is no concept of an established "funeral home" business in India because death and dying rituals are handled by the family members.

GENERAL ISSUES HINDUS FACE

There are some unique issues that arise in dealing with death and dying in the United States. Many American Hindus feel frustration that family members do not play a direct role in taking care of the body of the deceased or the organization of the funeral. They feel that they do not have the same level of control over the entire ritual that they would have in India. For example, they cannot cremate the body *within* twenty-four hours after death to facilitate the *atman's* journey. In most cases, U.S. law does not permit the body to be cremated until *after* twenty-four hours of the death. Also, because family members may be scattered across the United States, local family members may have to wait an additional day or two to perform funeral rites. In addition, U.S. Hindus have to deal with hospitals and commercial funeral homes. The hospitals and the funeral homes take control, thus charging fees for care and individual activity that is traditionally performed by the family. Because of government regulation, the body is only released from the hospital when the death certificate is ready, not when the family wants to take the body, and the body is not released directly to the family but only to the funeral home.

Some funeral homes in the United States have been making an effort to make this difficult time easier for Hindu communities. A few funeral homes and mortuaries have started to adopt Hindu death and dying rituals and address concerns that Hindus have within the limits of law and regulations. For example, several funeral homes in the New Jersey area that serve New York City have a division within the funeral home that is dedicated to serve Hindus and the broader Indian population. Bongiovi Funeral Home in Raritan, New Jersey, also operates as "India Funeral Home," specializing in funerals for Asian Indians, most of whom are Hindus. The owner, Anna Bongiovi, has been serving Hindu communities for over sixteen years. Similarly, Fresh Pond Crematory and Columbarium in Flushing, New York, one of the oldest crematories in the United States, works very closely with Hindus and even constructed a special crematorium room for them.[45] Garden State Crematorium in North Bergen, New Jersey, also set aside a special room for Hindus. Before the creation of this room, Hindu mourners felt rushed when conducting their funeral rites. They were asked to leave the room more quickly than traditional rituals allow. The crematory manager consulted a local temple before creating this room to meet the needs of Hindus. This special room can accommodate 200 people and is fully carpeted with low benches rather than standard chairs or pews. This room contains a main shrine with a central image of Shiva and is fully decorated with Hindu deity images, such as Ganesha, Hanuman, Durga, and Krishna.[46]

One of the first mortuaries in California to make efforts to facilitate Hindu practice is Fremont Memorial Chapel in Fremont, California, in the Bay area. The ritual washing of the body and subsequent application of water, milk, yogurt, butter, or honey to the skin can take two to three hours. This makes the ritual longer than Western funerals, and Hindu mourners felt rushed as they performed the ritual washing. After coming to understand the importance of having ritual washing as a part of the body's preparation, Fremont Memorial Chapel set aside special rooms for Hindu ritual washing.[47]

Specific funeral homes in other metropolitan cities are also sought after by local Hindu communities. Wages and Sons in Stone Mountain, Georgia, was contacted by members of a Gujarat Samaj community about twenty-five years ago. The community members were looking for a funeral home with a crematory; at the time, Wages and Sons was one of very few in the Southeast. Set in the heart of the Bible Belt, no other funeral home was willing to deal with an Eastern religious community. However, Wages and Sons took on the challenge and became the most popular funeral home for Hindus in the Greater Atlanta area.[48] One Hindu expressed his gratitude for their caring attitude, especially when he lost his father and was unable to take the ashes back to India for quite a while. Wages and Sons told him, "Do not worry about the ashes. We will keep them here until you are ready to fly back to India." When he went to pick up the ashes to take them back to India, they had a certificate and customs clearance forms ready so that he could carry his father's ashes as a carry-on without being questioned at the airport.[49]

As the first generation (those who immigrated to the United States after the 1965 Immigration Reform Act) grows older, their children are becoming adults without having experienced the "traditional" rituals that accompany life cycle events in India. It is interesting to note that when a first-generation Hindu passes away in the United States, the spouse or friends know exactly what to do because they have participated in numerous death rituals back in India. They are prepared to organize the ritual in America with help from relatives and friends. However, when the organization or preparation lands in the lap of second-generation Hindus, who have had no exposure to death rituals in India, they do not know what needs to be done. In response to this problem, the Gujarati Cultural Association of Bay Area in California created the *Cremation Services Guide for Indo-American Community*, with a list of funeral homes in the Bay area where cremation services are available and provide a guideline how the ritual should be conducted. This guide explains what needs to be done when a loved one dies for Indo-Americans in the Bay area. Similarly, Oregon Marathi Mandal in Portland published "Practical Aspect of Death, Funeral, and Last Rites" on their Web site.[50] This guideline not only outlines the necessary procedures but also provides an excerpt from the *Bhagavad Gita* and information on funeral homes and crematoriums that are familiar with Hindu rituals. Some Hindu communities, such as many BAPS Swaminarayan Temples throughout America, provide the names of local people to contact when a death occurs in the community.

INDIA/UNITED STATES VERSUS TRADITION/MODERN

This chapter has pointed out differences between traditional Hindu funeral rites in India and modern Hindu funeral rites in the United States. However, many of the adaptations that Hindus have to make are not just occurring in the United States. In modern Indian metropolitan cities, there are many changes that parallel those in the United States. For example, many Hindus in Indian metropolitan cities die in hospitals now because of the inability of family members to provide home care for sick and elderly family members. Although the basic attitude toward death remains the same—not wanting to extend the life by administering a feeding tube or feeding a dying person intravenously and allowing many people in the hospital room when the person is dying—the shift in practice is significant. In addition, people use crematoriums rather than the burning *ghat* (cremation bank) or the cremation ground where they can have an open funeral pyre because of the pollution caused by cremation. Even in the sacred city of Banaras, crematoriums are being used. People transport the body in a white van from the hospital to the home of the deceased and then to the crematorium instead of placing the body on a bier and walking to the burning *ghat* or the cremation ground to display the funeral procession. Therefore, there is a growing polarization between traditional and modern practices within India herself. As a result, Hindus in the United States and Hindus in the metropolitan cities in India may adapt the changes in similar ways.

CONCLUSION

Traditionally, Hindu funeral rites are performed to facilitate the deceased's soul in the transition from this world to the next world, from *pretaloka* to *pitrloka*. It is an opportunity for the individual soul to obtain *moksha*. By performing funeral rituals, Hindus are also ensuring the continuity of family lineage. In addition, the death ritual is performed for the living, so that they can go on with their lives. By going through the meticulous actions prescribed in the *Garuda Purana*, family and friends have the chance to grieve, and at the same time, the ritual motions provide the opportunity to take their mind off their grief.[51]

Also, as with other life cycle events, immigrants realize they want to keep their cultural tradition alive. Many Hindus consider the death ritual the most important life cycle event.[52] They may choose not to perform other *samskara* such as a naming ceremony, or a sacred thread ceremony, but they do not want to miss the death ritual. By performing the death ritual, Hindus are confirming their belief that death is a part of life that happens to everybody, and they try to maintain their Hindu identity as distinct from traditional American (i.e., white Anglo-Saxon Protestant) identity.

NOTES

The inspiration for this title is Karen Leonard's article, "Mourning in a New Land: Changing Asian Practices in Southern California."

1. Jonathan Parry, *Death in Banaras* (Cambridge, UK: Cambridge University Press, 1994), 158.

2. Hindus believe that a physical body is made up of five elements: air, light, earth, ether, and water, which correspond to certain deities associated with each element. When a human dies, they believe that these elements go back to their origin. See Terje Oestigaard, *The Deceased's Life Cycle Rituals in Nepal: Present Cremation Burials for the Interpretations of the Past. BAR International Series 853* (Oxford, UK: Archaeopress Gordon House), 344; http://www.svf.uib.no/sfu/oestigaard/ArtiklerWeb/BAR2000/Oestigaard_%20Kap.%205.pdf.

3. Gavin Flood, *An Introduction to Hinduism* (Cambridge, UK: Cambridge University Press, 1996), 23.

4. Thomas Hopkins, "Hindu Views of Death and Afterlife," in *Death and Afterlife; Perspectives of World Religions*, ed. Hiroshi Obayashi (New York: Greenwood Press, 1992), 145.

5. Back then, India was not an independent country. India, as a country, gained its independence in 1947.

6. Karen Leonard, "Mourning in a New Land: Changing Asian Practices in Southern California," *Journal of Orange County Studies*, 3/4 (1989/1990): 64.

7. Prema A. Kurien, *A Place at the Multicultural Table: The Development of an American Hinduism* (New Brunswick, NJ: Rutgers University Press, 2007), 100.

8. A rite of passage for boys, which marks the beginning of their formal education.

9. For detailed explanation, please refer to Lola Williamson's chapter in Volume 1.

10. The most famous story out of a long epic, *Mahabarata. The Bhagavad Gita*, is considered to be one of the sacred texts in Hinduism. See Barbara Stoler Miller, trans., *The Bhagavad-Gita* (New York: Bantam Books NY, 1986), 32.

11. Children are buried instead of cremated. How death should be handled is prescribed in the *Garuda Purana*, a sacred text in which Lord Vishnu gives instructions to a mythical bird, Garuda.

12. For a detailed account on Hindu traditional death and dying rituals, please see Jonathn Parry's *Death in Banaras* and Christopher Justice's *Dying the Good Death: The Pilgrimage to Die in India's Holy City*.

13. Information regarding these examples was gathered by the author during research conducted on death and dying rituals of Hindu American communities. For more, see Kyoko Murata, "'Who Does Karma for This Body?': Death and Dying in Hindu Communities in Metropolitan Atlanta," master's thesis (Atlanta: Georgia State University, 2004).

14. Although his daughter is married and does not live with Mr. Patel, for the ritual purpose, his daughter belongs to Mr. Patel's household.

15. According to Kurien (101), BAPS (Bochasanwasi Akshar Purushottam Sanstha) makes up a large proportion of Swaminarayan Sect overseas.

16. Bhavi Patel, interview by author, Atlanta, GA, April 10, 2008.

17. Ardith Z. Doorenbos, "Hospice Access for Asian Indian Immigrants," *Journal of Hospice and Palliative Nursing* 5 (2003): 27–33.

18. Pittu Laungani, "Death in a Hindu Family," in *Death and Bereavement across Culture*, ed. Colin Murray Parkes, Pittu Laungani, and Bill Young (London: Routledge, 1997), 54.

19. Kyoko Murata, "'Who Does Karma for This Body?': Death and Dying in Hindu Communities in Metropolitan Atlanta," master's thesis (Atlanta: Georgia State University, 2004), 36.

20. Ibid., 35

21. S. Cromwell Crawford, *Dilemmas of Life and Death: Hindu Ethics in a North American Context* (Albany: State University of New York Press, 1995), 126.

22. Christopher Justice, *Dying the Good Death: The Pilgrimage to Die in India's Holy City* (Albany: State University of New York Press, 1997), 230.

23. Water from the Ganges is available in South Asian grocery stores throughout the United States, according to Lavina Melwani, "Life and Death in the United States of Little Indias: Life and Death in the USA," *Little India* January 31, 1996: 10.

24. Many Hindus grow the *tulsi* plant at home.

25. A highly revered mantra.

26. In some cases, Hindus are asked not to light the *ghee* lamp because of the fire code.

27. Gillian Evison, "Indian Death Rituals," Ph.D. dissertation (Oxford, UK: University of Oxford, 1989), 9.

28. Bhavi Patel, interview by author, Atlanta, GA, April 10, 2008.

29. Because of the fact that most of the time the deceased's family is grief stricken, they do not desire much food.

30. This is not done in India.

31. If the family member were to enter the embalming room, they need to sign the waiver form for the Occupational Safety and Health Administration, U.S. Department of Labor, stating that they are aware of the fact that they are exposed to formaldehyde, which may trigger respiratory irritation, eye irritation, skin irritation, dermatitis, respiratory sensitization that could lead to asthma, and possibly cause cancer.

32. Of course, there are many variations. In South India, men are dressed in their traditional clothing.

33. Evison, 23.

34. Kurien, 99.

35. A scholar of Hinduism in America.

36. Lavina Melwani, "Hindu Rituals for Death and Grief," Beliefnet http:// www.beliefnet.com/Faiths/Hinduism/2003/02/Hindu-Rituals-For-Death-And_ Grief.aspx.

37. Shirley Firth, *Dying, Death and Bereavement in a British Hindu Community* (Leuven, The Netherlands: Peeters, 1997), 183.

38. Another famous epic about Rama, an incarnation of Vishnu.

39. Richard Gatrad et al., "Palliative Care for Hindus," *International Journal of Palliative Nursing* 9 (2003): 447.

40. Sri Siva Vishnu Temple, "Vision," http://www.ssvt.org/About/Vision.asp and Susheelam Center for Community Counseling, "Resources," http://www.suheelam.com/indexphp?section=7.

41. Firth, 171.

42. Bhavi Patel, interview by author, Atlanta, GA, April 10, 2008.

43. In modern days, taking the bath is done symbolically.

44. For more information on pollution issues regarding Hindu's perspectives, see Pittu Laungani's article, "Death and Bereavement in India and England: A Comparative Analysis," *Mortality* 1 (1996): 191–92.

45. Lavina Melawani, "Life and Death in America: When Yama Comes Calling," *Little India* (2007): 30.

46. Lavina Melawani, "Death in Little India: A Death in America," *Little India* (1997): 21.

47. Arthur J. Pais, "Ashes to Ashes," *India Abroad*, November 18, 2005.

48. Hank Wages, interview by author, Stone Mountain, GA, April 22, 2008.

49. Ravi P. Sarma, interview by author, Riverdale, GA, April 27, 2008.

50. Oregon Marathi Mandal, http://www.oregonmm.org/docs/cremation-guide.pdf.

51. Shoba Narayan, "Saying a Traditional Good-Bye," Beliefnet, http://www.beliefnet.com/story/172/story_17203.html.

52. Ravi P. Sarma, interview by author, Riverdale, GA, April 27, 2008, and Rajshekhar Sunderraman, Atlanta, GA, May 26, 2008.

CHAPTER 8

The Great Matter of Life and Death: Death and Dying Practices in American Buddhism

Jeff Wilson

BUDDHISM OVERVIEW

Death and dying can rightly be called central concerns in Buddhism. Buddhists have been far more inclined to ritualize death than birth or marriage, and Buddhist monks and priests are the specialized ritualists for death in many Asian cultures. For example, in Japan, death and dead bodies are seen as polluted and are shunned by Shinto priests; therefore, Buddhists—who have no such taboos—naturally came to be the experts on funeral and memorial matters. This has been a tremendously productive strategy—after all, everyone dies, meaning that sooner or later every family will call on a Buddhist specialist for help after the death of a loved one (and frequently pay for such services). At the same time, there have been negative consequences as well because Buddhism's linkage in the popular mind with death has caused some to shun its other teachings out of fear or superstition, and truly life-affirming Buddhist philosophies have been slow to develop. This has particular implications for Buddhism's transmission to the United States, a culture characterized by optimistic, active embrace of life, which expects religion to be relevant to this world and also tends to shun or ignore issues of death and dying.

According to traditional Buddhist legends, death was a prime motivating factor in the creation of Buddhism. Siddhartha Gautama, an Indian prince who lived approximately five hundred years before the Common Era, was a sheltered and pampered young nobleman. Venturing into the city one day, he was shocked to encounter a corpse being carried to the charnel ground, a sick person, and an old man. Confronted with the realities of suffering, he renounced his throne and went into the wilderness to seek a solution. After years of searching, he had a great breakthrough and became known as the Buddha, the "one who has awoken." His subsequent teachings became known as Buddhism, and they are in many respects concerned with the issue of death and how to manage it.

The key to understanding Buddhism is to grasp its cosmological worldview, which is intimately tied to ideas of death, transmigration of the spirit, and rebirth. Mortal, unenlightened beings may be born into any of six conditions: as beings in the hells, as hungry ghosts, as animals, as human beings, as violent demigods, or as gods in the heavenly worlds. Time is eternal, without beginning or end, and in this infinite time span, sentient beings have been born over and over into these various realms, going from life to death to new life elsewhere in an unceasing cycle. Each new destination is determined by moral and immoral actions in previous lives: karma, a principle or law of nature, compels beings with merit accumulated through good actions on towards relatively positive rebirth, whereas beings who have committed serious evils are pushed toward birth in one of the undesirable realms, such as the hells. However, all realms are seen as containing suffering (even the heavens); therefore, one hopes to ultimately escape from this endless cycle by achieving perfect wisdom, cutting off the generation of new merit and demerit, and passing instead into the permanent, peaceful state of nirvana beyond birth and death. Moving beings off of the wheel of life and into nirvana is the highest goal of Buddhism; to escape from life and death is to become equal to the Buddha, who is believed to have achieved the ultimate religious goal precisely by defeating death (indeed, at his moment of awakening, he was confronted by and conquered the Buddhist devil, Mara, literally "murder"). The process of dying, the moment of death, and the interregnum before new birth have often been seen as particularly fruitful times for breaking the chain or at least influencing future rebirth so that it takes place in a relatively comfortable circumstance. These are the moments when one's attachments to life and the body break down, when karma begins to most actively kick in, and when one's mental state—calm and focused or desperate and fearful—can affect the life to come.

Buddhism's focus on death can be seen in the rise of what are known as the pure land practices. After the death of the Buddha, many Buddhists feared that they would be unable to achieve liberation because the path was so arduous, and they had no teacher to guide them. One solution to this was the rise of belief in multiple buddhas throughout the universe—the buddha known as Siddhartha Gautama had died, but in an infinitely large universe full of sentient beings, surely there were other buddhas elsewhere who could be petitioned for help. In particular, one buddha, Amitabha, became popular because he was viewed as a sort of universal savior. In the traditional stories, Amitabha had vowed to become a buddha and create a pure, blissful land where beings could be reborn. In this realm of ease, without worry or challenge, they would be able to swiftly achieve buddhahood and finally escape from birth and death for good. This pure land of Amitabha was located far, far to the west, the direction where the sun sets and, thus, is symbolically linked to the end of life. Beings who called on Amitabha for help, especially at the time of death, would be enabled to go directly to his land. This teaching and practice spread through most forms of Buddhism, eventually creating sects entirely devoted to Amitabha worship as a way to use the moment of death as the stepping stone to enlightenment itself. Today, pure land practices dominate death-related rituals in much of Buddhist Asia, and they were imported early in the history of Buddhism's arrival in America, as Asian immigrants sought the reassurance of traditional rituals amidst the hardship and discrimination of a new land.

It is worth noting that at the same time that Buddhism was drawing attention to issues surrounding death and dying, it was also being influenced by other religions around it. Buddhism has always been a relatively porous religion, lacking centralized authority and more interested in practice than orthodoxy, which often made it open to other ways of approaching death and other concerns. Thus, we find that Buddhism often mixed with local traditions it encountered such as Daoism, Confucianism, Hinduism, Shinto, and the Tibetan Bon religion. These admixtures resulted in new configurations of Buddhism and often influenced its understanding of death and the afterlife. Thus, we find mixed in with originally Buddhist practices other ideas such as veneration of deceased ancestors, worship of deities to become immortal and cheat death, and similar things that, although practiced by Buddhists, do not strictly speaking come from Buddhist origins.

BUDDHISM COMES TO AMERICA

Buddhism is a relative newcomer to the American religious landscape. Fragmentary information on Buddhism began seeping into America via trade ties and European scholarship, but sustained contact with Buddhism did not develop until well into the mid-nineteenth century. A watershed event was the California Gold Rush. Starting in 1848, it brought tens of thousands of Chinese to the West Coast in search of fortune. In San Francisco's Chinatown in 1853, the Sze Yap Company founded America's first temple, which offered a mix of pure land Buddhism and other common Chinese religious elements. As the Chinese moved up and down the West Coast, carrying Buddhism with them, they encountered ever more racial and religious discrimination. Finally, in 1880, Congress passed the Chinese Exclusion Act, banning most Chinese immigration.[1]

Japanese Buddhists began arriving in America and Hawaii starting in 1868. A majority of these early immigrants were members of the Jodo Shinshu denomination of pure land Buddhism, and by 1889, they established the first Hawaiian Buddhist temple, with their first temple on the mainland coming in 1899.[2]

American interest in Buddhism also developed in the latter part of the nineteenth century as a few Euro-Americans began to identify themselves as Buddhists. During a ceremony in Ceylon in 1880, Henry Steel Olcott (1832–1907) and Helena Blavatsky (1831–1891) become the first Americans to formally pledge their allegiance to Buddhism. Olcott and Blavatsky were the founders of theosophy, an eclectic religious movement that incorporated Hinduism and Buddhism into its beliefs and helped to introduce ideas about reincarnation into American culture. An important early interpreter of Buddhism was the German immigrant to America Paul Carus (1852–1919). Carus identified Buddhism as one of the closest approximations to his vision of a rational, investigative approach to universal spirituality. In 1894, he published *The Gospel of Buddha, According to Old Records*, a popular book that helped to introduce Buddhism and the life of the Buddha to a general American audience. Although Olcott and Blavatsky represented a type of convert interested in mysticism and the exotic nature of Asian spirituality—and thus were open to ideas about reincarnation and other realms—Carus represented a second common type of American convert that tended more towards skepticism and would be far less interested in death rituals or the afterlife.[3]

During the first half of the twentieth century, Buddhism in America was dominated by Japanese traditions because Japanese Buddhist sects founded many of their first American temples during this time, including the influential denominations Nichiren Shu, Shingon, Soto Zen, and Jodo Shu. During this period, Japanese Buddhism began to make a visible impact on the American landscape through its death-related practices. Not only did the Buddhists develop their own cemeteries where statues of favorite buddhas and other figures were placed to look after the dead, but in Hawaii, Japanese fishermen erected public statues of Jizo (a protector of travelers and the dead) at spots where people were swept away by the sea, offering both an act of memory and a warning for others.[4]

Hard times loomed for the Japanese-Americans, however. The Immigration Act of 1924 blocked most Japanese immigration. With the flow of Japanese immigrants cut off, pure land Buddhism's growth slowed, and few other sects experienced further development. Worse yet, war with Japan was brewing, and the day after the Japanese attack on Pearl Harbor of December 7, 1941, federal agents began to detain Buddhist priests and other community leaders as possible spies and saboteurs. Within a year, more than 120,000 Japanese-Americans and immigrants had been forced from their homes into concentration camps because of such suspicions of their loyalties. Buddhist temples were ransacked during the process, and many families lost their homes and land; the Jizo memorial statues also became targets of vandalism. In the camps, makeshift Buddhist centers formed, and the younger generation began to push for adaptations that would make Buddhism seem more "American."[5]

Although these fifty years of American Buddhism largely belong to the Japanese-Americans, a few notable milestones were achieved by others as well. In 1927, Walter Yeeling Evans-Wentz (1878–1965) produced one of the most famous American Buddhist texts, a translation and commentary of the funerary text *Bardo Thodal* entitled *The Tibetan Book of the Dead*. This was a notable early example of American interest in Buddhism's teachings around death. The *Bardo Thodal* describes the symbolic and strange visions that one encounters in the state between lives.[6] Its vivid imagery would become a gold mine for psychoanalysts, scholars of myth, and later counterculture people drawn to alternate views of the mind and afterlife than the American mainstream.

In the 1950s, a new cycle of non-Asian interest in Buddhism began to appear. Most visible was the rise of the Beats, a loose collection of avant garde literary pioneers who explored Asian traditions in an effort to find meaningful art and spirituality. Buddhism played a large part in these explorations, findings its way into many of their works, such as Allen Ginsberg's (1926–1997) poem *Kaddish*, which draws on Jewish mourning rituals to express his feelings after the death of his mother. Probably the most famous of the explicitly Buddhist-related works produced by the Beats was Jack Kerouac's (1922–1969) 1958 novel, *The Dharma Bums*, a semiautobiographical account of hitchhiking literary Buddhist wanderers roaming the highways of America.[7]

Undeniably, the 1960s were the breakout decade for American Buddhism. The future of Buddhism in America was assured with the passing of the Immigration Act of 1965. This landmark legislation lifted the racist immigration laws that had largely choked off Buddhism's growth, allowing a new tide of Asian immigrants to reach the United States. The Chinese came again, as did the Japanese (although in smaller numbers), and they were joined by Sri Lankans, Koreans, Vietnamese, and the first trickle of Tibetans. These newcomers brought new forms of Buddhism, either as baggage to be transplanted along with their lives or as religious commodities to market to a new mission field in America. A number of new Zen missionaries were offering Zen practice as well. Significantly, these Zen teachers included not only Asian immigrants but also white Americans who had trained in Asia. Both types of Zen missionaries tended to focus their efforts specifically at non-Asian Americans, who were more interested in meditation than in Buddhism's traditional services for the dead.

A perception of Buddhism as ancient, wise, peaceful, and esoteric pervaded the 1960s and 1970s counterculture, with concepts like karma and reincarnation reigning side by side with free love and widespread drug use in the growing network of new convert Buddhist centers. Some missionaries did little to discourage these combinations. One example of this is Chogyam Trungpa (1939–1987), a Tibetan guru who founded the Tail of the Tiger practice center in Vermont in 1970. Charismatic, insightful, traditionally trained, sexually promiscuous, and alcoholic, Trungpa embodied a form of "crazy wisdom" highly compelling to the baby boomer seekers investigating Buddhism and other Asian religions. And the flow of immigrants continued, bringing the first Thai (1971), Korean (1973), and Cambodian (1979) temples.

The counterculture began to wane in the 1980s, as the baby boomers aged, and the Reagan era shifted the culture in a more conservative direction. Nonetheless, Buddhism continued to expand in America during the Reagan and first Bush presidencies, largely along the same established trajectories. This was also an era of disillusioning scandals in many Buddhist communities, perhaps the most serious being the announcement that Trungpa's successor Osel Tendzin (born Thomas Rich, 1943–1990) had knowingly spread the AIDS virus in his community through unprotected sex, allegedly believing that his status as an advanced Buddhist practitioner gave him power to defeat illness and death.[8]

Buddhism once more became trendy in the 1990s, with major movies (including *Little Buddha*, about a white American child who is discovered to be the reincarnation of a dead Buddhist saint), best-selling books such as Sogyal Rinpoche's *The Tibetan Book of Living and Dying*, and seemingly endless amounts of media buzz. The first major English language Buddhist magazine, *Tricycle: The Buddhist Review*, appeared in 1991, oriented toward elite Buddhist converts involved in Tibetan, Zen, and Vipassana Buddhism. Initially concerned with meditation and basic Buddhist teachings, magazines like *Tricycle* and *Buddhadharma* have expanded their offerings to include a variety of topics, including feature articles on dealing with death and information about the place of mourning rituals in Asian society.

As the millennium turned, Buddhism seemed to have made itself comfortable in America after long last. By the end of the second Bush presidency American-trained teachers led most of the convert-oriented temples and meditation centers founded in the previous four decades, and groups affiliated with major lineages were operating in every part of the country. As Buddhism diversified and aged, death-related issues and practices achieved an ever higher visibility in American temples and meditation centers.

DEATH PRACTICES AMONG THE NEW BUDDHIST IMMIGRANTS

Because Buddhism is so highly diverse, and practices and beliefs may differ even within specific Buddhist groups, it is impossible to present all the varied Buddhist practices related to death that can be found in the United States. Therefore, some representative practices among important groups will be described.

Death is so prominent an issue in Buddhism that virtually all traditional public gatherings include some reference to the dead through the practice of transfer of merit, arguably the most common and widespread of all Buddhist activities. These death-related rituals in Buddhism most often involve complex relationships between the laity and the monks because it is the monks who act as the ritual specialists. These Buddhist clergy in most countries are a special class of practitioners: celibate monks (in some countries, also nuns) who shave their heads, wear special robes, undertake hundreds of vows regulating their behavior, and engage in the bulk of the ritual activity on behalf of the entire Buddhist community. These religious orders, known as the sangha, live in a tight symbiotic web with the greater number of lay Buddhists. Monks are discouraged from working and are expected to concentrate on religious rather than worldly concerns; thus, they are reliant on the laity to provide them with food, shelter, clothing, and other needs. The laity, meanwhile, rely on the monks to teach about the doctrines of Buddhism and especially to maintain their precepts-based purity, which enables them to perform Buddhist rituals accurately and effectively.

In many traditions, a typical Buddhist service involves laypeople (often women) serving food they have cooked to a monk or monks. By giving to these holy men, the laypeople generate merit for themselves. Furthermore, the monks express their gratitude by chanting holy scriptures and generating further merit, which they then can dedicate to the laypeople and, most importantly, to the ancestors of the lay patrons. This high-powered monastic merit is believed to benefit the dead in the afterlife, allowing them to escape the hell realms and be reborn in a good situation as a human being or even a god. Thus, concerns over the fate of deceased relatives draw the laypeople to the monks, where they can learn about Buddhism and be comforted by benefitting their loved ones, and the monks are provided for and given the opportunity to fulfill their role as guides and protectors of the people, in this life and after. Such food offerings and merit dedications often take place during hours-long services amidst a constellation of other practices, such as sermons, affirmations, vows, and worship of the Buddha and various saints, yet the merit dedications are clearly the climax of the event for the participants—Buddhists do many other things than just focus on death, yet death and the dead are undeniably the greatest concern.

Dedication of merit to ancestors occurs in virtually all traditional forms of Buddhism; thus, it is particularly interesting that this form of memorial rite actually violates "orthodox" Buddhist doctrine in certain ways. In Buddhist thought, a dead person goes through a period as a disembodied spirit (often believed to last forty-nine days) and is then reborn in a new body.

However, in the merit dedication ceremony, deceased loved ones are typically treated as though they are still in the spirit state and not yet reborn,
even if the ceremony takes place years after death: in many Southeast
Asian countries, for instance, special services one hundred days after
death, one year after death, and on the anniversary even a decade or later
are common. Here, we see the ambiguity around ideas about the dead:
they are not visibly present; thus, they can be simultaneously imagined as
spirits and as having taken on new bodies and identities, depending on the
needs of the situation.

For many of the newer Buddhist immigrants, merit dedication services
take on special meanings in the American context. Cambodians, Lao-
tians, Vietnamese, Tibetans, and many Chinese came to the United
States as refugees escaping horrific war, violence, and sometimes religious
persecution in their native lands. Cast adrift in American society, they
are far from the resting places of their ancestors and in some cases are
unable to ever return. This is agony for members of the tight-knit family-based societies most Asian Buddhists hail from, cultures that explicitly venerate elders and ancestors as the wisest and most important
protectors of the community. In these situations, it becomes especially
incumbent to patronize monks and get them to dedicate merit to the
deceased. Doing so conserves central religious practices, which help to
maintain identity in a shifting, uncertain situation. But even more to the
point, they help to reestablish across boundaries of space and time the
damaged connections to the beloved dead, allowing refugee Buddhists in
America to assert that they have not forgotten their roots and that they
wish to continue demonstrating their love and devotion to those who
were left behind. Even for Buddhists who arrived more willingly, there is
a need to maintain the connections that merit dedication services help
to promote.

Ties to the Old World (and the next world) are also maintained
through the celebrations of the liturgical calendar, which are often concerned with death. For example, most immigrant Buddhist temples celebrate the death of the Buddha, in some cases in tandem with celebrations
of his birth and enlightenment, and there are usually festival days dedicated specially to remembering people who have passed away. Chinese and
Vietnamese immigrant Buddhists hold large services dedicated to feeding
hungry ghosts. By coming together for these communal memorial services,
the temples also strengthen the bonds between the individuals and families
of the Diaspora. Memorial services at American Buddhist temples allow
people an opportunity to cook the traditional foods of their homeland,
socialize with one another, speak their native languages, and to reinforce
bonds with those who have passed away. Thus, Buddhist death ceremonies
in America have the ironic additional function of improving the conditions of *this life* that the living are still engaged in.

Differences between the various forms of Buddhism are also important in relation to how death-related rituals are carried out and, thus, what their meaning and impact are for the community. For example, Vietnamese temples in America typically hold lengthy memorial services for the community on a monthly basis. Large numbers of laypeople gather at the temple, where they make donations of food, money, flowers, and other gifts. The monks chant many holy scriptures and chant mantras, special phrases believed to be endowed with magical powers. The names of all the dead being honored are read aloud, and often the services begin by inviting all the ancestors to join with the community in the temple, thus collapsing the distance between far-off Vietnam and the Vietnamese-American descendants. If the memorial day falls on a significant date in relation to a loved one, such as the forty-ninth day after their passing, then the mourners may wear white headbands (the color of death in East Asia) in commemoration, making their bodies a site of further connection with the dead.[9] In most cases, the activities take place at least in part before large communal altars festooned with pictures of the dead and memorial tablets, providing a visual connection with the deceased (and the homeland) as well, and the gifts placed before these images help to demonstrate continued commitment and care on the part of the living. The dedication of merit is often especially intended to help the deceased gain entrance to the pure land, and Vietnamese-Americans hope to go there themselves after death to rejoin their lost families and friends once more. This means that even practices performed for oneself in this life, such as repeating the name of Amitabha Buddha in a mantra-like fashion, which is often believed to help generate merit, have implications related to both death and the extended social group simultaneously.

At the same time, it can be difficult to completely reestablish traditional practice in America. In many cases, there are shortages of traditional ritual implements, food, or other important items, and fewer monks are available to lead rituals. Time, too, can be a precious commodity in short supply—refugee Buddhists often work long hours at difficult jobs that leave them far less time than they would have had in the Old World to sponsor and attend services. Monks compensate by shortening some services and omitting parts that cannot be reproduced, in some cases condensing events that might have taken place over several days into a single day or even just part of one day. Not uncommonly, major services cannot be held until a sufficient number of monks can be brought in from other temples, sometimes even from other states or even the other side of the country. This can have a significant economic impact on lay donors, who would not have nearly so much trouble rounding up sufficient numbers of local monks in their native lands. This forces some American Buddhist communities to become even more closely knit because it takes the combined efforts of many families to reproduce rituals that a single family or a handful of families would have been able to sponsor in Asia. It also has the effect of helping to maintain networks of Buddhists spanning the entire country because monks move about from region to region, weaving the scattered temples and their lay communities together.

Besides strengthening community ties, Buddhist memorial services in America can have important implications for the mental health of individuals. As refugees, many of whom have personally experienced violence and loss, large numbers of Asian Buddhist immigrants are prone to psychological problems. For example, Cambodian-Americans suffered through the torments of the brutal Khmer Rouge regime, and when they dream about their lost loved ones, they often interpret such visions as evidence of haunting by ghosts. These spirits may be angry that they were left behind without proper memorialization by those who fled. Symptoms such as depression, anger, aches, and so on are seen as evidence of the haunting. If possible, traditionalist Cambodian-American Buddhists will seek out monks to exorcise and appease the ghosts of their abandoned ancestors, offering them merit through ritual to help them rest peacefully and move on to a new rebirth.[10] Buddhists who lack access to such traditional cultural means of dealing with trauma may develop more serious mental illnesses over time, with the attendant physical illnesses that often follow in their wake.

Memorial services remember someone who has died at some point in the past, whereas funerals deal with the immediate aftermath of a death. Many Buddhist cultures have developed special ceremonies and practices to be performed to help usher the newly dead through the spirit world and, in the process, comfort the living that their loved one has been properly attended to. An example are the "fireside monks" (moke-pluhng) of Cambodian Buddhism. When a Cambodian-American Buddhist dies, his family calls upon fully ordained monks to perform the funeral services, but often a male relative will also serve for a short period as a fireside monk. Such temporary monks don a white robe (symbolic of mourning) instead of the usual orange monastic garb and stand watch over the corpse during its cremation. For the next few days, the fireside monk accumulates merit on behalf of the deceased through meditation and other practices and then dedicates it to him to help the spirit pass through the transition of death to new life smoothly. The fireside monk then relinquishes his white robe and returns to normal lay life.[11] This halfway form of ordination allows family members who are not full monks to take on greater responsibility in the funeral process, without the need to fully renounce their regular lives and retreat into the monastery. Vietnamese Buddhists, too, use specially empowered laypeople as ritualists at times: for instance, the ban ho niem are a class of elders who recite scriptures and perform some memorial rites if no monk can be found, a sadly common situation in America.

Cremation raises a number of issues specifically in the American context. Asian Buddhist burial practices differ, but the most widely practiced one is cremation. This was the method whereby the Buddha himself was laid to rest, and it is seen as a good act that symbolizes the sort of nonattachment to the body which Buddhism emphasizes. In Buddhist Asia, it is often customary to stay up all night with the corpse in the home where it has died, in some cases even waiting for several days as mourners arrive to pay their respects. However, in the United States, strict laws based on health codes govern how bodies can be treated, and usually, a corpse must be removed from the home swiftly, processed by a funeral home, and disposed of as soon as possible. Until relatively recently, cremation was not even a widely available practice in many parts of the country, necessitating changes in how Buddhist communities dealt with their dead. It can be difficult for Asian-Americans to find funeral homes willing to let them sit up all night with the corpse and conduct additional services. For example, many Cambodian Buddhists ritually rinse the mouth of the deceased with holy water blessed by monks. Such practices can run afoul of unsympathetic (often Christian) funeral homes or local laws dealing with how bodies can be interacted with, complicating the ritual practice and thus the mourning process for Buddhists.

Tibetan Buddhist funeral services are particularly elaborate because of the tantric nature of this form of Buddhism. Tibetan Buddhist monks chant for hours beside the corpse, going with it as it is processed through the medical system. These chants are intended to guide the spirit on the long process of passing through the bardo, the in-between state that Tibetans believe spirits must brave on their way to a new life. The experience of the spirit in this state affects where it will be reborn, and the magical powers and teachings transmitted by the monks' chanting can enable it to move on to a better rebirth or even become a buddha. In many cases, Tibetans who have sufficient time will prepare themselves for this bardo experience for months or years through mental training directed by Buddhist monks, once again demonstrating how practices related to death actually impinge directly on activities during life in the Buddhist religion.

Tibetan Buddhist funerals in America are affected in serious ways by their new environment. Many Tibetan Americans do not have regular access to a trained monk who can guide them through the preparatory predeath exercises. Even if a monk is able to be called in to conduct the funeral, time constraints often force bardo rituals to be shortened—these can last as many as forty-nine days in Tibet, but American Buddhist monks are often able to give no more than a few hours to the task. Most conspicuous is the change in how the body is finally disposed of. A common postmortem Buddhist practice in Tibet is "sky burial," wherein the corpse is ritually chopped up, mixed with grain, and ceremonially fed to vultures. This graphically demonstrates the value of nonattachment,

generates merit by feeding living beings, and avoids the necessity of cremation in regions of Tibet where wood is scarce. Such treasured practices are
absolutely impossible to carry out in the United States, where surrounding
cultural prejudices and laws prevent this type of disposal.

DEATH PRACTICES AMONG THE OLD-LINE BUDDHISTS

Newer immigrant Buddhists are often still in the thick of transition
from Old World to American cultures. Their death-related rituals have
not been strongly shaped yet by the new culture of the United States. A
useful contrast, therefore, is to look at the Japanese-Americans, who have
been in America for five or more generations at this point and are fully
assimilated. They may point toward the direction in which more recent
arrivals will eventually move as they reassess the importance of death practices and the practicalities of their performance in North America. And
because the Japanese have been here so long, their services have become
standardized and allow us the opportunity to examine the entire cycle of
memorial rites in detail.

Most of the Japanese-American Buddhists in the United States have
been involved with the Jodo Shinshu denomination of pure land Buddhism, often simply called Shin Buddhism. This is the largest form of
Buddhism in Japan, with approximately one in three Japanese connected
to the Shin tradition. Early waves of Japanese immigrants actually arrived
from regions characterized by particularly widespread devotion to this
denomination, increasing its representation in the new Japanese-
American communities. Arriving in the nineteenth century as manual
laborers on plantations in Hawaii, farm workers in the fields and orchards
of California, and fishermen in both areas, these pure land Buddhists at
first were without priests and thus had no access to funeral and memorial
rituals. This was a serious concern for these Buddhists forced to work
hard, sometimes dangerous jobs in poor conditions, where mortality rates
were high. By the 1880s, they were petitioning the head temples in Japan
to send them missionary priests, and soon temples were built that
provided some of the familiar rituals in Hawaii and the United States.

Jodo Shinshu differs from most other forms of Buddhism because it was
founded with noncelibate priests in the thirteenth century and, therefore,
has a greater lay orientation in keeping with the family-based nature of its
clergy. Priests who marry and raise families, keeping fewer precepts than
celibate monks and rarely shaving their heads, naturally have a higher
degree of integration with the daily concerns of ordinary Buddhists. Yet,
Shin Buddhism has become largely funereal in practice, similar to other
sects. Part of this is because of the inherent otherworldly nature of pure
land Buddhism. The focus of this branch of Buddhism is on devotion to

Amitabha and the hope that one will be welcomed into his pure land after death. In medieval Japan, torn by plague, famine, natural disasters, and civil war, the thought of escape to an idyllic land after death was a great comfort and helped Shin expand to its present dominant size.

American Shin Buddhists have tried to transplant their funeral and memorial customs to the United States, although at times these must be modified. The first death-related rite comes shortly after someone has passed away. As soon as possible, and certainly no later than the following day, the temple priest is called in to perform the makuragyo, literally "pillow scripture," service. This is a relatively short ceremony that involves chanting by the deathbed and burning incense. Members of the temple may gather to be with the bereaved family, particularly those who are involved in funeral arrangements. Once the makuragyo is completed, the priest, family, and temple representatives plan the official funeral rites.

Normally, the next Jodo Shinshu service would be the wake (otsuya), conducted the night before the funeral. This is considered an important practice in Japan, but it has been abandoned in the United States. Early immigrants, exhausted from work, were unable to stay up all night long with the body as tradition dictated, and priests usually were not numerous enough to justify the practice. Instead, services at the temple were often called "funeral and wake," suggesting that the single ceremony was intended to encompass both rituals. Even now that Japanese-Americans live more comfortable lives and have a greater number of priests to draw on, this combined practice of wake and funeral persists as an American form of Buddhist ritual.

The funeral itself takes place in the temple, not the home, typically about five or six days after the date of death. Preparations differ; in Hawaii, which has the oldest continuous Buddhist traditions in America and a much larger percentage of Japanese-American inhabitants, the family follows the Japanese tradition of washing the body themselves and dressing it in white funeral clothes. In the continental United States, on the other hand, such preparations are typically handled by the funeral home without the direct involvement of the family. For this reason, Japanese-American Buddhists often do their best to patronize funeral homes owned by other Japanese-Americans, ensuring the rites will be conducted properly and respectfully.

Funerals (*soshiki*) are a highly orchestrated affair, involving many members of the temple, in keeping with the greater degree of lay participation in this denomination and reflecting the absorption of American, mainly Protestant, approaches to handling death. Flowers are offered by attendees, a reception desk is manned by volunteers, and ushers hand out program sheets. Most people arrive in dark suits or dresses, no different from attendees at a Christian funeral. The temples themselves have adapted to American sensibilities by including pews, whereas the altar itself remains traditional in layout, displayed on a raised stage-like area. Pallbearers will bring the casket into the front of the worship hall so that the body can be viewed.

The service itself begins with the ringing of the temple bell, as the priests in special ceremonial robes process into the worship hall. They line up before the casket for preliminary chanting. Depending on regional variations, this may begin by calling on all the buddhas of the universe to enter into the hall and witness the service, followed by hymns from the tradition that extol the virtues of Amitabha Buddha. The priests offer incense and then move into the altar area.

The next phase of the ceremony, if necessary, is homyo juyo, the bestowal of a special Buddhist name. In Jodo Shinshu, unlike in other denominations, this ritual is often undertaken during life. It involves affirming one's commitment to the Shin Buddhist path and receiving a dharma (Buddhist truth) name, believed to represent the name the person will be called by when they are reborn as a spiritual being in the pure land after death. If no dharma name has been received before death, the priest will now give one to the corpse, presenting it with a copy of the name to keep in the casket and a second copy to the family. The dharma name is read aloud, along with the deceased's regular name and his date of death and age. More hymns are chanted by the priests, and the three refuges are recited. This act is ambiguous—ostensibly, it is a devotional act by the congregation, but it also seems to suggest that the priest is taking the refuges in the place of the deceased, in case he or she did not do so during life. Taking refuge (proclaiming one's reliance on the Buddha, dharma, and sangha) is a fundamental act in Buddhism, often perceived as the practice that demonstrates one's identity as a Buddhist.

Next, the congregation and priests chant a scripture known as *Shoshinge*. Unlike in other Buddhist funerals, this is not taken from the words of the Buddha. Instead, it is a song composed by Shinran, the founder of Jodo Shinshu, which describes the Shin tradition's lineage and central tenets. While the chanting is being performed, the attendees will come forward to offer incense, beginning with the family of the deceased. Incense offering (oshoko) is made by taking a small pinch of powdered incense and dropping it into a burner before the altar. This also affords the mourners a further chance to view the body and say their goodbyes.

When the chanting is finished, the merit generated is offered to all beings. Technically, this ends the funeral ceremony, but there are still more events to come. The congregation sings the first part of a hymn ("Nadame") in Japanese, set to Western-style music, about how the deceased has left their sufferings behind and gone to the pure land. Then, a short biography of the deceased is read to the congregation, and representatives of various organizations that he or she belonged to burn additional incense. A short eulogy may follow as well, and then the remaining verses of "Nadame."

The priest then prepares to give a sermon. First, he reads or chants an epistle from Rennyo, one of the major past leaders of the Shin denomination. Known as "White Ashes," this letter describes how life is fleeting and enjoins the listeners to take refuge in Amitabha Buddha. The sermon itself will be in English and perhaps also Japanese if a sufficient percentage of Japanese-speakers are present. For Shin priests, the sermon is often seen as an opportunity to spread correct dharma to the congregation, some of whom may only come to the temple for funerals or special holidays. The event comes to an end with thanks for those who helped in the ceremony.

Besides the ritual events of the funeral itself, an important element is the koden. Koden are offerings of money that are made to the family of the deceased. These are comforting because they demonstrate the care and concern of the community, and they help to offset the costs of the funeral and burial. Koden are collected at the temple during the funeral. Such gifts are always wrapped in plain white paper and put into a white envelope, often with the donor's name and address so that thank you notes can be sent later. Thus, even the monetary aspects of Buddhist funerals are ritualized to some extent and become a practice that helps the community support its members during crises such as death.

The next day after the funeral, the actual burial or cremation will take place, along with a service. The lead priest chants a hymn and everyone places flowers on the casket. If it is a burial, this is performed in the cemetery; if it is a cremation, it will be carried out at the crematorium. The group then moves on to either the temple or the home of the deceased for the shonauka service, commemorating one week since death. This also affords the mourners a chance to have a meal together, emphasizing the social nature of the mourning process. The service will include offering flowers, sweet bean buns, and incense, chanting scriptures, reading one of Rennyo's letters, and a sermon. Some temples hold services at the end of every week for the first seven weeks (i.e., forty-nine days), but in America, the usual practice is only to hold services on the seventh and forty-ninth days.[12]

On the forty-ninth day, it is traditional to erect the gravestone. Shin gravestones have specific sectarian markers on them. They contain not only the name and dates of the deceased but his dharma name as well. They also contain the mantra "Namu Amida Butsu," a chant that forms the most basic practice in Jodo Shinshu. It translates as "I take refuge in Amitabha Buddha" and traditionally has been said by those who hope to go to the pure land after death, and they may also bear crests that demonstrate that the deceased belonged to a particular Shin denomination. If the person was cremated, a portion of the ashes will be placed in the hollow base of the gravestone. The grave then becomes a site of future ritual, as family members return to it during the summer Obon season to clean the site, offer flowers, and remember those who have passed away. A portion of the ashes will also typically be interred in the columbarium (*nokotsudo*) at the temple, where periodic rites will be performed. And some American Shin Buddhists send ashes to be housed at the main mausoleum of the sect in Kyoto, where the founder Shinran is buried. This allows them to rejoin their Japanese ancestors in death even if they were far away from them in America during life.

Even now that the deceased has been disposed of and the immediate aftermath of death dealt with, the memorial rites are far from complete. In fact, this is only the beginning of services that will recur more or less perpetually as long as people are still alive to remember the deceased. The family will hold private memorial services (*hoji*) on the hundred-day day anniversary of the death, again on the one-year anniversary, on the two-year anniversary, and, if they are able to maintain the traditions of the sect, will hold yet more services on the sixth, twelfth, sixteenth, twenty-fourth, thirty-second, forty-ninth, and ninety-ninth anniversaries. Services may even continue perpetually, being held for the deceased every fifty years thereafter. These services are similar in form to the seventh-day memorial ceremony.

And there are yet more services to be conducted. Jodo Shinshu temples in Japan do not hold regular weekly services, but in America, they have adapted to the prevailing customs and hold services every Sunday morning at the temple. On the first Sunday of the month, these services are designated as *shotsuki hoyo*, meaning they are memorial services for people who died during that month in previous years. These *shotsuki hoyo* services are often the most heavily attended services of the month, other than those that fall on special annual holidays. There is also the Obon service, conducted during the midsummer festival period. Anyone who has died in the year since the previous Obon service is memorialized at this time.

Finally, the home also becomes a site of death-related rituals. Shin Buddhists, like other Japanese Buddhists, maintain a small home altar known as a *butsudan* (literally, buddha shelf). This shrine contains an image of Amitabha Buddha, and people are encouraged to chant before it daily and make offerings of candlelight, rice, incense, and flowers. The altar arrangement will also contain a *kakocho* (family death register). This is a small book wherein are written the names of deceased members of the family. Pictures of the dead may also be placed near the altar, and their dharma name will be kept in a drawer below the altar. Specific memorial services may be held on the dates of death of past family members, and it is traditional to invite priests to conduct annual memorial services here in the home during the Obon season.

The liturgical year of Jodo Shinshu Buddhists in America also includes specific memorial rites. The three most important of these are Hoonko (January 16), which honors the death of Shinran; Nirvana Day (February 15), which honors the passing of the Buddha; and Eitaikyo (typically in

November), for the honoring of all who have passed away. Of these three, Hoonko is the oldest and most important and is often a date that draws large numbers of people to the temple, even those who rarely attend otherwise.

As can be seen, Shin Buddhist practice in America includes tremendous amounts of ritualization around death. Yet, these rites are often contested by the members and even the priests themselves. In fact, they seem to violate central doctrines of Jodo Shinshu as a unique form of Buddhism. Ostensibly, the purpose of such rituals is to generate merit that can be dedicated to the deceased, helping them to move on to the pure land. Certainly, that is how similar rituals are structured and understood in other Japanese Buddhist denominations. However, Jodo Shinshu insists that there is ultimately nothing that one can do to achieve or deserve admittance to the pure land: it is solely brought about by the compassionate gift of Amitabha Buddha. Furthermore, Shin Buddhists often claim that Amitabha forsakes no one and that there is no need to worry about being denied entrance to his land. These doctrines would seem to radically undermine the need for such services.

Officially, Shin Buddhism attempts to get around these problems by declaring that the purpose of funeral and memorial services is actually for the *living*, not the dead. The reason they hold services is to comfort those left behind and especially because it offers a chance to preach orthodox Jodo Shinshu doctrine to the congregation during the sermon. Yet, it is undeniable that these elaborate, frequent rituals are an influence from other Japanese sects that see them as efficacious, and although Shin ceremonies differ in some details, they are largely similar in overall form. In Japan, this is not too serious a problem because the Japanese are used to this form of memorialization and tend to accept it unquestioningly. However, in America, the tradition can run into trouble. Here, Shin Buddhists are exposed to many other forms of funeral practice, both in non-Japanese lineages and the surrounding (mainly Christian) culture that treats funerals and memorials quite differently. This raises questions not often voiced in Japan about why Shin forms and doctrines seem at times to be odd and especially why so many time-consuming (and at times expensive) services must be performed when they are technically considered to be unnecessary for the salvation of the deceased. In response, American Shin priests must stress all the harder that they are for the benefit of the living and, thus, tailor their sermons to pastorally counsel the mourners. And they have to be careful about insisting too strongly on extended memorial practices, especially those for people long dead, because they could lead the laity to demand an end to most memorial services, which are not only a main raison d'être for the temple but often an important source of income.

In other ways, memorial rites are affected by the American situation of Jodo Shinshu. One of the most interesting of these is the role of Obon. In

Japan, Obon lasts several days in mid-July or August, when the spirits of the dead are believed to return to the mortal world to be with their families. Japanese people travel to their ancestral homes to renew bonds with the living and the dead, participating in services that honor the visiting spirits. In the United States, Obon has taken on a greatly expanded meaning and observance. During the summer American Shin Buddhist temples hold huge Obon festivals, with stalls that sell traditional Japanese foods, crafts fairs, games, taiko drumming performances, and much socializing. Obon becomes a way not only of honoring the dead but of celebrating Japanese culture itself, and it is a significant fundraiser. The climax of the event is Obon odori, a type of folk dance. Participants clad in Japanese work garb (often decorated with the name of their local temple) form large circles and perform synchronized dances around a tower atop which musicians and singers stand. The songs are mostly Japanese folk tunes and pop songs from the past, with a mixture of new songs written in the United States or Brazil (another country with significant amounts of Japanese immigration). This dancing goes on for hours, and in places with a large concentration of Japanese-Americans—such as southern California— people will travel from temple to temple on successive weekends because they all hold their Obon festivals in staggered fashion. This transforms Obon from a singular event to an entire season, creating a virtual Japanese-American Buddhist world. Although the point of Obon is respect for the dead, the actual effect is to revivify life and celebrate the community. Significantly, Obon odori was not practiced at the head temple in Japan until a couple of decades ago. Shin has traditionally resisted Obon as superstitious, but in America, Japanese immigrants found in Obon rituals a way to reaffirm their lives and culture, and in time, these rituals were adopted back in Japan under influence from overseas.

Jodo Shinshu is not the only Japanese-American form of Buddhism in America, although it is the oldest and largest. Other traditions are also present in smaller numbers, and their death-related rituals are worth mentioning. Most follow a format more or less the same as that of the Shin funeral, and to the degree that they have become assimilated to the American situation, they will show similar patterns of somewhat shortened services, pews for mourners to sit in, monthly Sunday memorials, and so on, but there are some noteworthy differences. For one, all other traditional denominations of Buddhism believe that merit transference is actually effective and necessary. They also hold to the practice of creating memorial spirit tablets (*ihai*). These are wooden tablets that bear the posthumous names of the dead and are enshrined either in the home *butsudan* or the temple (or both). These *ihai* actually provide a substrate for the spirit to live in, meaning that the ancestors in some sense actually remain in the temple or home with the living. This clearly violates the doctrinal Buddhist understanding that the spirit moves on to a new life, either in one of the six realms or in the pure land. The origin of such spirit tablets is actually from Confucianism, which lacks ideas of reincarnation and has been a huge influence on Buddhism in East Asia. Nonetheless, in actuality, *ihai* are a normal part of the hybrid Buddhist funeral and memorial practices of Japanese Buddhists. Because Japanese-American Buddhists have far less access to traditional ritual implements than people in Japan, *ihai* must be specially ordered through the temple from one of the few Buddhist supply shops in America, which in turn often receive their materials from overseas. This also limits the number of other trinkets and good luck charms that Japanese-American Buddhists can use compared with their Japanese counterparts, such as votive plaques designed to send messages to the dead. Only a very small number of Japanese-American temples are able to supply these to their members, whereas virtually all non-Shin temples in Japan sell many varieties of such items.

Another important difference in ritual understanding is that in non-Shin Japanese-American Buddhist temples, people are far less likely to receive a Buddhist name until the funeral, and when they do, such names are called *kaimyo* (ordination names), instead of dharma names. This is because the funeral rites are actually designed to ordain the deceased as a monk or nun in the afterlife, the better for them to become a buddha.

DEATH RITUALS IN CONVERT BUDDHISM

So far, we have looked at death-related rituals in the old and new Asian Buddhist immigrant groups, but there is another important segment of the American Buddhist community that has not been discussed: new Buddhist converts. Since the 1960s, the number of adult converts to Buddhism in America has grown steadily, and although it is still very much a minority faith, temples and meditation centers patronized almost entirely by converts (usually white) can be found in every corner of the country.

These groups have been slow to adopt funeral rituals. In fact, they have been characteristically slow to adopt rituals of any kind. Many people who converted to Buddhism did so because they wanted to get away from religions that they felt were too invested in the "trappings" of religion, including ceremony. Instead, they were attracted to a radically pared-down form of meditation-oriented neo-Buddhism, substantially different from traditional Asian practices. These new Buddhists wanted a rational, modern form of individualistic contemplation, shorn of the sorts of "baggage" they imagined had been attached to Asian Buddhism over the centuries (just as Christianity and Judaism had come to have seemingly irrelevant accretions). In such an atmosphere, it was difficult to justify elaborate rituals of any type, and because most initial converts were young baby boomers rarely touched directly by concerns over mortality, death rituals were slow to develop.

Over time, however, this has begun to change. In part this is because the baby boomers have aged and are approaching retirement, and their parents' generation has begun to pass away. New concerns about their loved ones and their own health naturally lead people to investigate areas of Buddhism previously believed to be unimportant. Another reason for the appearance of greater ritualization around death is that over time, some Buddhists have come to feel that meditation alone is not adequate as a basis for a well-rounded spiritual life and, therefore, seek to develop a richer ritual approach to religious practice. It also can be observed that as greater and more accurate information about Buddhist tradition has become available to Westerners, it has gradually dawned on newer Buddhists that ritual is an authentic, perhaps even central part of Buddhism, and they have discovered that some death-related rituals actually offer spiritual resources missing from mainstream American religion.

An example of this rise in rituals is the water baby ceremony, which has recently become popular in many convert Zen centers. It is based in part on the Japanese postabortion ceremony known as mizuko kuyo. This is a widespread ritual that calls on the savior figure Jizo to protect the spirits of aborted (and sometimes miscarried) fetuses, ushering them through the afterlife to the pure land. In America, female convert Zen priests have championed a modified form (the water baby ceremony) as a way of dealing with grief and loss. Women (and sometimes their partners) who have terminated or lost a pregnancy are invited to the temple for a special ritual. They sit in a circle and quietly sew red bibs (a traditional offering to Jizo) or manufacture other offerings. Often, they are encouraged to tell their stories about who they are memorializing and why, with the belief that voicing one's pain actually helps to heal it. When the bibs are complete, the participants will ritually offer them to tiny, infantile statues of Jizo, which act as surrogates for the lost, never-born child. Many such rituals also include some chanting and merit dedication. The female priests who promote these rituals see them as a uniquely Buddhist response to the abortion issue, which neither condemns nor approves of the act itself but rather cuts through the divisiveness to bring healing to women in pain. Increasingly, non-Buddhists too are allowed to attend such events, which means that Buddhism is finding ways to impact the larger American culture around selected death issues.[13]

A second area of innovation for convert Buddhists has been the development of hospice programs and practices related to sitting with the dying as they pass away. The first of these was started in the late 1970s, but they became more popular in the 1990s, especially after the much publicized example of convert Zen priest Issan Dorsey's Maitri Hospice in San Francisco for people dying of AIDS. Convert groups that start hospice programs hope that they can be an active expression of the great compassion that Buddhists are enjoined to cultivate. Over the long process of dying, whether from AIDS or other illnesses, the practitioners care for the sick, tending to their needs and encouraging them to learn meditation techniques that help to deal with pain and fear. The final step in such practices is to actually be present with the person as they die, offering a calm presence and hopefully allowing the passing to be relatively stress-free. These programs are seen by their Buddhist staffers as a partial remedy to the American predilection for ignoring death and hiding the dying away in hospitals or nursing homes.[14]

Of course, convert Buddhists have developed regular funeral services as well. Often, these have to be reinvented when the need arises because the first generation of converts tended not to seek instruction in traditional rituals from their Asian missionary teachers, most of whom have passed away. As new inventions, these ceremonies vary widely but tend to be based on forms already present at the meditation center, such as the evening service. For example, the Vermont Zen Center has a funeral service that consists of chanting several standard scriptures and mantras, closely mirroring the standard evening service, with the only significant change being the addition of a memorial prayer. Other centers may include some time for eulogies from attendees. Significantly, ongoing memorial services have not emerged as a widespread practice in convert Buddhism, despite being a feature of all Buddhist lineages. Converts continue to hold to American notions of when and how often a person should be ritually memorialized, such that the common pattern is to hold a single funeral (and perhaps a wake), and, less often, a later memorial service for people who could not attend the funeral, but thereafter to dispense with yearly or other periodic ceremonies. The sense that traditional Buddhism is overly ritualistic continues to impact such decisions.

CONCLUSION

American Buddhism is so diverse that few generalizations can be accurately made—but one undeniable truth is that all Buddhist communities and individuals must eventually face the issues of death and dying. A second truth is that Buddhist funerals and memorial rites in America are always impacted by two different sets of forces: Asian Buddhist tradition and American cultural circumstances. Thus, they are rarely exactly identical to how such practices are conducted in the Old World, yet also differ in recognizable ways from mainstream Christian, Jewish, and secular rituals around death. Whether in assimilated, newly immigrant, or convert forms of Buddhism, Buddhist rituals are always responding to these forces in varying degrees. Even the most ritual-phobic convert center must find ways to navigate the great matter of life and death, and even the most conservatively traditionalistic ethnic temple must grapple with the realities of reproducing rituals in a radically different setting.

NOTES

1. Sylvia Sun Minnick, "Never Far From Home: Being Chinese in the California Gold Rush," in *Riches for All: The California Gold Rush and the World*, ed. Kenneth N. Owens (Lincoln: University of Nebraska Press, 2002).

2. Buddhist Churches of America, *Buddhist Churches of America 75 Year History, 1899–1974* (Chicago: Nobart, 1974).

3. Thomas A. Tweed, *The American Encounter with Buddhism, 1844–1912* (Chapel Hill and London: University of North Carolina Press, 2000).

4. John R. K. Clark, *Guardian of the Sea: Jizo in Hawaii* (Honolulu: University of Hawaii Press, 2007).

5. Duncan Ryuken Williams, "Camp Dharma: Japanese-American Buddhist Identity and the Internment Experience of World War II," in *Westward Dharma: Buddhism Beyond Asia*, ed. Charles Prebish and Martin Baumann (Berkeley: University of California Press, 2002).

6. W. Y. Evans-Wentz, *The Tibetan Book of the Dead* (Oxford, UK: Oxford University Press, 1927).

7. Jane Falk, *The Beat Avant-Garde, the 1950s, and the Popularizing of Zen Buddhism in the United States* (Ph.D. dissertation, Ohio State University, 2002).

8. John Dart, "Buddhist Sect Alarmed by Reports that Leader Kept His AIDS a Secret," *Los Angeles Times*, March 3, 1989.

9. Janet McLellan, *Many Petals of the Lotus* (Toronto: University of Toronto Press, 1999).

10. Thomas J. Douglas, "The Cross and the Lotus: Changing Religious Practices Among Cambodian Immigrants in Seattle," in *Revealing the Sacred in Asian and Pacific America*, ed. Jane Naomi Iwamura and Paul Spickard (New York and London: Routledge, 2002).

11. Penny Van Esterik, *Taking Refuge: Lao Buddhists in North America* (Phoenix: Arizona State University, 1992).

12. Description of the funeral services taken from Masao Kodani and Russell Hamada, *Traditions of Jodoshinshu Hongwanji-ha* (Los Angeles: Pureland Publications, 1995); Jodo Shinshu Hongwanji-ha Hongwanji International Center, *Jodo Shinshu: A Guide* (Kyoto: Hongwanji International Center, 2004); Shoyu Hanayama, *Buddhist Handbook for Shin-shu Followers* (Tokyo: Hokuseido Press, 1969); and personal observations.

13. Jeff Wilson, *Mourning the Unborn Dead: A Buddhist Ritual Comes to America* (Oxford, UK: Oxford University Press, 2008).

14. Patricia Sheldon, "The Great Work of Life and Death," in *Buddhism in America*, ed. Al Rapaport and Brian Hotchkiss (Rutland, VT: Charles E. Tuttle, 1998); David Schneider, *Street Zen: The Life and Work of Issan Dorsey* (New York: Marlowe and Company, 2000); Joan Halifax, "The Lucky Dark," *Tricycle: The Buddhist Review* 67 (2008).

CHAPTER 9

Diné (Navajo) Narratives of Death and Bereavement

Lawrence Shorty and Ulrike Wiethaus

DINÉ HISTORY AND TRADITION

We begin this chapter with the harsh and impersonal numbers of public health and other statistics, with a communally experienced history that shaped Navajo identity and attitudes, and we will close it with shared stories about grief and its many lessons for cultural survival and the continuance of traditional lifeways in a multireligious modern world. Today, the Navajo Nation is one of over 560 federally recognized tribes in the United States.[1] The Navajo Nation land comprises 27,000 square miles in the states of Arizona, New Mexico, and Utah. As such, it is the largest reservation in the United States. It is largely rural, with a population density of 7.1 persons per square mile.[2] It also comprises the second largest American Indian population, at approximately 290,000 enrolled members.[3] The 2000 median age for residents living on the reservation was twenty-four years.[4] In comparison, the median age of the U.S. population in 2000 was 35.3 years. In the last decades of the twentieth century, the population growth was approximately 1.84 percent for Navajo citizens living on the reservation and approximately 4 percent overall. The quest for jobs has caused many young Diné to move to nearby cities. This demographic shift has contributed significantly to lower population growth for Navajo residents on the land of Navajo Nation. Educational disparities impact the quest for jobs as well. For example, in 2000, 80.4 percent of the U.S. population over the age of twenty-five had a high school degree, and 24.40 percent had a bachelor's degree or higher. In contrast, 55.93 percent of the total population living on the Navajo Nation's homeland over the age of twenty-five had a high school degree, and 7.29 percent have a bachelor's degree or higher. Furthermore, 12.16 percent of the Navajo population is recorded to be without formal education. In comparison, 1.44 percent of the U.S. population is reported to be without formal schooling.[5] A lower level of education is considered a risk factor for a number of diseases and the potential for death because of its association with poor diet, lack of physical activity, and limited access to medical care.

The top public health priorities in 2008 were injuries, heart disease, cancer, diabetes, pneumonia and influenza, alcoholism, infectious diseases, and emergency/disease outbreak planning and preparedness.[6] Each category is present in Diné families and communities.

- Injury is a major concern for the Navajo Nation and includes motor vehicle accidents, homicide, and suicide.
- The diabetes rate among Diné is three times higher than the U.S. population and is increasing.
- Heart disease is a major concern because of the recognition that many Diné consume a high-fat diet; diabetes is a major concern and can contribute to heart disease and increasing obesity among this population.
- The cancer mortality rate is decreasing among the U.S. population but is increasing among the Diné.
- Death because of alcoholism is eight times higher than that of the U.S. population as a whole.

Additionally, the Diné population has had a lower per capita income and resided in fewer homes with phone service than the U.S. population.

Diné history comprises oral history and contemporary statistics that serve as reminders of the struggle that exists to achieve *hózhó*, the possibly most important guiding principle of Diné lifeways. Hózhó is a state of harmonic balance that includes happiness, sadness, and beauty. It affects our mental, spiritual, and physical well-being. Diné existence and the struggle to achieve hózhó against the perils of life are reflected in our creation stories and the strife our ancestors encountered and continue to encounter as we have developed as a people.[7]

It is said that our history in this world began after a passage through three previous worlds. First Man and First Woman imagined and sang into existence life-supportive elements of the fourth world, the world in which we live now. This was necessary to support not only themselves but the nonhuman beings who accompanied them from previous worlds and who had helped to make the passage into the fourth world possible. First Man, First Woman, and the nonhuman beings were accompanied by holy people. Through the contributions of the nonhuman beings, First Man and First Woman, and the holy people, passing into this world was made possible. The holy people established a viable lifeway for this world that promoted harmony through teachings of peace, serenity, and balance that supported coexistence with all of the earth's inhabitants.

First Man, First Woman, and the holy people created four sacred mountains to remind the people of the sacredness of life and of hózhó. In addition to symbolizing the cardinal directions, they also represent and are represented by sacred stones and their associated colors, and the cycle of life. Their importance is illustrated well by the description of the sun's path across the sky. For example, the daily sunrise represents the beginning of hózhó and life and is represented in pictorials as a white mountain, known as Sis Naajiní or Mt. Blanca, and is represented by a white shell. Spring is also represented by this sacred mountain. As the sun blazes across the south sky, it reaches toward Tsoodził, or Mt. Taylor in New Mexico. This sacred mountain is represented by the color blue and the blue turquoise stone. It represents the adolescent period of all living things and the summer season. The sun sets in the west, represented by Dook'o' ooslííd, or San Francisco Peaks in Northern Arizona, the color yellow, and symbolizes an adult maturity. The abalone shell represents this direction. The sun is believed to rest in the North. The sacred mountain is Dibé Ntsaa, or Mt. Hesperus, symbolized by the color black representing the night, when life must rest. As such, it also represents the elderly and the completion of life. The north also represents winter, and its stone is black jet.

It could be argued that these cardinal directions and their representation of Diné beliefs describes an indigenous respect for death but has also contributed to the stereotype that native peoples are not fearful of it as a natural part of life. This stereotype is described by Germans simply as being "ein Indianer"—that is, the dehumanizing notion that "an Indian feels no pain" and experiences the world in a state of harmony that is without strife. In contrast, the stories that accompany the shorter narratives of Diné creation stories indicate a more complex understanding of humankind's struggle with the knowledge that we will perish against our desire to live.

For example, before the creation of the fourth world and the sacred mountains and its associated colors, seasons, and life cycles, a proposal was made for life to continue without end. The first beings sought to ensure this through a ceremony that involved a piece of wood, water, and an anxious crowd. The proposal was that if a selected piece of wood did not sink when dropped into water during the ceremony, then life would continue without end, which is what the first beings in this world wanted.

Coyote, a trickster figure in Diné cosmology who is sometimes called "one who can do nothing right," contested the wisdom of this desire and action. Coyote argued that the earth would not be able to support an uncontrolled population nor have the area for enough cultivation to feed everyone. Coyote produced a stone, and subverting the words of First Man and First Woman, said that if the stone sank, life would need to end. In the midst of panicked protest and lunges to thwart his action, Coyote plopped the stone into the water and the cycle of life with birth, adolescence, adulthood, old age, and the afterlife that is known as death was established.

According to the Diné creation story, this world is perilous, and the potential for illness and death is great. For example, uncontrollable beings frequently described as "monsters" existed in the fourth world before the first humans arrived. These "monsters" were and continue to be things that can kill. Additional monsters, borne through the acts of the first humans against the holy people's prescribed teachings for living cooperatively in this world, ravaged the Diné and gravely threatened their existence in this world. Warrior Twins borne to Changing Woman, one of the holy people, eliminated most of the monsters. Those monsters that were permitted to remain supported the need for humankind to have some struggle to work continuously to improve their lives. Among the remaining monsters include Old Age, who provided a rationale for his life being spared. Old Age is reported to have explained that killing him would strengthen the desire to live forever, which would be in conflict with the order established by the holy people. It would likely result in there not being a need for future births. The first beings had become accustomed to the joy that new births brought and death had already become accepted as a necessity for the order of the world.

Changing Woman created more humans and organized them within distinct familial ties that became the four original clans. These clans are matrilineal and provide prohibitions to ensure the cooperation within the group, encourage genetic diversity, and provide support for the physical, mental, and spiritual health of the Diné.

The Diné homeland, known as Diné Bikéyah, encompasses an area the size of West Virginia and extends from Arizona into New Mexico and Utah. The geography of Diné Bikéyah includes the sparseness of the buttes and sandstone that is depicted in the background of the Coyote and Roadrunner cartoons spotted with brush and piñon trees, mountainous areas with tall pines, and canyon areas typified by photographs of Cañon de Chelly. Across this area, Diné have hunted game, gathered plants as food and medicine, and engaged in agricultural practices for both existing foods from the Americas and of introduced "Old World" foods. As a result, the Diné Nation developed an economy and wealth based on sheep and other livestock.

Modern Diné history includes the milestones of a forced march (known as the Long Walk) and the subsequent internment at Bosque Redondo in New Mexico (also known as Fort Sumner) from 1864 until 1868. In 1868, a treaty was ratified by the U.S. Congress to return the prisoners within the areas of the four sacred mountains. Warfare between the U.S. troops and the Diné before this march and the death from starvation and disease during the Long Walk forced many to deal with the difficulties in honoring the rites for the dead while under extraordinary duress.

Beginning in 1934, Diné witnessed a federal livestock reduction plan that included mass shootings of whole herds. The livestock reduction plan altered the economic foundation for the social, psychological, and physical people of the nation. In addition to the shootings, whole herds were removed without just compensation and sometimes resold to a non-Indian. who was then permitted to graze the sheep over the same land from which they had been taken originally.[8]

Yet another Diné history milestone includes participation in an elite Marine unit that coded and decoded messages during World War II. This group of Marines, known as the Code Talkers, saw firsthand the results of a war that involved great losses on both the Axis and Allied sides.

As an unintended outcome of post-World War II politics, the Cold War and the race for the development of nuclear weapons and the opportunities for uranium companies to make money created yet another milestone. Federal policies and uranium mining companies converged to exploit both Diné lands and its people in search of uranium ore. Systems to protect the miners were not put into place, nor were they informed of the risks of working with the hazardous ore. The small mines in which the men worked typically lacked lighting, ventilation, and supplies of water. The results of the manual labor and the explosive blastings without protective ventilation caused many to inhale harmful silica-laden dust and radon gas. Furthermore, miners lived their lives fully encapsulated within the uranium industry, eating their meals and drinking water from groundwater sources within the mines.

Showers were not provided, and workers brought their dirty clothes home with them into the realm of their family homes. Miners and some family members suffered from the exposure to radiation that manifested itself as cancer and emphysema, among other diseases.

Later, in an attempt towards justice for the uranium miners, the Radiation Exposure Compensation Act of 1990 was enacted. However, many Diné were deemed ineligible because their job had been as uranium millers, and this job was not included in the legislation. Miners and their survivors, too, had difficulty in receiving compensation because the questions associated with a claim, some of which centered on ceremonial tobacco use, nullified the claims.[9]

TRADITIONAL LIFEWAYS, THE NATIVE AMERICAN CHURCH (NAC), AND CHRISTIANITY: A HARD-WON COEXISTENCE

Today's ceremonial and spiritual responses to the departure of loved ones may include elements of multiple traditions. Every family and every individual family member may practice one or more religious tradition, mixing and matching practices, beliefs, and convictions as one may see fit. Traditional lifeways, as alive and vibrant as ever, coexist with Christian and NAC rites, prayers, and songs. Such frequent experience of coexistence is a profound expression of hózhó, but Diné did not arrive at this state without struggle. Christianity was first encountered as the religion of enslavement and abduction during the Spanish colonial era (1598–1750), when Catholic colonists attempted to subjugate the Pueblo peoples. The Diné resisted Spanish oppression and challenged their brutal treatment of the Pueblos; the Spanish responded by taking Diné as captives to enslave them. The first Spanish baptism of a captive Diné is recorded for the year 1705. The enslavement of Diné captives continued under Catholic Mexican rule, and thousands of slaves, men, women, and children, were traded with Protestant Anglo-Americans.

The genocidal policies that led to the forced march to Bosque Redondo and intentional murder and enslavement sanctioned by General James Carleton also included plans for conversion to Christianity and schooling in agriculture while in captivity; from a Euro-American perspective, Christianity and Western civilization were seen as synonymous. For the Diné, it meant the intentional destruction of their identity as a people. The first missionaries moving to the post-Bosque Redondo communities back in their homeland were Presbyterians, yet neither they nor other denominations could claim noteworthy success in competing with or eradicating traditional lifeways. A third religious change was brought about in the 1930s through the increasing visibility of the NAC, an indigenous religious practice with roots reaching thousands of years into the past that could successfully absorb new elements into its spiritual matrix, including Christianity. Initially, NAC split Diné communities into oftentimes hostile sections. It was a Diné Tribal Council act, passed in 1967, that affirmed the right of every Diné to freely choose and exercise their religious preferences and thus created a stronger foundation for peaceful religious coexistence. Nonetheless, NAC is still struggling to pursue its ceremonies freely because of the U.S. government's power to regulate the possession and use of peyote. As is illustrated in the stories below, Christian, traditionalist, and NAC practices are used in carefully synchronized fashion to assist families and communities in coping with grief and loss.

DODGING THE MONSTERS' BULLETS

Early federal policies about death and dying for American Indian peoples may have focused on the best way to achieve and hasten both. The infamous statement of Rep. James M. Cavanaugh (1823–1879), often attributed to General Philip Sheridan, "I have never seen in my life a good Indian ... except when I have seen a dead Indian," and Brigadier General Richard H. Pratt's (1840–1924) boarding school motto, "Kill the Indian, Save the Man," help to make this point. The impact of U.S. policies, geared toward the destruction of First Peoples sovereignty and culture, shapes the way American Indian peoples today navigate their lives against the starkness of historic trauma and destruction. One of the ways I had heard this expressed was through a statement by well-known artist Jaune Quick-To-See Smith (Salish, French-Cree, and Shoshone), shared with me by her son. Jaune Quick-To-See Smith is known to address a non-Indian group about her art by saying, "By all rights I should not be here with you today." This opening line is an acknowledgement that despite a history of federal policies intended to decimate or assimilate "the Indian," she has managed to find success. Her son, Neal Ambrose Smith, explains that in her work as an artist, she continually manages to dodge "her bullet," a potent symbol of what would stop not only her life, but also her work. Simply put, every Native person in the United States has a bullet with his or her name on it.

A CULTURAL FRAMEWORK FOR DINÉ GRIEF NARRATIVES

Resonating with Jaune Quick-To-See Smith's remarks, my people have a similar belief about the inevitable impact of destruction. In the traditional Diné way of thinking, there is little doubt that we will feel pain or perish from one of the afflictions that have been around since this particular stage of our world began. These afflictions include disease, hunger, and war. They represent forces of which we must be mindful as Diné because they impede our highest form of contentedness or hózhó. Hózhó represents the entirety of our notion of balance, happiness and sadness, and beauty. How these entities interact and our response as Diné to them is of great interest to me. It contributes to my own understanding of hózhó while dealing with the dying and death of Diné loved ones.

I approached relatives and friends to help provide clarification on Diné beliefs and to describe the task of writing this chapter. In at least one instance, it was received by "Why would you want to write about that (death and dying)?" Furthermore, "Why would you want to talk about the depths of our traditions when you know these things should not be shared with non-Indians?" The second answer is easiest to answer: I really do not have the most esoteric understanding of our spiritual traditions, and, as I have learned, many Diné do not. Furthermore, it is readily apparent that the Diné embrace religious and spiritual practices that originated in other cultures, such as Christianity. As a result, our contemporary belief systems include the ancient lifeways of our ancestors, the modern adaptation of these, and new non-Diné beliefs and practices. From a practical perspective and as a qualitative researcher and public health practitioner, I am both curious and concerned about what we chose to discuss in preparation for this chapter. I am also concerned about the impact on health outcomes when we are not thorough or inclusive in the descriptions of our culture.

With this in mind, I recognize that there will be criticism of this chapter because of the deeply held belief that we as Diné should avoid discussion about death and disease. Diné are taught to avoid talking about these topics to prevent any disease becoming overly familiar with the discussants or with those they care about. I recall hearing this as a reason for why we should not talk about diabetes and cancer and their great potential for causing death within Native communities. Growing up I heard, "Don't talk about that (disease) or you will cause it to happen." Similar direction was given whenever I would tease a family member about growing older and becoming bald or in having to wear glasses that would eventually become as thick as soda bottle bottoms. Criticism of my actions helped me to become more empathetic and supportive of friends and family who did become bald or, more seriously, suffered from a painful illness.

It is important to explore the core reasons why American Indians and Alaska natives have some of the greatest health disparities in the United States, many of which lead to death. This means that there are many bullets to which American Indians and Alaska natives are vulnerable. Frequently cited statistics give an overview of likely Indian killers. According to the U.S. Commission on Civil Rights, Native Americans are 770 percent more likely to die from alcoholism, 650 percent more likely to die from tuberculosis, 420 percent more likely to die from diabetes, 280 percent more likely to die from accidents, and 52 percent more likely to die from pneumonia or influenza than the rest of the United States.[10]

Thus, this chapter seeks to explore Diné experiences of bereavement and ritual practice from a Diné perspective that integrates contemporary realities. In doing so, I will use the format of storytelling and personal experiences, a technique that supports those engaged with end-of-life issues with empathy and compassion.[11] It has been my experience that sharing similar stories creates stronger connections with friends and family. The format of sharing stories allows for other stories with valuable coping wisdom to emerge, following the lead of the first story being told. It is not to say, however, that choosing this format to encourage increased connections and sharing will always be without challenge for cultural prohibitions about discussing death to come into play. The following scenario of working through tobacco-related mortality threats in American Indian communities will illustrate my point.

TOBACCO-RELATED MORTALITY THREATS: BREAKING THE TABOO

Roughly 40 percent of all deaths in American Indian and Alaska native communities are tobacco related.[12] As a public health practitioner and tobacco control advocate, I utilize storytelling to create a participatory narrative about how tobacco use creates addiction, disease, and death in indigenous communities. In doing so, I seek to challenge the common American Indian notion that we should not be critical of tobacco, which is considered a sacred plant, product, and industry, and the widely shared attitude that we should not talk about disease and death. I argue that not explicitly talking about how tobacco products create addiction within indigenous communities only keeps tobacco-related illnesses and death operating in our communities with disastrous effects.

Breaking the taboo was necessary to support the development of policies to protect community health. It allowed for the emergence of empowering narratives by utilizing historic and contemporary stereotypes of "the Indian" with irony and humor. I would ask groups to collectively create a list of what they would consider the most notorious Indian Killers.[13] The list would fill up with topics such as small pox blankets, the U.S. cavalry, Generals Custer and Sheridan, President Andrew Jackson (illustrated once by a participant holding up a U.S. twenty dollar bill), the white man, other Indians, and alcohol. Further questioning would broaden the list to include drugs (in general), methamphetamines, and additional emphases on alcohol. I would then ask for them to share stereotypes of "the Indian" that they had heard or were told to them that had "made them mad" and to explain why. Among those things that were upsetting were many of the standard depictions of "the Indian," which include: living in a tipi, making war whoops, and being or acting wild and savage-like. At least once, a participant said that one saying from his generation that people knew well and repeated often, especially in the racially conscious Southeast, was "the only good Indian is a dead Indian." Many of the stereotypes manifested on historic tobacco advertisements served to reinforce a demeaning tradition of the American Indian and depictions of other people of color. The resentment of past stereotyping and social injustice would turn into personal anger and frustration upon recognizing tobacco products their family had used and embraced. A certain somberness would settle in knowing that they had never, before then, really talked about it within their family or community. With this framework, it was possible to explore taboo topics, in this case sacred plant materials, disease, and death, and to have one person's story be the catalyst for other stories.

DINÉ FUNERAL PLANNING: CARING FOR THE BODY

The classic Diné prescription for a funeral comes from the holy people's actions. When Coyote dropped the stone into the water and it sank, it is described that that is where those who die will go. In this case, it is to the previous world that provided for a clear separation from people in this world.

Contact with a body was highly regulated and functioned to protect individuals and the community from illness or premature death. Only persons who were willing to accept the possibility of getting sick and were required to perform an internment participated in burial rites. The body would be dressed well in the clothes considered to be his or her finest and adorned with the jewelry and goods that would serve them when they returned to the previous world.

The body would be transported to an area where the burial would occur. Those supporting the burial rites would have typically kept their conversation minimal and their actions subdued and reserved. Once the body was buried, the shoveling tools were destroyed. The people who buried the body would then disguise their tracks or erase them with a brush to keep the spirit of the body from following the footprints back to their home in this world.

Before preservative mortuary practice, when the body needed to be buried soon after a death occurred, it was commonly the practice for the family to avoid eating until the body was interred. One public health effect was to reduce the potential for a contamination of food sources. The deceased's clothes would be burned, and the burial participants would purify themselves and then remain reserved, quiet, and without a bath or contact with water for four days of mourning after a death.

After the four days of mourning, Diné are instructed not to speak the deceased's name or recount her or his life. This helps the deceased's spirit to not be drawn back into our lives in this world, and it serves a practical purpose of forcing the living to attempt to proceed with their lives. These practices have their basis in our creation stories to inform Diné that specific practices must be observed, or a life-threatening event may occur.

Modern funeral practices include many of these elements. One informant reflected that during the period of preparation after her relative's death family meetings, planning for the funeral, remembering the individual in formal Christian wakes and Diné storytelling, and burial took place together. Contemporary Diné funeral planning is systematic and reinforced through repetition from close and extended family members' passing. A source commented that "sadly, it seems that by the time we have reached our twenties, we know the entire funeral planning drill from previous experiences. Within the last few years, we've lost my great-grandmother, my brother, my cousin, and two of my uncles."

Funeral planning includes convening family meetings to organize burial details and is an integral part of the grieving process. Preliminary tasks include identifying a site for the family meetings, which typically take place at family homes, and coordinating arrangements with the funeral home, local church, or community center for a wake and a service. Requests from family for food and monetary and firewood donations are also made to support these activities.

During these meetings, stories about the deceased are shared and are carefully moderated to preserve the dignity of the person who passed away and the people who experience grief. There is crying that can quickly change into laughter as an attempt to strike a balance between sadness and joy in recounting the deceased's life and contribution to our own lives.

Roles to support the funeral are delegated. One informant said that she would sometimes be charged with watching children while their mothers were busy preparing food and preparing the home or a central meeting place such as a community center or house for many visitors, all the while being supportive of the closest relative or relatives of the person who passed away. Another informant told me of how an adopted niece was the primary support for her aunt/mother when her uncle/father passed away.

Support for the service and the family meetings are demonstrated in different ways. Family members living a great distance from the deceased person's home area are asked specifically for monetary donations as their contribution to supporting the funeral activities when their physical labor is not available, although all who can provide money as well.

In addition to the Christian wakes and memorials that occur, the NAC has also been incorporated into Diné households. For example, blessings in a Diné NAC household include cedar needles and water. A man, using eagle feathers made into a fan, distributes smoke created from dried cedar needles being placed upon smoldering coals, towards the attendees as a group. Water is also dispensed from the tips of the fan on the attendees as a collective group. Individuals are invited to bless themselves using the cedar smoke.

A FAMILY GRIEF NARRATIVE SHARED

HIV/AIDS: A Constant State of Dying?

My uncle was a self-described misanthrope who died with his partner in an auto accident in 2002.[14] I had thought of him as a brother because he was only a year older. As a child, he was a hero of mine. He died just a few days before I got married. I reflected on what I heard about the strong bond between him and his partner. I wondered whether the two had discussed formalizing their commitment in any way and wanted to believe that he had found some peace and love.

In thinking of a contemporary Diné concept of death and dying, I frequently think of him and the family's reaction to his death. I feel that he often acted like a person in a state of dying. I had learned about this idea from speaking with a Nahuatl-speaking descendent who told me about how she believed that at the point of birth, we begin our process of dying and that both should be an obvious expectation. She said it helped her not fear death. My uncle had engaged in many life-threatening behaviors and could be self-destructive. The scars on his wrists were testament to the lengths he could go that were in strong contrast to his upbringing. He had been a Roman Catholic altar boy assisting in the celebration of Mass and was the son of a man who practiced a way of life that had been used by many to fight their addictions.

My uncle's bullet came in the form of an auto accident as he rode in the passenger seat with his partner after losing control in a curve. I tried to make sense of his death and the moment-by-moment process of his dying by obsessively trying to affix blame to the truck or to the negligence of someone, anything for me to have a reason to explain his death. His death was tragic because after much struggle, he was able to find a partner. Did they not sleep enough before going on the trip? Were they speeding? Was there a mechanical failure as the result of negligence?

Many Diné believe that disease and illness can be attributed to the breaking of a taboo. The cumulative result of actions that upset our hózhó can lead to death. We can correct this imbalance through either ceremonial or physical manipulation or a combination of both. In doing so, a Diné would be provided a clarifying lesson for future conduct describing how we should be within this world and how we should be inclusive in our relationship to others.

Here is a relatively current Diné example of a way to offset a series of missteps. I recently returned from a bus tour of the U.S. Southwest with a diverse group of people. Paved roads are somewhat bumpy and are not designed for travel by a bus with the rises and dips and curves in some places. In a rushed afternoon that included two meetings separated by over sixty miles of scrub brush, red earth, and many sheep and cows lining the roadway, this writer nearly perished with thirty distinguished colleagues. In our rush, we nearly careened out of control as the result of attempting too great a speed for a fifty-passenger bus over a bumpy reservation road negotiating between two curves. We had been told that it was possible to drive over the speed limit to get back on schedule. The speed limit was 55 and we attempted to go faster than this. After a hard bump and cursing among the bus driver and the two first rows, we insisted the operator reduce his speed to drive safely to our next destination. When we reached an official-looking sign that appeared to indicate that we had arrived, we drove triumphantly onto the parking lot of the local graveyard. Everyone on the bus seemed to have some kind of reaction to this: fear of sinking into the soft sand, appropriately fearful of driving off the parking lot and into the graveyard, and amusement.

We finally found our way to the meeting. At its conclusion, we were invited to another meeting ninety minutes away. This meeting was about to start and we were most likely to be late if we did not leave at that moment. With the sun setting, we drove the speed limit following another attendee to the meeting site.

When we arrived at the site, we found it quiet, dark, and abandoned. Thinking that the directions we received were wrong, we then tried to find the meeting by going to every major meeting site in town. We finally decided to call off our search after we gleefully walked into a meeting that turned out to be a funeral reception.

In short order, we were nearly in a bus accident, visited a graveyard, and then interrupted a funeral. On the bus were people, both Indian and non-Indian, who were very uncomfortable with the extent to which we came in close contact with the dead. The following day, our host was a Diné who, upon hearing about our near-death experiences, rolled a smoke, shared water, and then fanned us off to help correct our imbalance. Other Diné joined the host in singing corrective songs and used an eagle feather fan to disperse cedar smoke on everyone. Everybody joked about the predicament we had found ourselves in and the intent of his work to protect us from any negative effects of a near brush with death.

When my uncle died, I first wondered if alcohol, drugs, or a combination of both were contributors.[15] I wondered if we could have done anything to help him. In my experience with my family and among some Diné friends and colleagues, someone's poor health outcome is understood to be a result of not living correctly. Our family was trying to explore the "bullets" he tried to dodge that we knew about to help us understand his death. A complicating factor in our understanding his dying was his self-destructiveness, which colored our fondest memories. Obvious questions included whether he had the support of any mental health provider, whether he felt comfortable in seeking assistance, and whether he felt the need for any assistance. How did he reconcile his earlier attempt at suicide[16] with his Catholic upbringing? Complicating his living/dying was his sexual orientation and his admission that he was HIV-positive. This bullet is described in stark statistics by the Department of Health and Human Services: American Indians and Alaska natives ranked third in rates of new HIV/AIDS diagnosis.[17] Furthermore, among diagnosed persons suffering from AIDS, American Indians and Alaska natives have survived for a shorter time than other population groups. Socioeconomic disparities account for increased risks of infection, as does a lack of access to high-quality health care. During the time period of 1997 to 2000, more than 50 percent of American Indian and Alaska natives reported that they had not been tested for HIV/AIDS, often because of a concern for confidentiality.

Sixty-eight percent of diagnosed women became infected because of high-risk heterosexual contact, whereas sixty-one percent of diagnosed men contracted the disease through male-to-male sexual contact.

The bullet reaches even deeper, however. Traditionally, gender diversity was often considered a highly valued asset for Diné communities. For example, Hosteen Klah (1867–1937) was a famous *nádleeh* ("one who is transformed") who worked as highly skilled and respected medicine man and artist. The contemporary pan-Indian two-spirit movement works to reeducate native communities about preconquest traditions of respect for gender-diverse men and women and to strengthen spiritual aspects of gender diversity. It is also supporting AIDS/HIV testing in American Indian communities and the care of those suffering from the disease.[18] American Indian women and men do not only suffer disproportionately from HIV/AIDS infections, but they have a colonialist Euro-American fear and hatred of gender diversity that has also severely damaged the ability to appreciate and value the identity and contributions of two-spirit persons.

At my uncle's funeral and burial, I was a pallbearer for his casket. It is customary to bury a body and to spend money on a coffin. A Catholic mass was said primarily in English with some words spoken in Diné. At his burial and during the lowering of his casket into the ground, one of the pallbearers' straps slipped, and one end of the casket crashed crookedly to the ground. I wanted to help and purposely evoked the other side of my ancestry, which is Mississippi Choctaw, even though I know nothing about Choctaw taboos regarding burial practices. Fully aware that I was putting myself in danger, I built up the courage to jump into the hole and right the casket so we could proceed. I remember the gasps and shock of my aunts who could not believe what I was doing. However, I was pleased I could help my family support my uncle one last time. I was pleased, too, for my relatives who were unafraid to help me climb out.

In retrospect, I realize that I employed a common coping practice by seizing the moment to attempt to make up for the things I was not able to do for him before he died. I found some comfort in realizing that he died after finding peace and a partner, which I had hoped could help him avoid a violent death. I felt that he at least would not die alone were he to die from AIDS.[19] I wished that we could have provided more support to him. One of the lessons I have taken away from this experience is the belief that mental health services need to be both improved and increased to balance the loneliness and anguish someone with HIV/AIDS might experience.

CANCER: PREPARING FOR DEATH WITH DIGNITY

When my paternal grandmother died, and my dad passed away from cancer, I understood the causes and was witness to their dying.[20] My Grandma C. had cancer that developed in her bile ducts. It was almost expected that she would die from cancer because most of her siblings had died from it. Cancer was her family's bullet. Likewise, when my dad was diagnosed with esophageal cancer, my brother and I made sense of it by scouring the Internet and medical texts to understand its cause and his prognosis.

In contrast to my uncle's sudden death, when Grandma C. and Dad were dying, both shared and described to us their means of coping with their illness. Grandma was resigned to her dying from cancer. Dad spoke of what he intended to do when he was healed. In the months before she died, Grandma C. described what she wanted to see. She wanted to visit the Blue Ridge Mountains and drive along its Parkway to view the changing leaves. Grandma also wanted to have a family member come to help her with her transition in the same way she had helped her mother-in-law when she was dying. I never knew whether she got to see the Blue Ridge Mountains foliage, but I knew that she died in the hospital without the assistance she wanted. Because of this, it was important for me to support my dad when he was dying. Dad died a day before my mother's birthday in 1999 after a six-month fight with esophageal cancer. When he finally allowed himself to be diagnosed, his cancer was already at stage four and had metastasized in his bones. Like many men, he chose to ignore the possibility of a serious illness and chose to self-medicate the burning in his throat with sore-throat medication. It seemed Dad believed he could overcome cancer in the same way that he was able to beat pneumonia a decade earlier. When he told me about what he wanted to do when he got well, I listened and helped him flesh out his dreams by asking questions and suspending my belief to help him create his world of hope. At around this same time, my paternal grandfather, Grandpa S., was praying for Dad using his deep relationship with the NAC. As it turned out, the way of the NAC had been invoked by weekly offering prayers for the entire family.

When Dad died, I was alone with him and made the calls to my brother, Dad's father, and other family members to inform them of his passing. Shortly thereafter, I told my mother who returned from her errands. My brother's reaction to the news was to quiz me about whether I should have called the hospice nurse who could have helped save him. My mother's reaction was to bless his body with Holy Water she had received when a family friend priest had come earlier to pray with them both. The older folks, Dad's dad, a great aunt, and Dad's cousin appeared to simply accept the news.

Some years later, I came to better understand my Dad's strong belief and self-motivation. He was a skilled (and sometimes ham-handed) mechanic servicing his British cars and early twentieth-century motorcycles. I think of his skills as a mechanic as an ongoing testament to his belief that he could fix any and all problems himself. As a soldier in the Vietnam conflict, he faced critical life or death situations, which required him to believe in himself.

When my Uncle J., mom's sister's husband, also a Vietnam vet, heard that Dad had died, he came to the house and brought over a Pendleton blanket. He carefully wrapped Dad with it. It was during this moment that I started recognizing my fear of death while watching this man conduct this ritual. I thought about whether my mom should ultimately abandon the home, as had once been the Diné practice when someone died within it. I wondered if in helping with the ceremonial act, I should leave through the window, a practice explained to me about how people should abandon a home in which someone had died as had been a traditional practice when death occurred or, less dramatically, an infestation of lice made inhabitation impossible.[21] I wondered, too, if my recollection was correct. I realized that since the moment my Dad had died, I had not touched him, although I had recognized the importance of touch to others while a loved one is dying. I decided that I would help to carry Dad out of the bedroom and did so with my Uncle J. when the funeral service arrived.

LESSONS FROM OLD LODGE SKINS

Most recently, my paternal grandfather died. Grandpa C. was the first to have a deep discussion with me about death and dying, especially about the dignity of death. He was a farmer, livestock owner, and hunter. Grandpa C. had witnessed his father suffer from diabetes, which took his legs. He saw his first wife die after his only son was born, saw his son die, and then his brother, again from complications related to diabetes. He was also witness to death in war at Pearl Harbor. I had seen him kill pests and other animals for food. I had seen him kill his dogs when they had become injured and watched him grieve whenever he lost one to his own hand or to a car.

As a child, when I would visit over the summer, Grandpa C. and I would watch old movies. While watching the scene in *Little Big Man* where Old Lodge Skins prepares to die outside in the bitter cold of winter, he asked me if I thought I was strong enough to do that. I mentioned that being a Diné, I thought separating myself from my family to die a peaceful death in the woods would be preferable to dying at home. Grandpa C. explained to me that he understood that dying of extreme exposure to cold, if I could not will myself to die, would be very, very painful. He told me then that if he became too decrepit and burdensome, he would shoot himself. When he lost his leg to diabetes and later, when his health began to decline, I received a call from my brother that Grandpa's friends and he had removed the guns from his home. I wondered whether that was the best way to honor his wishes and his desire for autonomy. He died while hospitalized. He had prepared for his death by prepurchasing a service agreement with his cousin that included his removal, cremation, and funeral by setting aside money for the church service. His careful preparation seemed unusual. I saw this as a way for him to reassert his autonomy.

Of those who have died in my family, only my paternal grandparents had wills. It appears that the feeling among many Diné is that the probate process is the acceptable means for distributing property.

When my Navajo grandfather, Grandpa D., died, it came after a trip with him to arrange an NAC membership renewal for him and one of his sons and to secure firewood for an upcoming NAC meeting he was sponsoring.

I had just begun to document some of the stories he told and asked if he would let me record our conversations as we traveled to and from the Navajo Nation headquarters of Window Rock, Arizona. Grandpa told stories of his youth and of his cousins attending the Gallup Ceremonial. He spoke of their kindness in asserting their kinship by letting him ride their horses. He was going to school in Santa Fe, New Mexico, and had been away from his relatives. He talked about how people would camp in the area around Gallup, New Mexico, for the Ceremonial.

We stopped at his favorite café for what I saw was a ritual homecoming breakfast of western New Mexican "Mexican" food at a town near the Navajo Nation border. For lunch, we ate a mutton and fry bread sandwich at a food stand in Window Rock and later stopped for an ice cream milk shake.

Grandpa had diabetes. He told me he recently had his medication changed, which would permit him to indulge more frequently in foods he most wanted to eat. In fact, we had a very good time together enjoying foods we both loved. Two days later, he was hospitalized with a failing liver and signs that his other organs were beginning to fail.

Despite being eighty-eight years old and having had a very full life as an adventurer, Navajo Code Talker, NAC religious freedom advocate for the Navajo Nation, well-respected silversmith, and avid participant of the most ancient Navajo ceremonial activities as a child, he was not immediately resigned to die, nor were his family and friends ready either.

I am reminded of the version of our creation story where the first beings in the fourth world were not entirely convinced that death should be their fate, and many were angry with Coyote for being successful in his action and argument for why it is necessary. Likewise, my grandfather's friends and family include Diné and other Indian people and non-Indians who shared many of his values of ancient traditional beliefs, of the introduced NAC, of Catholicism, and of other Christian religions, and each were not ready for his death.

Grandpa died on his birthday. A wake was held, and a mass was said for him at the burial site. Clan relatives attended his funeral. His adopted children through the NAC and his blood children who believed in this way sang for him before his coffin was lowered into the earth. As part of our family meeting on our last night of mourning, we witnessed his eldest son lead an NAC song, something that at the time seemed incongruous because the youngest son had embraced these ways most completely.

CONCLUSION

Being a modern Diné means having relatives and Diné friends who embrace the rites of Mormons, Roman Catholics, Baptists, Bahai, Jews, and Buddhists, among others. We share similarities in negotiating our beliefs as Diné along with our other beliefs and practices and share an authentic connection as a result.

When the holy people began developing a framework for Diné to live in this world, it was in response to lessons learned from the collective journey from previous worlds into the one we reside today. From our creation stories, we are provided with a protocol for Diné supportive of those who are living and, thus, struggling to stay alive in a treacherous world where illness would be commonplace and death a certainty. Despite this order being established, this decision was not wholly embraced, and there was fear and uncertainty amongst them that have persisted until the present.

Although our symbolic representations of our lifeways include death as a certainty, I have met few vibrant and healthy people who embrace it. I recall a relative who was close to dying look me in my eye and exclaim in a hushed, boyish whimper, "I'm going to die" and then cry. He was not entirely sure what awaited him after he would pass. In contrast, I recall his wife being ready and wanting to die because of the pain from cancer and, I believe, from the prayers of her faithful Methodist church society reinforcing that the Kingdom of Heaven awaited her.

So despite the order being set, one could argue that the residual energy from those first fearful discussions about death remains and persists to the present. This fear and uncertainty must be especially complex for Diné Christians who may expect a heaven shared with their loved ones, but who recognize they may be without those who never embraced Christianity. Although Diné stories imply that we will return to the previous world, it is not a world easily accessible to modern people. Shared grief and shared knowledge about the causes of premature death build bridges across religious boundaries. Through working on this chapter, I have also found new connections within my family. I shared earlier drafts with an aunt who recently celebrated her forty-third birthday. She remarked that it was a timely piece because she had been thinking about her mother who died at the age she is now. My brother and I spoke about Dad and the letter he had never seen. We also talked about our shared memories of Grandpa C. We laughed about Grandpa C.'s opinion of Methodist funerals and his desire to see drama during the service. We spoke about new lessons in obligation from other cultures. I witnessed my German father-in-law binding his just-deceased mother's jaw with one of his scarves to set it in place before rigor mortis set in. Witnessing this made me think of it as a last act for a loved one and one that I would employ if possible.

Which brings me to share my perspectives on hózhó. My notion of hózhó is reached and maintained when I am being able to feel and experience fully the emotions of a person who is present. It is reached and maintained when I am able to function cooperatively with my friends and family. When I think of how it is expressed, I think it is expressed well during those times of mourning where we experience all these feelings and articulate them in stark contrast to one another. Outside of the context of grief work, my notion of hózhó remains the same, except that it is present with fewer relatives and friends than during times of shared grief, and the struggle is often job specific and related to stress. Being able to engage with my colleagues, friends, and family and being able to be open to their emotions, to be empathetic, and to be able to function well in all I do is hózhó.

One informant related that for her the awareness of death appears to be closely held as a reminder that our loved ones could perish at any time. Though this could be a cause for panic, it is also a stark reminder of the preciousness of our relationships. Through the process of sharing and reflecting on stories of how we cope, without dwelling on those who have passed beyond their lives in the fourth world, the authors have tried to navigate and negotiate a means for building bridges and improve the well-being of modern Diné. This practice, we believe, is affirming a tradition and teachings with which Diné can live more fully in this treacherous world.

NOTES

This chapter emerged from many conversations, phone calls, readings, and other research. Many people, past and present, near and far, have contributed to its content. Whenever the first pronoun (singular and plural) appears in the text, it is Lawrence Shorty's voice. Both authors dedicate the essay to the health and well-being of the Navajo Nation.

1. Also known as the "Navaho" and referred to by many within this tribe as Diné.

2. Evelyn Acothley, testimony, "Navajo Nation Public Health Priorities," Centers for Disease Control and Prevention Tribal Consultation (Atlanta, Georgia), February 28, 2008.

3. Ibid.

4. See 2002–2003 Comprehensive Economic Development Strategy of the Navajo Nation Report, http://www.navajobusiness.com/pdf/CEDS/CEDS%20 2002-03.pdf.

5. Ibid.

6. Evelyn Acothley, testimony, op. cit.

7. Different versions of the creation story exist. For example, the Navajo Curriculum Center in Rough Rock, Arizona, makes an important point about disagreements in regard to the specifics within the creation story with respect to the exact periods when events occurred, the number of worlds, and the

colors associated with them. See Ruth Roessel, *Navajo Growth and Culture II: Growth of the Navajos to 1960, Navajo Studies at Navajo Community College* (Many Farms, AZ: Navajo Community College Press, 1971).

8. See Ruth Roessel, op. cit., 15.

9. Maureen Schwarz provides an interesting analysis of how the displays of grief of the surviving miners contributed to an increased interest in and advocacy for justice for the Diné miners' claims. See Maureen Trudelle Schwarz, *Navajo Lifeways Contemporary Issues, Ancient Knowledge* (Norman: University of Oklahoma, 2001), 134–141.

10. U.S. Commission on Civil Rights, *Broken Promises: Evaluating the Native American Health Care System* 15 (2004).

11. See Robert E. Goss and Dennis Klass, *Dead but Not Lost: Grief Narratives in Religious Traditions* (Walnut Creek: Altamira Press), 2005.

12. Centers for Disease Control and Prevention, "Prevalence of Cigarette Use Among 14 Racial/Ethnic Populations, United States, 1999–2001," *Morbidity and Mortality Weekly Report* 53 (2004): 49–52. http://www.cdc.gov/ncipc/osp.indian/indians.htm.

13. Today's four major killers of Indians include heart disease, cancer, unintentional injury, and diabetes. See "American Indian and Alaska Native (Both Sexes, Males or Females) 1995–97, Ten Leading Causes of Death," http://www.cdc.gov/ncipc/osp.indian/indians.htm.

14. Mortality because of motor vehicle injuries among Diné is five times higher than the United States. See Evelyn Acothley, Testimony, "Navajo Nation Public Health Priorities," Centers for Disease Control and Prevention Tribal Consultation, Atlanta, GA. February 28, 2008.

15. Death because of alcoholism is eight times higher among Diné than the United States. See Evelyn Acothley, Navajo Nation Testimony, February 28, 2008.

16. Suicide among Navajo is 1.6 times higher than the United States. See Evelyn Acothley, Navajo Nation Testimony, February 28, 2008.

17. Department of Health and Human Services (updated report, August 2008).

18. See Brian Joseph Gilley, *Becoming Two-Spirit: Gay Identity and Social Acceptance in Indian Country* (Lincoln, NE: University of Nebraska Press), 2006.

19. Of persons who had received a diagnosis of AIDS during 1997–2004, American Indians and Alaska natives had survived for a shorter time than had Asians and Pacific Islanders, whites, or Hispanics. See Centers for Disease Control and Prevention, "HIV Fact Sheet, HIV/AIDS among American Indians and Alaska Natives," http://www.cdc.gov/hiv/resources/factsheets/PDF/aian.pdf.

20. Cancer is the second leading cause of death for AI/ANs nationally and the leading cause of death among Alaska natives. See Centers for Disease Control Report, http://www.cdc.gov/mmwr/preview/mmwrhtml/mm5230a4.htm, 704–7.

21. See Clyde Kluckhohn and Dorothea Leighton, *The Navajo* (Cambridge, MA: Harvard University, 1974), 89.

CHAPTER 10

Mourning in America: Civic Ritual, Public Remembrance, and Saving Grace

Stephen Johnson

It is often said that weddings and funerals are "the only times you see everybody together anymore." Most people would not think of missing them, so attending is something they "do religiously" even when the ceremonies are not officially religious. That old phrase means secular occasions or everyday practices not explicitly religious but taken as seriously. Whether solemn and sad like funeral home ceremonies or fun like tailgate parties before big sporting events, they are shared with fellow mourners or fans whose religious affiliations and beliefs are quite different from our own, or nonexistent. If fights erupt, they are not about religious diversity but about some old family feud, or another's treatment of the person who has died, or their having switched allegiance to the rival team, etc. Although anyone might privately merge personal religious beliefs or practices into the shared activity (praying for the dearly departed or their team's success), public funerals and sporting events in multicultural times and societies are essentially secular ceremonies.

Some such occasions are important civic rituals. The operationally "religious" nature of national holidays like Memorial Day, of political gatherings like conventions, and family celebrations like birthdays and anniversaries was shown by sociologists like Durkheim and Malinowski. They saw how it is through such special days and functions that the group's collective sense of self and purpose is celebrated and passed on. Thus, these occasions serve the nation or party like holy days, and liturgies serve officially religious communities. Similarly, it is at birthdays, anniversaries, weddings, and funerals that family origins, characters, and events are mostly recalled and learned.

This passing on of memories and traditions is essential to any group's identity and survival. Whatever official religions your kin may follow or have converted to, it is only when they no longer come even to weddings and funerals that you will have no meaningful family or clan left. Likewise, whatever official religions our fellow citizens may (or may not) follow, if ever the time comes when Americans no longer celebrate Memorial Day and the Fourth of July or reduce their observance to merely beer and fire-crackers, we will have lost national memory and identity.

Such insight forty years ago led American sociologist Robert Bellah to describe the importance of what he called "American Civil Religion." The discussion he began provides useful perspectives for the history and meaning of America's public dealings with death, disaster, mourning, and memorials. Because our first volume showed the development(s) of medicalized death and its unintended challenges to traditional responses, and our second volume explored multiplying issues of morality and meaning thereby involved, this volume has surveyed the ritual responses of religious traditions to bereavement and death. We close by reviewing America's "civil religious" responses to grief and loss, the challenges and occasions of public mourning and meaning shared by Americans of different (and no) religious affiliation.

For many, alas, the same 1960s that revealed to Bellah the critical potential of American civic tradition also began that tradition's loss of credibility. That echo of Lucy Bregman's introduction to this anthology is no coincidence. Previewing the consequences of dying's "medicalization," she stressed that one "very un-nostalgic fact about 'traditional' vs. 'modern' dying is that the demographics [are] utterly different." Relevant demographics in the area of "civil religion" and public mourning relate to the political and cultural empowerment of American minorities. Recent decades have seen more people than ever identifying not primarily (or at all) as Americans but as members of their ethnic or other groups. This tendency, compounded by speedily growing numbers who self-identify as "not religious, but spiritual," challenges America's explicit religious communities *and* our traditional civic ways of ritualizing loss. In the realm of public meaning and mourning, too, although not totally, older practices have "disappeared massively—and fast."[1]

Our capacities for responding to any changes in American death and dying depend importantly on whether and how "we" survive as a national community. Whatever one's politics, that is a huge challenge in our multi-religious, multiethnic, multiracial, multigendered, multi-life-styled twenty-first century. Sharing the physical land and social setting whose smaller group and individual dynamics seem increasingly centrifugal, postmodern varieties of attending (or ignoring) public mourning and civic rituals impact us all and our neighbors—citizen or visitor, native or immigrant, religious or otherwise.

AMERICAN CIVIC TRADITION

Bellah showed how understanding traditional religious communities sheds light on the dynamics of America's national history and identity. Amid the turmoil and hopes of the 1960s, he meant to highlight the best of the cultural inheritance of Americans, something deeper than the smug materialism and triumphalism Will Herberg had decried a dozen years earlier in *Protestant, Catholic, Jew*. Although sharing the lament about the shallow American way-of-life-ism that Herberg called our unacknowledged "fourth religion," Bellah saw the saving silver lining. He showed how Americans had inherited and still shared a deep core of nondenominational ideals and commitments. It was their official and everyday faith in these ideals and shared commitment to key ways of collectively working toward them that had enabled Americans to function as a multireligious nation. This is very important because otherwise, our history might have replicated old Europe's endless religious wars.

Bellah saw that the ideals proclaimed in the nation's founding documents and echoed in presidential inaugural speeches were historically drawn from Judaism, Christianity, and eighteenth-century Deism but were identical with none of them. Thus, when American presidents speaking in their public role mentioned God (which was not often), they did so in ways that traditional church goers and deists could share. Hardy skeptics had no problem with presidential inaugurals referencing the "Hand that shapes the universe," an "overruling Providence," or other open-ended ways of naming "God." Most church and synagogue goers heartily affirmed the exceptional role given America by that divine providence, adding that American exceptionalism was subject to God's judgment. Swearing "before you and Almighty God the same solemn oath our forebears prescribed," John F. Kennedy's memorable inaugural was very traditional in nondenominationally asking "His blessing and His help, but knowing that here on earth God's work must truly be our own." That theme and spirit of our individual and collective obligation had run deep as any in our civic tradition, as had JFK's open-ended way of referencing the deity.

"Our forebears" had prescribed oath, ideals, and pursuit of them via separation of governmental powers, no established religion, constitutionally guaranteed individual freedoms, etc. For all their personal hypocrisies and later governmental self-contradictions, Bellah pointed out that founding words and ideals like Jefferson's remained hard to twist into support of slavery and inequality.[2] This made them powerful for Lincoln's use in 1863 and, a century later, for Martin Luther King Jr.

Bellah's preliminary 1967 sketch could be easily filled out by anyone with wit and rudimentary knowledge of Jewish and Christian religions. "Founding fathers" like Jefferson, John Adams, and Patrick Henry were the new nation's early prophets, whose better voices still resonate. As Torah

and Bible served Judaism and Christianity, so have the Declaration of Independence and the Constitution (and amendments) served this country,
guiding our later development. The preamble to the former provided the
nation its best "prophetic" ideals, the provisions of the latter its basic "law"
(norms for all particular laws). As traditional religions have their saints
and martyrs, so too does American civic tradition.[3] As traditional religions
have their sacred places and memorials of their beginnings and key events,
so American civil religion has its sacred monuments and shrines. As the
holy days of traditional religions are their sacred times, powerful for ritually sharing mythic memories and meaning, so for Americans are their
great public holidays and memorials.

As traditional religions employ special liturgical discourse, sing holy
songs, and perform particular rituals, so American civic tradition speaks in
secular ceremonial ways, sings the national anthem and other patriotic
songs, and prescribes precise ways for properly handling the flag. As traditional religions reverently handle and gaze upon saintly relics or other holy
objects, Americans respond "religiously" to the Liberty Bell, original copies
of the Constitution, and other secular holy objects. As traditional religions
stress the religious education of their adherents and obligations, traditional
civil religion pledged allegiance to the flag in public school classrooms
where national history and "civics" were taught, stressing such citizen obligations as voting. As surely as traditional religious communities ritually
grieve their disasters and mourn their departed, so too have Americans of
multiple and no religious affiliation gathered together for public mourning
while remembering and reaffirming communal meaning and resolve.

From Protestant, Catholic, and Jewish pulpits, throughout the rebellion,
"General Washington" was prayerfully proclaimed as "our Moses." This
made stirring sense in biblically steeped colonies picturing their defiant
secession from the British Empire as like the Israelites' exodus from Egypt.
(Having militarily succeeded, Washington shocked the rest of the world
by retiring to Mt. Vernon. That did not last because he was called back to
chair the 1787 Constitutional Convention.) Astonished at their success,
the founding fathers considered adopting as their national seal the image
of Moses parting the Red Sea or the wandering of the Israelites in the de-
sert. Their eventual choice of a Masonic divinely eyed pyramid with the
Latin "New Order of the Ages" showed how their civic faith and mood
were more humanistic and rational than Catholic or Protestant founders
would have allowed and way more optimistic than sober rationalists should
have been in "reading" America and Americans as God's newly "chosen
people" and land.

Besides combining biblical with deist imagery for their new national
life, they produced a basic governance document that thirteen very different states could all agree to. The resultant Constitution was inevitably a
compromise formation and a very different document from the Declaration

of Independence. The Declaration's Preamble had flung to world and heavens the new Enlightenment ideals of "nature's God," by whom "all men are created equal" and, therefore, possessed of such "inalienable rights" as "life, liberty, and the pursuit of happiness." Void of all such idealistic rhetoric, the Constitution simply (but enduringly) laid out a "law of the land" as the best foundational procedures they could agree on for beginning to live together. Although we are thankful that they provided for later amending the Constitution, they were thankful Washington was available to become the first president. Neither they nor the general populace could imagine or agree on anyone else to carry such symbolic weight and set such enormous presidential precedents, which he did for two terms, then once again retired to his plantation.

CIVIC DEATH, REBIRTH, AND GETTYSBURG

In the last month of the last year of the eighteenth century, Philadelphia (still the national capital) heard of George Washington's death. First Lady Abigail Adams canceled her regular receptions, asking that black gloves be worn by ladies thereafter attending. The Senate wore black for its remaining sessions, and bells tolled every day.[4] Ten days later, a slow military procession through the city's brick streets honored their country's "Father" (whose political heritage was being torn apart by their emerging political parties, about to wage one of the country's dirtiest presidential elections).

Although political fragmentation continued, American religious groups flourished, energetically joining hands with enlightenment-guided civic reform movements back east while evangelically harvesting the expanding west with raucous revivalism and camp meetings. By the 1850s, though, reform optimism had dissipated. The expanding nation's many sectional issues, increasingly glued to hardening contradictory commitments about the morality of slavery and the legality of secession, could no longer be politically compromised. Therefore, national faith, identity, and political union shattered, with northern Unionists and southern Secessionists both laying full claim to Washington as their nation's Father and to the Declaration and Constitution as their guides. In effect, they went to civic-religious war over the meaning of their national scriptures.

Seeing themselves as fighting "the Second American Revolution" (against a tyrannous North's "War *Against* the States"), Southerners were as sure as Northerners that God was on their side. Unlike all other politicians (and all but two theologians), Abraham Lincoln saw the war as divine judgment on *both* sides because all had long been accomplices to the sins of outsized states' rights and human slavery. Taking the Bible as seriously as he took organized religion lightly, the president saw nothing unrighteous about a divine judgment that would end up costing more

American blood than all the nation's wars before and since combined. Although the war still raged, its conclusion very much up for grabs, this president used an intended partisan occasion to transcend sides and teach a suffering nation how to mourn.

Not the featured speaker but invited to add a "few appropriate remarks" at Gettysburg, Lincoln powerfully honored the Union soldiers killed there months earlier, consoling their survivors *and* reinforcing those still fighting the war by transforming the meaning of their sacrifice. In elevated language ("Four score and seven years ago" rather than a prosaic "eighty-seven"), he invoked not "delegates" to the Constitutional Convention or their "documents" but rather "our fathers," who had "brought forth" a "new nation, conceived in liberty and dedicated to the proposition that all men are created equal." By the end of his second sentence, the Civil War was dedicated to testing whether "that nation or any nation so conceived" can long endure. Although he came to dedicate a "final resting place for those who here gave their lives that that nation might live," he said we cannot consecrate what they already had by their struggle and death. "It is for us the living rather to be dedicated here—to the unfinished work which they who fought here have thus far so nobly advanced. . . . that from these honored dead we take increased devotion to that cause for which they gave the last full measure of devotion. . . . that this nation under God shall have a new birth of freedom."

Without uttering the words "reunion" or "slavery," he enhanced need of the first while more clearly than ever committing the latter to ultimate extinction. He concluded national dedication to this "new birth of freedom" by recalling America to become what the Bible would have called "a light unto the nations," but Lincoln cast in terms of civic faith commandment "that government of the people, by the people, for the people shall not perish from the earth."

Taking him as seriously as he took the ideals of the founders and the "the brave men living and dead who struggled here" meant raising the nation's commitments.

The *fact* of the July 1 to 3 military victory at Gettysburg, combined with Grant's finally taking Vicksburg that same July 4, mortally wounded the cause of secession. The *meaning* of Gettysburg as memorialized on-site that November 19 effectively guaranteed the death of legal slavery while rhetorically renewing higher ideals of national unity. "Everyone in that vast throng" departed with the "new constitution Lincoln had substituted for the one they brought there with them." They walked "into a different America" (whose thirteenth, fourteenth, fifteenth, and nineteenth amendments were now implied), into a wholly different future.[5] Only after the war, as Shelby Foote observed, did Americans start referring to the United States as a singular entity (instead of, in British fashion, "the United States *are* . . .").

This was and would remain hugely important. Mourning rituals traditionally get the community through their loss by ritually absorbing the departed into the community's lasting meaning and identity. Lincoln raised the felt civic sacredness of the war (and of the federal casualties) by *changing* the Union's (and ultimately the nation's) very meaning and identity. Like the slow evolution of explicit religious traditions, this national process would prove a long struggle. A full century later, Lincoln's use of the Declaration's prophetic ideals to effectively transform the federal cause would need a later prophet's powerful reinvocation to further that transformation. However, that lasting power of Lincoln's civil religious rhetoric and memorial dedication made him the preeminent prophet of American meaning and community.

Therefore, Gettysburg, the physical land, became secular holy ground, a sacred shrine of American civil religion. As with explicit religion's holy days and places, American memorial holidays and consecrated places are power times and spaces. They are powerful for head-and-heart *representing* (getting deeply "in touch with" *now*) Gettysburg *the event's* mythic meaning. On its battle fields and through its cemetery's dedication by Lincoln, the promise(s) of America began to be redeemed. Despite later regression and repressions, the nation was firmly redirected in pilgrimage toward extending equality and broadening inclusiveness.

However, his small part of one day's much larger ceremony also reflected what countless Americans everywhere do whenever, in churches, funeral homes, or public squares, they pledge themselves to carrying on the departed's values, carrying on "her" exemplary work, embodying "his" spirit in our lives. This common function of grieving rituals calls us to absorb the best qualities or commitments of the loved and lost as our best tribute to them, the most helpful way of assimilating their loss while enabling our own moving on. Properly mourning the dark nights of their passing prepares us to rise to our mornings after.

Also universal is any tribe or nation's lamenting while praising the "heroic" deeds and dying of their warriors and heroes. Memorial gratitude and praise of those "who died for us" is powerful and common because, like weddings, funerals and mourning bind us together—to the lost ones we mourn, to each other, and to our gods. When the mourning of the lost coincides with celebration of their/our victory, memorial naturally tends to triumphalism, boastfully self-congratulating "our" collective selves and proud call to carry on. In earlier history, however, such triumphalism was always of a tribal or ethnic (or religiously "chosen") people. It is here that authentic American civic tradition differed, as did Lincoln's rebirthing of it.

Already from colonial days multiethnic and multireligious, the "we" Americans were called to become could only be those born into or entering its historical meaning, committing to its civic ideals and constitutional ways. The founders created a civic tradition powerful enough to bind multicultural descendants as a people, with ideals and practices that *could* even empower collective self-correction of their worst practices. "For better and for worse" (the worse too often painfully slow in getting made better), Lincoln's recreative civic mourning leading the way, it has so far worked.

Eighteen months after the Gettysburg Address, on Good Friday of 1865, just five days after Robert E. Lee's surrender, Lincoln was assassinated. The following Wednesday, April 19, final services were held in the East Room of the White House, where his body had been lying in state, the coffin on a flower-covered catafalque. Six hundred Washington officials were there, with General Grant only one of many openly weeping. After four ministers had spoken and prayed, the casket was closed and then carried out by twelve veteran corps sergeants. Church bells tolling and bands playing slow, the funeral procession went up Pennsylvania Avenue, a detachment of black troops leading the way. Right behind the casket carriage, in the way that would too often be repeated (most memorably for my generation with JFK), the first assassinated president's boots sat eerily empty in the stirrups of his riderless horse. Columns of mourners followed, then battalions and regiments with arms reversed, then wounded soldiers, followed by 4,000 black citizens in neatly ordered lines of forty, curb to curb, dressed in dark coats and shiny white gloves, clasping hands and quiet. Arrived at the Capitol, Lincoln lay in state on another catafalque. All the paintings and statues round him were covered, save for George Washington's, which bore a black sash. The rest of that day and the next, thousands of people poured through to pay their last respects.

Then, April 21, his nine-car funeral train began the roundabout two-week journey that would carry Lincoln back to Springfield, Illinois. As their descendents would do for Franklin Delano Roosevelt eighty years later, people gathered by the tracks all along the route, silently watching their dead president's train carry him home. There, after yet another city's hours of ceremony and citizens passing by, "Father Abraham" was buried. At his gravesite was birthed a new tradition that has ever since grown, as countless Americans laid bouquets of flowers.[6]

Ralph Waldo Emerson eulogized the slain Lincoln as the only American comparable with George Washington. Politically guiding and holding together the federal side during that war (at the price of being the most hated politician even in the North), successfully transforming the meaning of the war's horrors and suffering, Lincoln midwived the nation's resurrection. Dying as and when he did prevented his overseeing the country's reunification but magnified his symbolic stature. If Washington had been creative Father in the country's mythic memory, Lincoln became its redeemer Son. His faith and works saved the country, leaving behind its spirit to become more truly united and equal. Thus, Christian redemptive death and resurrection symbolism entered American civic tradition's story.

Lincoln became what literary types call a "Christ figure," and his Gettysburg Address became the start of national "New Testament" writing, built on the civic "Old Testament" of the founders.

MEMORIAL DAY AS CLASSIC PUBLIC MOURNING

Meanwhile, more than six hundred thousand Americans had been killed. Besides the many needing burial or long search and reburial, all needed to be remembered. Therefore, Americans created Memorial Day, originally called Decoration Day. Northern historical credit for ordering its widespread observance on May 30, 1868, goes to the Grand Army of the Republic's General John A. Logan. However, the practice of decorating the graves and memorializing the Civil War fallen had started earlier. The very first such public ritualizing may well have been carried out in South Carolina. On May 1, 1865, Charleston's African-American community, protected by a full brigade of Union infantry including three regiments of U.S. Colored Troops, honored the federal dead with flowers, processions, and oratory.[7]

Throughout the Southern and border states, though, many of the bodies lay anonymously, very casually or not at all buried—and sometimes abused by locals still resentful of dead enemies. Except for the ancient republic of Athens, as James Russeling argued, no people or nation had ever designated a burial place for the common soldier, but surely the United States, newly dedicated to the proposition of human equality, should lead the way. Because "*dulce et decorum est pro patria mori* is a good sentiment for soldiers to fight and die by," the government should honor not only generals but "reciprocate that sentiment by tenderly collecting, and nobly caring for, the remains of [all] those who in our greatest war have fought and died to rescue and perpetuate the liberties of us all."[8] Propelled by Russeling's and Clara Barton's arguments, by the heroic efforts of Edmund B. Whitman, and fully approving the sentiment that "it's fitting and sweet to die for your country", the federal government took over the discovery, return, and proper reburial of its veterans, including those who remained nameless. This "program's extensiveness, its cost, its location in national rather than state government, and its connection with the most personal dimensions of individuals' lives all would have been unimaginable before the war and their mourners, who would change the very definition of the nation and its obligations."[9]

The ill-buried Confederates got no such attention from the national government their survivors had, by losing, been forced to rejoin. They had to privately find and reclaim their men's bodies from Gettysburg and from all the Southern and border states where they lay. When the 1866 National Cemeteries Act prohibited those new cemeteries' reception of Confederate dead, the Southern women who had lost those men took it upon themselves. Beginning on May 3, 1866, Richmond women accepted the challenge of caring for the thousands who lay neglected in the city's Hollywood and Oakwood cemeteries, and the tens of thousands more still scattered on the battlefields surrounding the city. Private donations were supplemented with contributions from legislatures of other Southern states, so many of whose soldiers lay in Virginia soil. Similar "Ladies Associations" in other defeated states did likewise, and their legislatures and local governments supported the cemeteries and (eventually) monuments in those cemeteries and town squares where Southern "Decoration Day" would be celebrated.

Dozens of cities and towns (North and South) claim to have invented Decoration Day, but as Drew Gilpin Faust tells us, the observances "seem instead to have grown up largely independently and, for at least half a century after the Civil War, to have continued to reflect persisting sectional divisions among both the living and the dead." In the South, the day's ceremonies featured flowers and flowery rhetoric praising the beauty of "sacrificial valor." However, Northern ceremonies were already reciting Lincoln's words while celebrating the victory of their sacrifices. In the South, where all the cost and labor of reburial and memorial was of, by, and for the people, white celebrations were nurturing "lost cause" sentiments of "defeated valor." For several decades, then, honoring Confederate dead overlapped with remembering and honoring the principles for which they had fought. In the 1890s, of course, some of those principles became legally established in the Southern system of legally forced segregation. The powers of civic mourning and memorial remained always powerful, although not always for the good. Not until World War I did the Southern states join the rest of the United States in sharing one national Memorial Day.[10]

Decoration/Memorial Day observances had most easily retained their original power where towns still had Civil War veterans to physically represent the war and its cost. By the time those survivors reached more natural deaths, later wars were adding new martyrs, memories, and veterans to spur grateful mourning and somber recollection. World War I replenished the supply of (now nationally united and victorious) veterans. Although that war's mechanized and gas warfare horrors led poet Wilfred Owens and others to reject valorous death for country as "the Old Lie," for most, it firmly established Memorial Day as *the* day for ritually enfolding the local community into grateful (and national) remembrance of all those who have given "the last full measure of devotion" in serving their country.

And so it remained through World War II, the Korean War, and into the early 1960s. Memorial Day observances flourished in cities and especially towns across the country, where four stages of civic memorial rituals were typically involved. First came the differently timed and placed memorial events held by all the separate local organizations throughout the year. Next, in the several weeks, all these groups of immediate preparations for Memorial Day weekend, building toward climax with the "scores of rituals held in all the cemeteries, churches, and halls of the associations" on that Saturday and Sunday. On Memorial Day itself, "all the separate celebrants would gather in the center of the business district [or town square] on the afternoon of Memorial Day. The separate organizations, with their members in uniform or with fitting insignia, would then march through the town, visit the shrines and monuments of the hero dead, and, finally, enter the cemetery. Here dozens of ceremonies are held, most of them highly symbolic and formalized," their rhetoric and rituals continually stressing "devotion in following the ideals of Washington and Lincoln and the Unknown Soldier." Sacrifice for one's country and Lincoln were repeatedly referred to "and the Gettysburg Address recited."[11]

Those were the days, of course, when public (and most private and parochial) schools began classes with the pledge of allegiance, and students (who were taught American history and civics) quite regularly memorized Lincoln's address. Thus, the first half of the twentieth century was what might be called the high tide of American civil religion's routine practice. Stadiums full of people would belt out the national anthem as lustily as in church they did their best hymns. Schools held ceremonies for Washington's and Lincoln's still-separate birthdays.[12] On the plus side, this included popular ethnic and religious buying into the "melting pot" goal of national family that enabled the massive civilian pulling together effort(s) of World War II. The negative side included quiet but large-scale forgetting by many immigrant families of their distinctive heritage; the entire nation's accepting, since its 1890s institution, Southern re-subordinating of African Americans via *de jure* segregation; and massive Northern racism and *de facto* ghetto-izing.[13]

Return home of "the greatest generation" to such ironic divisiveness after winning "the good war" against German and Japanese racist nationalisms planted seeds for American conversion. The 1950s "silent generation" started sympathizing with and even joining Southern blacks' (law-breaking) civil rights protest movement. By the mid-1960s, this righteous challenge to domestic self-righteousness expanded into simultaneous protest against the Vietnam War, eventually to the point that a foreign war still in progress became opposed by a majority of the folks back home. Aided by the postwar spread of television, the emerging political and cultural empowerment of America's many minorities challenged American civic life's most hypocritical domestic failure (racism) and civil religion's chronically weakest point (the temptation to foreign policy imperialism).

CIVIC CONVERSION, MARTYRS, AND MOURNING IN THE 1960s

Every historical religion has been and remains variously embodied (and its meaning fiercely fought over) by quite different followers, and so has

American civic faith and practice.[14] All of this is tough, exhausting, and sometimes scary. That is why it still includes Lincoln's Gettysburg use of the Declaration's prophetic ideals. Long the centerpiece of classic Memorial Day rituals, the Gettysburg Address could in its turn function prophetically, as its reinvocation by Martin Luther King Jr. showed. He began *his* most famous ("I have a dream") speech in front of the Lincoln Memorial, "Five score years ago, a great American, in whose symbolic shadow we stand, signed the Emancipation Proclamation."[15] He then persuasively interwove traditional American civic rhetoric with biblical discourse to spotlight and expose the contradiction between the claims of egalitarian American identity and the segregated identities of Southern practice. Segregationists could resist King's prophetic call with violent repression of self and others (and "priestly" blessings from their religious and local civic officials), but they could not ignore him. King compelled serious response because he invoked cherished American and biblical words against their Southern distortion. He presented the nation with the yet-uncashed "promissory note" of its best civic ideals. Through his powerful presentation, the Declaration's proclamation of all men's equality and the national motto "*e pluribus, unum*" once again empowered the forward march of inclusiveness over oppression in the *name* of America.[16]

Despite JFK's assassination that fall, the gathering momentum of the civil rights movement thus climaxed by King and others (plus LBJ's skilled handling of Congress) soon produced the 1964 Civil Rights and 1965 Voting Rights Acts that legally finished the South's *de jure* American apartheid. Too many years after his own assassination, King would deservedly join the official roll of American martyr saints by becoming the first African-American honored with his own federal holiday. Even as this essay is written, work has not yet begun on his monument for the Capitol mall. His first major memorial outside of Atlanta, it will stand on the banks of the Tidal Basin, between the Jefferson and Lincoln memorials. Like theirs, King's will feature his famous quotes engraved in stone walls, around a raised walkway and Lei Yixin's twenty-eight-foot "Stone of Hope" granite sculpture.

The assassinations of JFK in 1963 and of King in 1968 shook America, the more so because both were young, inspiring leaders seeming to move the country in better directions. National depth of shock was evident in the intensity of public mourning then and powerful recall ever after. Shot in Dallas on Friday, November 22, Kennedy's body was flown back to Washington on Saturday. Only after his casket was placed in the East Room, now draped with black crepe, did Jacqueline Kennedy, still wearing her blood-stained strawberry suit from the previous day's motorcade, leave her husband's side. While his casket lay where Lincoln's had, on the same catafalque used for the Arlington burials of the World War II and Korean War Unknown Soldiers, she reviewed a book about the aftermath of Lincoln's assassination and consulted with staff about arrangements.

On Sunday, the dead president's coffin was carried to the Capitol on the same horse-drawn caisson used for FDR's funeral. Three hundred thousand people lined Pennsylvania Avenue, but the only sounds were muffled drums and horses' hooves. For eighteen hours, a quarter million people, some of whom had waited ten hours in near-freezing temperatures, passed through the Rotunda to view the closed casket. On Monday, the official national day of mourning, a million people lined the route of the funeral procession, from the Capitol back to the White House, thence to St. Matthew's Cathedral for Mass, and finally to Arlington National cemetery. Thanks to television, many millions of Americans watched it all, long remembering Mrs. Kennedy's composure as she joined Robert and Edward Kennedy in leading the procession on foot to St. Matthew's, a route she had often walked with her husband. All the music, including "Hail to the Chief," was played at dirge-like pace.

Instead of a eulogy at the Mass, Bishop Hannan read several of Kennedy's addresses, including his entire inaugural. Only during Schubert's "Ave Maria" did Mrs. Kennedy sob. After the casket had been carried back outside to the caisson, she whispered to three-year-old John Jr., who saluted his father's coffin. Caught on camera, that moment (the children's final farewell) is still remembered. The procession passed the Lincoln Memorial, crossed the Potomac, and climbed up to Arlington for the burial, where the widow lit an "eternal flame."

Four and a half years later, spring of 1968, Martin Luther King was assassinated. Working to broaden the civil rights movement into a poor people's campaign, he had come to Memphis where, the day before, he had delivered his "I've been to the mountaintop" speech. He was shot the evening of April 4. Five days later, two services were held in Atlanta. The first, at Ebenezer Baptist Church (capacity thirteen hundred), was limited to family, friends, and dignitaries foreign and domestic. They all had trouble getting in, so great was the crowd around the church. Inside, the open casket was flanked by a cross of white chrysanthemums and lilies. Besides the eulogies, at Coretta Scott King's request, the service included a taped recording of the sermon in which Dr. King had described the simple funeral he (would have) preferred.

From Ebenezer, King's casket was carried three-plus miles through Atlanta to Morehouse College, in whose quadrangle the public ceremony would be held. As many as a hundred thousand people viewed or marched in the procession. The casket was carried on a farm wagon pulled by two mules, and several of Dr. King's aides had changed into farmer and laborer clothes for the procession. The segregationist governor had refused to declare a day of mourning (and had stationed state police to "protect" the statehouse), but the silent procession passed by the capitol entirely peacefully. Jesse Jackson carried the United Nations flag, and bystanders occasionally sang freedom songs. After the service and further eulogies at

Morehouse, the casket was carried by hearse to South View Cemetery, founded in 1866 by former slaves.[17]

The night King was shot, Robert Kennedy had been informed of the tragedy upon arriving in Indianapolis for a Democratic presidential primary appearance. Although advised not to, he went to the planned campaign rally site, whose large African-American crowd did not yet know of the tragedy. Kennedy broke the "sad news for all of you, and I think sad news for all of our fellow citizens." Instead of his prepared speech, he shared feelings:

> In this difficult day, in this difficult time for the United States, it's perhaps well to ask what kind of nation we are and what direction we want to move in. . . . For those of you who are black and are tempted to be filled with hatred and mistrust of the injustice of such an act, against all white people, I would only say that I can also feel in my own heart the same kind of feeling. I had a member of my family killed, but he was killed by a white man. . . . What we need in the United States is not division. . . . We will have difficult times in the future. It is not the end of violence; it is not the end of lawlessness; and it's not the end of disorder. But the vast majority of white people and the vast majority of black people in this country want to live together. . . . Let us dedicate ourselves to that, and say a prayer for our country and for our people.[18]

There was no violence that night in Indianapolis.

Two months later, the evening of June 5, Senator Robert Kennedy was assassinated in Los Angeles. As with Dr. King and his own brother, television brought the nation to the site of the shooting and to the days that followed. As he had for JFK, President Johnson ordered a national day of mourning for RFK. After June 8 Mass at St. Patrick's Cathedral in New York City, the body was brought by train to Washington, D.C. It arrived five hours late, going much slower than planned, in response to the many people lining the right of way to pay respects. Every station platform overflowed with young and old (and as with Lincoln and Franklin Roosevelt, especially racial minorities), giving "Bobby" their grieving farewell.

At Union Station, twelve friends and son Robert brought the casket off the train, while the Navy band played "Eternal Father, Strong to Save." After the president and other dignitaries spoke with Ethel Kennedy and her family, she and brother Ted and eldest son Joseph got into the hearse. The procession to Arlington paused at the Department of Justice (where Kennedy had served as Attorney General) and circled, then stopped at the Lincoln Memorial. There, the U.S. Marine Band sang "The Battle Hymn of the Republic," surrounded by thousands of people. Many of these were from nearby "Resurrection City," the symbolic shanty town erected by Dr. King's Southern Christian Leadership Council as part of the ongoing civil rights struggle. The funeral procession then went up to Arlington, where the new gravesite waited, just to the left of President Kennedy's. The funeral closed with John Glenn folding the casket flag and presenting it to Joseph, who handed it to his mother. The Harvard University Band played "American the Beautiful," while the family and other mourners, carrying lighted candles, paid their last respects.[19]

THE LATE TWENTIETH CENTURY

After the 1968 assassinations, in the context of racial, generational, and class antagonisms and a Vietnam war that seemed it would never end, the 1970s challenged every area of domestic discrimination. Bitterness blossomed in precisely the "God is on *our* side [*and against evil you*]" mode warned against by Lincoln and deplored by King. Liberal reactions to Nixon's Watergate abuses and conservative reactions to the *Roe v. Wade* decision were icing on the toxic cake that American politics and culture became. "Hard hats" spitting on "protesters" and the latter assaulting American servicemen returning from hellish service in the war previewed and bred fierce partisan bitterness that would spread and deepen.

As surely (and shortsightedly) as Southern moderates had let their extremist cousins monopolize the Confederacy's familiar "battle flag," antiwar protesters let the national flag be turned into partisan political statement by supporters of the Vietnam war. Consequently, the most familiar Southern flag became for most people a symbol only of slavery and racism, and the American flag for too many seemed only a banner of reactionary politics they could not salute. For conservatives, in turn, "liberal" came to mean anti-American, and "critical patriotism" or "loyal dissent" seemed some inconceivable contradiction in terms. Perhaps unsurprisingly, the 1976 bicentennial celebrations were more timidly exercised and tepidly participated in than could have been imagined a generation earlier.

In reality, American civic faith did not die from its 1960s "great awakening" and reactive aftermath. Even while continuing to fuel all sides of partisan fights over its interpretation, the nation's civic faith tradition just returned from prophetic fever pitch to normal temperature. Throughout the 1970s, everyday civil piety and practices continued. Traditional historical sites (Gettysburg, the Alamo, and countless others) continued to be visited, as did museums and civic monuments (from the Capitol Mall and Boston's Freedom Trail to newer sites consecrated in blood during various civil rights movements, whether in Selma and Birmingham or in Greenwich Village and San Francisco).

Hotly disputed before its opening, an important new American shrine grew powerful in the 1980s. The Vietnam Veterans Memorial in Washington turned out to provide a profoundly moving liturgical experience for those on all sides of arguments about that traumatically divisive war. Its sunken wall, which had seemed to some a slight, insulting institutional token, turned out to be multidimensionally fitting and ritually potent. The monument's architectural broken-ness "seemed fitting for a war that had no conventional narrative structure—a war without a clear beginning or end, without well-articulated goals." A visitor's loneliness reminded her that the cultural circumstances and military management of that war isolated with unique cruelty every soldier's working and fighting, living, and dying and being shipped home. And many visitors' unconventional and eclectic offerings, "like things washed ashore after years at sea," echoed the 1960s context that gave objects and appearances "heightened symbolic meanings."[20]

Visiting "the wall" and "connecting" with it still provides descent into pain and loss, frustration and betrayal, defeat without apparent meaning. The wall's inspired simplicity physically reflects mourners' faces with the names of honored dead. Searching and consciously communing with individual lost ones, each is united with others doing likewise. A Catholic might see such communion as a civil *sacrament* of atonement. A Protestant might rather stress the *witness* and renewed commitment in such faithful gathering. A Jew might stress the ritual's *making present* that it was not just "they" who suffered "then," but we here now. Our women and men "living and dead who struggled" there became us. As with formative events like the Exodus, as with history-bending struggles like Gettysburg, we the living must wrestle out the implications.

Will it or no, such struggling is communal. Architect Maya Ying Lin intended that only the visitors' physical passing could complete the "broken circle" of names, the beginning and end of whose chronological listing lies in the depth, at the juncture of west and east wings.[21] However, no one guessed that the monument's opening would bring the largest gathering of veterans in ninety years. No one expected the quantity, diversity, and unconventionality of the offerings they and the victims' families ceaselessly leave. From notes to clothing and food, from found objects to well-wrought icons, the offerings are made by veterans (who usually come alone) and by loved ones. Many families make yearly returns to the wall, multigenerational holy day observances. Nearby, starting on Christmas Eve, 1982, Vietnam veterans in booths kept alive the names and histories of thirteen hundred missing in action soldiers, solemnly passing them on with memorial bracelets to solemn-eyed youngsters, each ritually gaining thereby a new "uncle." This vigil witnessed the missing while initiating children into a personalized share of national history. It was not about one over another political evaluation, and the grizzled guys inducting the youngsters certainly were not peddling blind deference to government. From mixed personal motives, they were apprenticing a generation of children one-by-one into historical tradition, kids who were getting so little of it elsewhere.

All of this was and is civil religious experience. Physically visiting "the wall," participants ritually die and lose buddies, loved ones, and innocence yet again. They symbolically share the real blood and common tragedy so variously experienced in the national family. Former veteran for or against the war, demonstrator for or against, all emotionally represent that inexpressible time. Under Lincoln's gaze, one walks along the first few names on the wall (perhaps recalling how at first only a few "advisors" were sent into 'Nam); gradually, without quite noticing, you realize you have descended into symbolic hell, buried beneath ground level with fifty-eight thousand names, all our names, stopping at ones you know; how did we get here? For what? Terribly, gradually, finally we ascend, through so many more names, back up to ground. There, nothing overt has changed, and no shared analysis or new doctrine emerged, but all have ritually died, sharing the tragedy in silence, tears, and painful whispers with those there named and each other, all narrower politics be damned. "It remains for us the living" to be here reunited, Lincoln said. Something like that happens through experiencing this memorial.[22]

So serious healing had begun. Throughout the 1990s, many Americans came to further share (and argue over) national memory through viewing Ken Burns's *Civil War* documentary television series, whose public response to its first and multirepeated PBS showings exceeded all expectations. The number of visitors to Gettysburg and hundreds of smaller Civil War battlefields and burial sites set new records. Lee's Arlington home, first vengefully used only for Union dead but now including a Confederate section, had long since become our major national military cemetery. Whatever their politics, visitors flocked to its many subsites but always to its tomb of the unknown soldier(s).

Not without long and sometimes complex dispute, traditional battle/memorial sites and National Park Service presentations at places like the Little Bighorn have been expanded. As Confederate monuments and memorial plaques started rising at Gettysburg in the early twentieth century, by late century, what had begun as a triumphalistic memorial shrine to George Custer's troops expanded to include the last victory there of various Plains Indians against loss of their lands. Such expansion of memorial physicality and narratives to remember other of the "sides" once contending proceeds more slowly at the Alamo. Expanding civic memory to honor the patriotism of pain/loss and the patriotism of power/victory is itself a painful kind of national growth.[23] Notable and encouraging, too, were the enthusiastic opening and ongoing popularity of pilgrimage to refurbished Ellis Island.

True, most local Memorial Day observances were by century's end "thinner" than fifty years earlier—less heavily attended (with some needing to be taught to remove their caps when the flag went by); held in mid- or late morning (so onlookers could get to private picnics or activities in the afternoon); with the high school band and other local participants marching shorter distances along the main street (to shorter than used-to-be closing ceremonies); and the citizens' remembering (or not) to "buy a poppy for the vets." Still, every Memorial Monday evening since 1991, from the West Lawn of the Capitol building, PBS has broadcast the "National Memorial Day Concert," a medley successfully combining "uplifting musical performances, documentary footage and dramatic readings that honoring all Americans who have served or made the ultimate sacrifice for our country."[24]

MOURNING, MEANING, AND COMMUNITY SINCE 9/11

On September 11, 2001, the suddenly victimized United States felt like one huge community for the first time in a long time. Most people could see the event(s) and aftermath only via television. Thirteen miles away, many suburbanites looked down at the smoking pile from Eagle Rock Reservation. After calling the homes of any they knew who worked near the World Trade Center, these New Jerseyans gathered in stunned silence at the overlook. By the next morning, bouquets and flags had been left at its old granite wall. In the following days were added written remembrances and other hand-made mementos (like at the Vietnam Wall and at countless local sites nationwide). Essex County later formalized the spontaneous memorial, transforming what had been daytime scenic overlook and nighttime teenage hangout into a graceful, powerfully understated monument.

The centerpiece of its largest bronze sculpture, topped by an eagle in flight toward the city, is a girl facing visitors with her teddy bear. She represents all the children who lost loved ones. Behind her is a bronze book whose pages reveal the name, age, and town of the county's fifty-seven victims. This largest pedestal is flanked by the two shortest, topped by a bronze New York Fire Department (NYFD) helmet and a New York Police Department (NYPD) cap, respectively. Behind them all, inscribed on the now bronze-capped old wall, are the names, towns, and age of all who died at ground zero. Facing that way, to viewer's left of the bronze girl, is a medium-sized pedestal, "Remembrance and Rebirth," whose rescue-worker holds lantern high and a draped flag. Quietly off to viewer's right are seven trees. Each is dedicated "in living memory of the casualties of the September 11, 2001 attack on our nation who lost their lives on ... [one of the four airline flights, at One or Two World Trade Center, or the Pentagon]."

Across the country that horrific day, most Americans shared first grief by phone and visual participation through televised replay of the planes crashing and towers falling. Later came broadcast of memorial services. Foremost among these was the rookie president suddenly playing the role of national high priest at ground zero September 12. Although like other Americans they would later divide over the president's uses and invocations of "9/11," New Jerseyans still remember the tangibly different feel of things in those first days. We walked softer and spoke more with each other, even strangers. Whether or not participating in explicit religious communities' ritual responses to the disaster, common grief and mourning brought even the hard-wired, fast-paced metropolitan area *sense* of "being in it together" and that none of us could entirely be taken for granted. Even liberals flew flags on lapels or cars, whereas grumpy oldsters and loud teenagers joined most everyone in greater gentleness and politeness.

9/11 is, to be sure, still ritually commemorated in localities nationwide, with understandably special attention and attendance in lower Manhattan, at the Pentagon, and in Shanksville, Pennsylvania, where the fourth hijacked plane was brought down by its captives' heroic resistance. In 2007, the sixth anniversary but first to fall like the attack on Tuesday, the New York ceremony was not held at ground zero, now a construction site without public access. Allowed a quick visit there, where many still left flowers, letters, and mementos, the victims' immediate families were led a block away for their ceremony. Once again, it featured the national anthem and NYFD color guard, flutes and bagpipes, tolling bells, and brief readings by political figures, plus the names of all who died there. The three-and-one-half-hour reading of names (by 118 pairs of readers) went silent four times, starting with 8:46 a.m., the moment the first hijacked plane struck the North Tower. Aware of the symbolic 1,776-foot "Freedom Tower" that is to rise from the pit, relatives and other participants expressed hope the city would continue to solemnly observe the anniversary even after the planned tower, memorial museum, and plaza are finished.

Time would tell. "The first anniversary was a commemoration of an attack on a city and a country and the victims' families, all blended together," all attending together. However, now police separated the immediate families, whisking only them to the small nearby plaza for the official ceremony. The survivor families know the crowds will annually grow smaller, but hope the ritual still will be held. "This is where we need to be," said Gloria and Anthony Zabriskie, who have nothing else of their son Chris. "No headstone. No remains. ..." Only the other families. "We're here for Chris, sure, but we're also here for" them, all the "people we didn't know then but have come to know now because of this."[25]

These events received respectful but perfunctory coverage in print and television media. American civic tradition and identity's "natural" depth and underlying vitality were reassuringly manifest in New Yorkers' and other Americans' first response(s) to that day's traumatic attacks. But soon, the ease and danger of using such sense of unity to support foreign interventions and dubious domestic enactments tempted all into civically disastrous recycling of an earlier generation's false dilemma. Many proadministration officials and supporters politically self-identified as the (only) "people of faith" and true patriots. Many antiwar and antiadministration Americans responded with equally sweeping dismissals of both religious and civic faith.

There is, alas, nothing new about governmental manipulation of crisis, public grief, and mourning rituals for political purposes. The funeral train cortege that took Lincoln's body two weeks and the longest possible round-about way home was so directed by Secretary of War Stanton. Meanwhile, he created and spread as fact the rumor that the president's assassination had been planned from Richmond, the Confederate capital, by its desper-ate president Jefferson Davis. There never was a shred of evidence for that charge, but Stanton was vengefully seizing opportunity to obliterate Lin-coln's announced plans for peaceable reconstruction of the Union "with malice towards none." Effectively running the government the first weeks after Lincoln's death, "Stanton and the other bitter-enders saw to it that no one in the North was allowed to get over his grief quickly." They suc-ceeded. It soon became clear that Booth had no direction from Richmond, but "in the terrible revulsion of feeling that swept across the North few people would bother to speak out for the sort of peace Lincoln himself had wanted."[26]

The analogy to George W. Bush's use of 9/11 to justify his Iraq invasion and occupation seemed obvious to many. Even as the war's opponents carefully expressed support for the young men and women fighting it, they saw the administration as cynically betraying the troops and American public in a variety of ways. Among the least covered but long-term most threatening was the government's failure even to acknowledge the American dead.

From the beginning, the administration, whose president photo-op vis-ited "the troops" in dining halls (rather than in hospitals as Lincoln regu-larly did), sneaked in the bodies of those killed in action, through Dover Air Force Base in the middle of the night without cameras. When Ted Koppel once dedicated a special edition of "Nightline" to reading all the names of the American war dead, he and ABC were blasted as traitors. Only PBS continued their practice, at week's end, of silently picturing and naming each latest fatality, with rank, unit, and hometown.

Far from mourning the war dead and honoring their "last full measure of devotion," by 2004, the government was firing military contractors who gave photos of flag-draped coffins to newspapers. Those coffins were some-times hidden in larger cardboard boxes, lest passengers see them loaded into cargo bays. Mourning was left to the fellows and families of those killed in action, privately aided by a "casualty assistance calls officer."[27] Arlington National Cemetery demoted and fired public relations officers who worked to enforce the families' (Army-regulated) rights of choosing whether and how close to have media at their lost one's burial.[28] Although this chapter is not the place to argue the merits of the Iraq war's choosing and management, hiding the bodies of its heroic dead was a decidedly dishonorable slap at their comrades and families. Their persistent burial without wider public mourning abused and injured American civic faith.

Meanwhile, as in other areas of death and mourning covered by this anthology, the effects of broad cultural challenges were increased by technological changes. Although civic habit and political usage saw to it that Ronald Reagan received a six-day state funeral (June 5–11, 2004), public mourning was quietly suffering ironic diminishment from the very media that made it so accessible. The same television that had joined us in mourning assassinated presidents and the crew of the exploded space shuttle Challenger (1989), had become a 24/7 multichannel cable industry giving similar saturation treatment to the loss of media and entertainment figures.

The ways of the "info-tainment" industry could superficialize anything, even while our use of it for viewing important public mourning and other civic rituals could dangerously privatize our own observance.[29] Television sets and internet monitors had by 2008 long since spread to many rooms of many homes, and the Internet was increasingly accessed through hand-held MP3s, iPods, and iPhones. With its ever-increasing options, media-viewing was becoming ever more fragmented and individualistic. Getting the daily news or viewing national mourning might be shared with actual family members, but just as easily and often only with the cable or network personalities and Internet bloggers functioning as the viewer's "virtual" family.

A FUTURE FOR NATIONAL MOURNING, MEANING, AND COMMUNITY

Across the country, lively local memory of losses to, and the active presence of veterans from, the nation's recent wars still nurture powerful memorials. Thickly layered rituals and recollection still unify American communities. Just one example has been Bayonne, New Jersey, where "for every young person who 'paid the ultimate price,' there is a family left behind that continues to pay. 'It never goes away,'" were the words "spoken yesterday by every survivor of the Bayonne men killed in Vietnam." Their names are etched on the granite wall of a manicured hill in the waterfront park. "The names on the wall, like Bayonne itself, read like a poem to the demographics of America. Duffy and Chwan. Martorella, Maczulski and McGuire. Mione and Negron, Jackson and Jacobs. White, black, and brown. All red, white and blue. Nothing brings this home like Memorial Day," wrote one reporter of these observances. Friends and families, children, and grandchildren gathered "at two weekend Memorial Day Masses, ceremonies at each of the town memorials for the wars of the twentieth century, and yesterday morning's parade." It was "like a sad Christmas. Everybody comes home—not for cheer, but for comfort," said Sal Mione. A surviving vet, he explained 2008 Memorial Day's old-time depth in the town where he was one of the high school's 1964 class of

684. From that class are "fifteen of us up on that wall. Bayonne had the highest KIA [killed in action] rate in the country. And we all knew each other growing up."[30]

So Memorial Day can still annually function like the local observances after any town's disaster or sudden slaughter. Grieving folk and their children leave flowers, notes, and pictures at the site and/or gather for spoken and sung eulogies, where we share shocking loss of the victims. In the immediate aftermath, neighbors talk more with each other. With others who knew and cared for the victims, we become a trans-denominational community. Although not sharing identical (or any) membership in explicit religious community, we are bonded briefly by the deaths and our memories. More precisely, we are bonded by the ritual sharing thereof. As we "get more out of giving than receiving," so through shared funeral and later memorial services "for" the slain or other departed we well-serve our private and our collective selves. These ritual occasions of gathering as civic "congregations" renew our sense of local (or larger) community. Physically shared mourning helps clan or town, region or nation face the next morning.

Besides their faith and prayer fellowship, religious congregations usually have a body or casket for hands-on processing their departed and focusing shared grief. So do nonreligious civic lodges, Veterans of Foreign War posts, and other local groups who turn out for occasions where "the remains" are not just remembered but physically buried. Together facing and actively ritualizing the deaths they do not want to be true, they survive as communities.

In our popular culture, however, death is becoming one more fast fact that consumer convenience prefers to disappear. Having already minimized its ritual expression and real sorrow in favor of celebrating the departed's life, Americans now turn to party planners to orchestrate some services. Such planners credit the growing popularity of cremation for the trend; the "body's a downer, especially for [baby] boomers," one "funeral concierge" explained. "If the body doesn't have to be there, it frees us to do what we want. They may want to have [a memorial service] in a country club or bar or their favorite restaurant. That's where consumers want to go."[31]

It is hard to get further from Gettysburg. There townsfolk for weeks carried bottles of peppermint oil to neutralize the smell of six million pounds of human and animal flesh stinking in July heat. As those bodies demanded unprecedented physical attention, so their death required commensurate meaning. Lincoln's rendering of it began redemptive rebirth for a nation rededicated "to the proposition" of *all* our peoples' civic equality. Ironically, the very success of 1960s to 1970s protests, followed by the rightful progress of minorities' political and cultural empowerment, has merged with other factors to produce (as history habitually does) unintended consequences. Among the most dangerous are contemporary feelings of boundless individualistic entitlement that ironically threaten any determination "that government of the people, by the people, for the people shall not perish from the earth."

Waking to this threat, we realize that, as historian Barbara Fields put it, we still can *lose* the Civil War. Because it remains "for us the living" to be dedicated "to the unfinished work" and "the great task remaining before us," we as a nation have needed the U.S. Holocaust Memorial Museum, the National Museum of the American Indian, and the new Museum of African-American History and Culture in the nation's capital. If and when "the stories of any substantial groups are untold" or "the groups turn exclusive about their histories and talk only among themselves," the nation is impoverished and endangered.[32]

Although our civic ancestors and national motto called this *e pluribus unum* (out of many, one), we can well update it by affirming *in uno, plures*: in, through, and by our common civic context, we are entitled and empowered to be, all we can, our many different selves. Thanks to our predecessors having so worked prophetic ideals and constitutional norms, "we the people" have become so proudly diversified that the old "melting pot" symbol feels counterproductive. Effective new symbols, however, grow not from private choices, political arguments, or abstract preferences, but from publicly shared practices. This is why active, interpersonal sharing of enlarged and interwoven civic remembrance(s) are more vital than ever, thus the enduring importance of American civic tradition *and especially its rituals*, including though not limited to those of national disaster, mourning, and memorial.

Religious traditions implode, disastrously dividing into warring parties and denominations, when they overfocus on particulars of doctrine (especially in Christian history) or regulation of proper observance (as usually in Jewish and Islamic history). Such evil dividedness is best avoided by communities remembering that, as Christian theologians put it, "lex orandi, lex credendi." This means that healthy normative beliefs (concepts, particular regulations) flow *from* the community's praying and liturgy, not vice versa. More simply, the religious "family that prays together, stays together." By analogy, our national community can sustain enormous disagreement over political ideas and conflicting behaviors, working out ways to live with our differences, so long as we remain a family of many who publicly express commitment to each other and our largest civic goals. In other words, to survive and thrive as the country we have meant to be, we have got to "show up" and sincerely "join in" to American civic ritual.

If we have no familiarity with each other, no sense of togetherness because we have ceased showing up even for "the weddings and funerals," then forget it. Meaningful national community needs nurturing by national and local observances of July 4 and Memorial Day. As celebration of this nation's unique birth, the Fourth is essentially recollection of national purpose/identity. The more this includes physical and televised attendance at music, remembrance, and fireworks, the better. Memorial Day remains a proud but sober recollection of ancestors, the price(s) they have paid, the value of our inheritance. Made an official national day by Lincoln, Thanksgiving is part of this inheritance simply because it has long been something "we always do" (whatever different families' foods). Even the Super Bowl and any sporting or other event where those attending pause to hear (better yet, to sing) the national anthem or "God Bless America," play their part—not least by our simply *being* and *seeing* each other there, so varied many *thus* gathered together.[33]

As with traditional religions, the reality and power of American civic tradition is no old idea unchanged but the living process of its inheritors using their past to make better today and tomorrow. As the plumber uses his line, we can (like Lincoln and King) use our country's heritage lines to better "true" their meaning in our living diversely but faithfully as a nation. That is the civic saving grace our "secular Scriptures" promise, but sure it is a faith that can only be delivered if we proactively remember with JFK "that here on earth God's work must truly be our own."

Americans as diverse as Ronald Reagan and Maya Angelou have agreed on our need for the gravitational sense of *being* "all in it together" gained by *doing* together the rituals of public mourning and remembrance. In the process, as the poet put it, we better find ". . . the grace to look up and out into the eyes of our sisters and brothers . . . And say simply . . . Good morning. . . ."[34]

NOTES

1. Lucy Bregman's "Introduction" to this anthology.

2. Robert N. Bellah, "American Civil Religion," *Daedelus* 96 (1967), 1–21. Often misunderstood, Bellah's insight and its discussion have provoked many academic controversies. For full introduction, see Chapter 13 of Catherine Albanese's textbook *America: Religions and Religion*, 2nd ed. (Belmont, CA: Wadsworth, 1992). More recent editions shorten treatment of this topic while more richly interweaving it with "Public Protestantism" and "Cultural Religion."

3. Even explicit religions of saints and sages vary from one locale to another in terms of who is much or less honored or has their holiness or ortho-doxy disputed, all the more so with any list of American civic tradition's her-oes. The fierceness of such argument itself witnesses the tradition's enduring vitality, over whose meaning (and appropriate embodiments) citizens argue.

4. Bernard A. Weisberger, *America Afire* (New York: HarperCollins Perennial, 2001), 227.

5. Garry Wills, *Lincoln at Gettysburg: The Words That Remade America* (New York: Simon & Schuster, 1992), 38, 145–47. Wills offers definitive and delightful literary, oratorical, and historical analyses of the speech.

6. Jay Winik, *April 1865* (New York: HarperCollins Perennial, 2002), 356–59.

7. David Blight, *Race and Reunion: The Civil War in American Memory* (Cambridge, MA: Harvard University Press, 2001), 68–71.

8. James F. Russeling, "National Cemeteries," *Harper's Monthly Magazine* 33 (1866), 311–12, 321–22.

9. Drew Gilpin Faust, *The Republic of Suffering: Death and the American Civil War* (New York: Alfred A. Knopf, 2008), 233–37.

10. The last three paragraphs (quoting her pages 232 and 241) merely suggest Faust's richly detailed Chapter 7, "Accounting" (210–49). In showing how the civil war birthed a federal system of national cemeteries, she establishes that by its 1871 completion the federal reinterment program had buried 303,536 Union soldiers in 74 of those cemeteries. She also reminds us that the 30,000 black soldiers, "separated into units of U.S. Colored Troops in life, . . . were similarly segregated in death" in their new country's new national cemeteries (236).

11. W. Lloyd Warner, *American Life* (University of Chicago Press, 1962), 8–9, 14. For Warner's fully detailed description of classic Memorial Day, see Chapter 6 of his *The Family of God* (New Haven, CT: Yale University Press, 1959), 216–64.

12. Even here, even then, American "civil religion" retained as serious a split as western Christianity's divide into Catholic versus Protestants. In the rival southern version of American faith, Washington's Birthday was ritually celebrated in the public schools, but Lincoln's Birthday was studiously ignored, with Robert E. Lee's birthday or Jefferson Davis's accession to the Confederate presidency being turned into alternative regional (and school) holiday.

13. Not coincidentally, the same closing decades of the nineteenth century included blossoming of the brutal "gilded age" and this country's "manifest destiny" involvements in colonialism. See Howard Zinn, *A People's History of the United States: 1492-Present*, twentieth anniversary ed. (New York: Harper-Collins, 1999). For legal segregation's paradoxical evolution, C. Vann Woodward, *The Strange Career of Jim Crow*, rev. ed. (New York: Oxford University Press, 1957). For how much worse it was until World War II (including re-enslavement to Southern factories), see Douglas A. Blackmon, *Slavery by Another Name* (New York: Doubleday, 2008).

14. Early during World War II (when Vicksburgers had not yet rejoined national celebration of July 4), H. Richard Niebuhr sharply observed these dynamics in both national and traditional religious faith. His *The Meaning of Revelation* (New York: Macmillan, 1941) implied all that Bellah, Marty, and others would later unpack.

15. Lincoln's right to be called The Great Emancipator has been contested for some years now. For good introduction to this debate, see Chapters 12 and 13 of James M. McPherson's *Drawn with the Sword: Reflections on the American Civil War* (New York: Oxford University Press, 1996). Indeed, had Lincoln or King lived long lives and/or failed at later causes, we might remember them very differently.

16. As George M. Marsden put it, the speech's power came from its "appeal to the republican, and even Puritan themes [being] interspersed with

quotations from the Bible." *Religion and American Culture*, 2nd ed. (New York: Harcourt, 2001), 242.

17. The body was eventually encrypted at the King Center. For photos of the procession, see http://www.jofreeman.com/photos/Kingfuneral2.html, accessed July 30, 2008.

18. http://www.historyplace.com/speeches/rfk.htm, accessed July 30, 2008.

19. http://jfklibraryorg/Historical+Resources/Archives/Reverence+, accessed July 30, 2008.

20. Leslie Allen, "Offerings at the Wall," *American Heritage* 46 (1995): 92–103.

21. For the architect's conception and implementation of the monument, see the Oscar-winning documentary film, *Maya Lin: A Strong Clear Vision* (Sanders and Mock Productions, 1995).

22. These last four paragraphs differ very slightly from their first appearance in my article "A Southern Sense of America: From Jackson Square, Gettysburg, and the Vietnam Wall Toward Tomorrow," *On the Culture of the American South*, ed. Dennis Hall (Louisville, KY: Popular Culture and American Culture Associations, 1996), 237–56.

23. For a rich and pictorial review of the memorial battles over Lexington and Concord, the Alamo, Gettysburg, Little Bighorn, and Pearl Harbor, see Edward Tabor Linenthal, *Sacred Ground: Americans and Their Battlefields*, 2nd ed (Chicago: University of Illinois Press, 1993).

24. Public Broadcasting Service, http://www.pbs.org/memorialdayconcert/features/last/html, accessed May 28, 2008. This Web site offers multiple screens and interactive links for historical information and features of previous years.

25. As reported by Bob Braun, "Do You Recall When We All Grieved as One?" *The Star-Ledger*, September 12, 2007, 1, 3.

26. Bruce Catton, *The Civil War* (Boston: Houghton-Mifflin, 1987), 270–71.

27. For these and other details, see Jim Sheeler's coverage of how American war dead have been treated. Neither muck-raking nor maudlin, *Final Salute: A Story of Unfinished Lives* (New York: Penguin Press, 2008) is based on his 2006 Pulitzer Prize feature writing for *The Rocky Mountain News*.

28. Dana Milbank, "Putting Her Feet Down and Getting the Boot," *The Washington Post*, July 10, 2008, A03.

29. For disturbing insight here, see Edward Hoagland, "The American Dissident: Individualism as a Matter of Conscience," *Harper's Magazine*, August 2003, 33–41.

30. Mark DiIonno, "In Bayonne, an Ever-Fresh Wound of War," *The [New Jersey] Star-Ledger*, May 27, 2008, 1 and 4.

31. Sandra M. Gilbert, "The Mourning after Death," *Los Angeles Times*, October 29, 2007.

32. Martin E. Marty, *The One and the Many: America's Struggle for the Common Good* (Cambridge, MA: Harvard University Press, 1997), 6 and 191.

33. See further Michael Kazin, "A Patriotic Left," in *Dissent*, Fall 2002.

34. Excerpted from Maya Angelou's poem for President Clinton's first inauguration, *New York Times*, January 21, 1993, A14.

ABOUT THE EDITOR AND CONTRIBUTORS

Lucy Bregman, PhD, is Professor of Religion at Temple University (Philadelphia). She is author of books and articles on death and dying, including *Beyond Silence and Denial: Death and Dying Reconsidered* (1999) and *Death and Dying, Spirituality and Religions* (2003).

Rebecca Alpert is Associate Professor of Religion and Women's Studies at Temple University. She is coauthor of *Exploring Judaism: A Reconstructionist Approach* and author of *Like Bread of the Seder Plate: Jewish Lesbians and the Transformation of Tradition, Whose Torah? A Concise Guide to Progressive Judaism*, among other works.

Tonya D. Armstrong, PhD, teaches pastoral care at Duke Divinity School and directs pediatric palliative and bereavement care initiatives with the Duke Institute on Care at the End of Life. She is a licensed psychologist in private practice and congregational settings.

Glenn H. Asquith Jr., PhD, is Professor of Pastoral Theology and Director of the Masters in Pastoral Counseling program at Moravian Theological Seminary in Bethlehem, PA. He is a Fellow in the American Association of Pastoral Counselors. He has authored numerous books and articles in the field of pastoral care, including *Vision From a Little Known Country: A Boison Reader* (1992).

Regina A. Boisclair, PhD, is Professor of Religious Studies and Cardinal Newman Chair of Catholic Theology, Alaska Pacific University (Anchorage, AK). She has contributed many articles to biblical and theological publications.

Kathleeen Garces-Foley, PhD, is Assistant Professor of Religious Studies at Marymount University. She is editor of *Death and Religion in a Changing World* (2006) and has published on hospice and contemporary funerals.

Stephen Johnson, PhD, joined the religion studies wing of the Department of Philosophy and Religion at Montclair State University in 1971. Now the senior professor there, he has published articles on "civil religion" and civic tradition.

Kyoko Murata, MA in Philosophy, also holds a Graduate Certificate in Gerontology from Georgia State University. Her research focuses on death and dying rituals among Hindu communities in the United States.

Lawrence "Lorencito" Shorty (Diné and Mississippi Choctaw) is a writer and American Indian public health advocate. He received a Robert Wood Johnson Foundation Fellowship, a W. K. Kellogg Foundation Fellowship for Emerging Leaders in Public Health, and a U.S. Department of Agriculture Fellowship. He served as Director of Public Health for the National Indian Health Board.

Gisela Webb, PhD, is Professor of Religious Studies at Seton Hall University, where she is Associate Director of the University Honors Humanities Program. She has published in the area of Islamic spirituality and is editor of *Windows of Faith: Muslim Women Scholar-Acitivists in North America* (2000).

Ulrike Wiethaus, PhD, is Director of Religion and Public Engagement and Professor of Religion and American Ethnic Studies at Wake Forest University (Winston-Salem, NC). She has been involved in community partnership projects with American Indian communities in South Dakota and North Carolina for several years.

Jeff Wilson is Assistant Professor of Religious Studies and East Asian Studies at Renison University College, University of Waterloo (ON, Canada). He is the author of *Mourning the Unborn Dead: A Buddhist Ritual Comes to America* (2009) and the founding chair of the Buddhism in the West program unit of American Academy of Religion.

INDEX